*Reiki: Transmissions of Light, Volume 1*

# The History and System of Usui Shiki Reiki Ryoho

Robert N. Fueston, M.L.I.S., M.S.O.M.
Reiki Master/Teacher, Licensed Acupuncturist
Founder of The Reiki Preservation Society
Member of The Reiki Alliance

LOTUS
PRESS
Twin Lakes, WI

*Reiki: Transmissions of Light, Volume 1*
**The History and System of Usui Shiki Reiki Ryoho**

The author has exhaustively researched all sources to ensure the accuracy and completeness of the information contained in this book. The author has strived to present the information in a neutral fashion and with respect to all parties involved. Any slights of people or organizations are purely unintentional. Readers should use their own judgment and inner discernment or consult a holistic medical expert or their personal physician for specific applications to their individual problems.

First Edition
First Printing March 2017

For more information, please contact
The Reiki Preservation Society
3175 Custer Dr. Suite 303, Lexington, KY 40517
www.TheReikiPreservationSociety.org

ISBN 978-0-9406-7644-2
Library of Congress Control Number: 2016963480

**LOTUS PRESS**

Published by:
Lotus Press, P.O. Box 325, Twin Lakes, Wisconsin 53181 USA
Web: www.lotuspress.com
e-mail: lotuspress@lotuspress.com
800-824-6396

## Additional Praise for
## *Reiki: Transmissions of Light, Volume 1*

*"I am well aware that some parts of this book could be considered contro-versial in the Reiki world. There will always be those who disagree with the idea of publishing a book about Reiki, and to them I say: Don't shoot the messenger or, in this case, the researcher. I have known Robert Fueston for several years, and I can confidently state that he researches and reports with integrity. If someone is to write about Reiki history (and someone al-ways will), then I am glad it is Robert. Robert comes from a place of great honor and respect for the Usui Shiki Ryoho traditions, supports teaching Reiki in a traditional oral format rich in student-Master interaction, and stresses the importance of students using discernment when choosing the Reiki Master with whom they will train. Robert also writes with both wit and clarity... two qualities I appreciate in a writer.*

*In spite of the decades I have walked as a Reiki Master, I've learned a few new things from Robert's research; all of which served to reconfirm for me my own feelings of self-confidence with the Reiki I teach. I invite you to read this book with an open mind. It can deepen your connection with the Reiki lineage and enrich your Reiki practice."*

**Kathy Harmony Gaston**
a Senior Member of The Reiki Alliance, U.S.A.

---

*"For a considerable part of my over 30 years as a Reiki teacher and practitioner I avoided reading books and articles about reiki. Aware that inaccuracies appeared I do not know how to distinguish between good and unreliable information. Meeting Robert and learning about his research not only affirmed my core experience and sense of Reiki, but also enriched my knowledge of its history. I feel grateful for this gift. Now this book shares this research with a wider audience."*

**Marcia Halligan**, M.A.
U.S.A.

# Foreword

*By Mary Goslen, Reiki Master Teacher*

*Reiki: Transmissions of Light*
*The History and System of Usui Shiki Reiki Ryoho*
by Robert N. Fueston, M.L.I.S., M.S.O.M.
Reiki Master/Teacher, Licensed Acupuncturist

The book, "Reiki: Transmissions of Light," by Robert N. Fueston, Reiki Master/ Teacher offers the reader a rare opportunity to gain insight into the history and practice of the System of Usui Shiki Reiki Ryoho brought to America by Mrs. Hawayo Takata. Transmissions of Light miraculously guided the author through the entangled jungle of an oral tradition to unravel the teaching practices and policies of Mrs. Takata. Without this research, the information would have been locked up in hidden archives, fading memories, and forever lost in the mists of time.

The reader is the benefactor of the one-pointed focus, determination, and a decade of intense investigation motivated by the burning desire to know exactly what Mrs. Hawayo Takata taught and passed on to teachers and other students she trained. Unprecedented discoveries gleaned from interviews with people who knew and studied with Mrs. Takata is of tremendous value to Practitioners and Master-teachers of the Usui-Hayashi-Takata Lineage and the extended Reiki Community worldwide.

Of particular interest are the stories of Mrs. Takata and the biographical data of the 22 Master-teachers whom she trained. The articles written in 1928 and Hawaiian newspaper articles written in 1937-1938 translated from Kanji to English provide insight into early publicity of the Reiki System.

There is a wealth of information for anyone seeking to understand the system of Usui Shiki Reiki Ryoho as taught by Mrs. Hawayo Takata and teachers whom she trained. Historians are provided with a version of Reiki history as told by Mrs. Takata. The translation of the story of Dr. Mikao Usui, founder of the Reiki System, written on the Memorial Stone erected in Japan after his transition in March 1926 provides another viewpoint.

The distinctions between traditional teachings and later versions of the system of Reiki serve to clear up misunderstanding, misinformation, and confusion prevalent throughout the world. The section on finding a Reiki teacher is beneficial for the novice and others seeking more training. Looking at the Reiki system from a larger historical perspective helps to build correct understanding, self-awareness, and preparation for the future.

The most intriguing and astounding discovery that came out of Mr. Fueston's painstaking research is the hand-written letters from Mrs. Takata to Doris Duke revealing her practice of remote initiations. Found in the Doris Duke Charitable Foundation Archives, pertinent parts of the correspondence are reproduced with permission from the Rubenstein Library at Duke University for the benefit of all.

Without boundaries or limitations, Consciousness, Universal Energy, and Transmissions of Light take multiple pathways and many forms. Transmissions of Light through Reiki Initiations set in motion the conscious, inner-awakening process that is unique for each individual. Awareness of Reiki and the Transmissions of Light empower all with the possibility of understanding that everything and everybody is inter-connected in the web of Life. Each person plays a vital role in the ongoing drama of living energy dynamics and the evolution of Consciousness. May this book serve as a reminder that the system of Reiki is about Light, healing, peace and harmony, health and happiness for all. The Light of Consciousness is the ultimate Master and teacher.

Review by
**Mary Goslen**, Reiki Master Teacher
The Usui Reiki System (Usui Shiki Reiki Ryoho, Takata Style)
Usui-Hayashi-Takata-Fran Brown-Mary Goslen Lineage

# Prelude

*"Laughter is the shortest distance between two people."*
~ Victor Borge

We have a fire pit on our farm here in Kentucky. This is where I had planned to burn all my Reiki research and Reiki "artifacts" a few years before writing this book. I felt I no longer needed them. I no longer had the need to research into the history of the system of Reiki. I understand, from a deep part inside myself, Hawayo Takata's statement to her students, "Reiki will teach you." At my wife's strong insistence (just short of tackling me), I agreed to abstain from transforming these documents back into energy. I realize now the responsibility for sharing with the community a deeper sense of our system's history.

# Acknowledgements

This book might not have ever come into being if not for Reiki Master Hyakuten Inamoto, who kept asking me to write a book on Reiki and simply would not take "no" for an answer. That was the initial spark for this book. He wanted a book written about Takata, her Master students, and the history of the system of Reiki. Since then, I have felt honor-bound by my word, so here it is.

This book would not have been possible without all the careful guidance and instruction I received from my Reiki teachers. They have each contributed in their own way to my understanding of Reiki and the system of Reiki.

The same goes for my students, from whom I am constantly learning. I feel every teacher is a perpetual student; teachers have just had more time to practice. I feel amazed when I hear a thoughtful question that I have never been asked before in all my years of teaching, or when a comment is made that allows me to view something from another point of view. Thank you.

A special thank-you goes out to my Reiki colleagues for sharing with me their insights, valuable time, and conversations: Rick Bockner, Fran Brown, Jone Eagle, Phyllis Furumoto, Kathy Gaston, Marta Getty, Mary Goslen, John and Lourdes Gray, Marcia Halligan, Hyakuten Inamoto, Jojan Jonker, Light and Adonea, Pamela Miles, Paul Mitchell, Susan Mitchell, William Allan Perkins III, William Rand, Amy Rowland, and Justin Stein.

Another round of applause goes to Justin Stein, who helped me with the Takata chapter. The initial manuscript Justin received from me of this chapter was a hodgepodge of written paragraphs, containing numerous notes to myself about thoughts, questions, further research that needed to be done, etc. I simply could not look at it anymore. Not only did he clean it up, but he also generously supplied some of his own research to be included in it. This helped immensely in piecing together a more accurate history and certainly improving the quality of the chapter.

Kathy Gaston selflessly went beyond what any ordinary, reasonable, and sane person would do. She spent countless hours editing this manuscript and spent many four-hour marathon sessions online with me, going over manuscript changes. Thank you, Kathy!

I would like to also thank Nancy Arnott and Beth Davis for their incredible editing skills.

Thanks to Miho Motono Cunningham for the calligraphy of the Reiki *kanji* depicted on the cover of this book.

Thanks to Miho Motono Cunningham, Michiko Gonterman, and Justin Stein for the various translations of Japanese text and for their insights into Japanese culture.

A big thank-you to the University of Chicago and to Duke University for their wonderful archive departments. These archives came fully equipped with a very valuable resource – their outstanding staff. Both the staff and their records in these two archives were a considerable help in my research.

Thanks most of all to my wife, Heather Bullock, who was *practicing* her daily self Reiki treatment, exemplifying an important aspect of the system, while I was sitting in front of a computer simply *writing* about the system of Reiki. She worked extra hours at her job to give me the time to spend researching, traveling, and writing. I will always be eternally grateful for this gift.

# Dedication

*"Therefore let us stop passing judgment on one another.*
*Instead, make up your mind not to put any stumbling block or obstacle in*
*the way of a brother or sister."*
~ Romans 14:13


For my Reiki brothers and sisters,
may we be the examples of peace and kindness in the world.

# Table of Contents

# Preface

This book is an attempt to convey my own understanding of Reiki and the system of Reiki called Usui Shiki Reiki Ryoho, in an accurate and complete way. I have tried to do my best to explain my views, but have determined that I am unable to do so to the degree to which I would like. Every time I have re-read a chapter, paragraph, or sentence, I have had an urge to change it in some way. This I have done countless times, enough for many different versions of this book. So what you are getting in this book is a snapshot of my views, which is a very static way of trying to fully understand another's views, at best. This also means that in a few years, I might have a different understanding of Reiki, as my understanding will deepen with more time and practice.

It is this discovery that has reemphasized my personal belief that it is best for students and teachers to be physically present with each other while learning and teaching about the Reiki system. The Reiki system is a dynamic force that needs a dynamic interaction medium for its transmission—something words printed on pages in a book, no matter how eloquently written, simply fail to do.

Best of luck to you on your Reiki journey,

*Robert N. Fueston*

P.S. Read the footnotes! They contain important information that would have been too cumbersome to be included in the regular text of the book. If you don't read the footnotes, you will miss out on some important information!

I also tried to always cite sources that are readily available to the reader. However, at times this isn't possible, as some source material remains unpublished at the time of this writing.[1]

---

1   For example, Iris Ishikuro's notes and the autobiography of Takata are currently unpublished. The latter was used as the primary source for the books *Reiki: Hawayo Takata's Story* by Helen J. Haberly (Olney, MD: Archedigm Publications, 1990) and *Living Reiki: Takata's Teachings* by Fran Brown (Mendocino, CA: LifeRhythm, 1992). I have been given permission by Phyllis Furumoto to use Takata's unpublished biography entitled *Reiki is God Power: The Story of Hawayo K. Takata* as a source for information found in this book. However, I will often reference Fran's and Helen's books for the reader's convenience in checking the information presented.

# Introduction

For me, history is not a fiction-writing exercise. I almost named this book *Usui Shiki Reiki Ryoho: An Accurate Historical Account of an Unnecessarily Complicated Simple Practice* as an example of how complicated we can make things in life that are, in reality, very simple. The system of Reiki is one such example.

I value the oral tradition of Usui Shiki Reiki Ryoho. However, this doesn't mean that nothing is to be written on this subject. After all, Hawayo Takata, the woman who is responsible for bringing Reiki out of Japan, intended to write a book about her own Reiki practice and experiences. Instead she ended up choosing a biographer to do this for her.[2]

Because the system of Reiki is about doing the practice, rather than writing, reading, or talking about it, I will try to keep this book as short as possible. I want you, the reader, to *practice*, not sit around reading books about the practice! (And I want to get back to my practice too!)

I understand the brain's desire to read as a way to acquire an understanding of a subject. But Reiki can't be learned this way. Through practice I have learned that insight bypasses the intellect. Books contain knowledge, but wisdom comes from insight. The insight and wisdom that Reiki has to teach us will come only through practice, not by reading about it. Reiki is an experience, not a reading exercise.

Reiki Master Earlene Gleisner passed on this advice to me: "Trust Reiki, shift happens." Over my more than 19 years of Reiki journeying, I have found that my viewpoint and relationship with the system of Reiki has changed many times.

On a few occasions when I have discussed Reiki with people, I have received a certain "look."[3] I can almost hear their thoughts—sung like the opening theme song from the 1960s television show The Addams Family—"They're creepy and they're kooky, mysterious and spooky, they're all together ooky, the Addams Family."

---

2  Takata's unpublished biography is entitled *Reiki is God Power: The Story of Hawayo K. Takata.*

3  On one of occasion, I was asked to explain Reiki and questioned about a Reiki conference I had flown in to attend, when trying to pass through customs in a Canadian airport.

However, since you are presently reading a Reiki book, I think it is safe to assume you at least have an open mind about this "Reiki" stuff when I tell you that Reiki is a mystical experience. The more you practice, the more you'll understand.

Let me express at the outset that this book is meant to be more informative than instructive. You should know that I was trained as a librarian/information specialist, graduating with a Master of Library and Information Science from the University of South Carolina in 1999. I was trained to gather, verify, and organize information using many independent and valid sources. Professional standards dictate that references to information be cited so the reader can track down the original sources for the stated information.

The funny thing about this book is that I spent many years doing research and traveling around the world, spending countless hours trying to learn exactly how Takata, the woman responsible for bringing the system of Reiki to the Western world, taught the system of Reiki to each of her 22 Master students. In my mind, one or two Master students were not enough of a sample for me to cross-reference the information. Again, I blame the librarian in me.

This has been a great adventure in my life, traveling around and meeting many Masters. But, once I had successfully accomplished my goal, and as I continued my practice of Reiki, a major internal shift happened in me. I no longer had that strong drive and desire to continue my research into the history of Takata, her master students, and their teachings.[4] Even now, as I reread some of the history I have accumulated over the years, I think, "How silly of me to have spent all that time researching instead of practicing."

In 2012, I read a passage from the *Hua Hu Ching*, a book allegedly written by Lao Tzu. It says, "Don't imagine that you'll discover the truth by accumulating more knowledge. Knowledge creates doubt, and doubt makes you ravenous for more knowledge. You can't get full eating this way." I eventually managed to figure this out on my own; it had taken me only a decade or so. Can you say "slooooooooow learner"?

A few Masters encouraged me all along to spend more time practicing Reiki and less time researching its history. An e-mail I received from Mary McFadyen,

---

4   I still get little flare ups of doing research, but they are more in spurts now than one long marathon.

one of the 22 Master students of Takata's, sums up this consensus nicely.

> *"Reiki has gone far beyond its early stages and any importance that the first Masters had more or less evaporated. It's true that we were all pioneers, and it was wonderful, but at this point Reiki is so vast and varied (and corrupted in many places), and there are so many dedicated people using it and spreading it all over the world that our significance has diminished radically.*
>
> *The history of Reiki is interesting, and nothing more. The only thing of importance is that Reiki was given to the world again, and the truth is that how, why, and through whom is not really of any significance. Masters will come and go, organizations will come and go, and each will have its importance in the moment, but the big picture is that Reiki has a life of its own and will do whatever it does.*
>
> *Blessings, Mary"*

I realize now that this was supposed to be my path to Reiki—to seek and to find. I sort of stumbled into researching its history anyway—something I'll explain in detail later. Due to numerous e-mails I received after posting some of my research on my website, I found that other people also had a great interest in the history of Reiki.

Today I am very happy just practicing and encourage my own students to *practice* Reiki over *reading* about Reiki; practicing Reiki takes us into the mystery. So I encourage you to find a good, qualified teacher and practice. If you want to learn the system of Reiki, Usui Shiki Reiki Ryoho,[5] as Takata traditionally taught it, I give some advice later in this book about how to find a qualified teacher.

Suffice it to say, I am very grateful for my first few Reiki teachers. Without them (and some of their non-traditional teachings), I never would have gone on my Reiki journey and never would have met so many traditional Reiki Elders. Along this journey, I discovered the word "Reiki" has lost its meaning, just like the word "vegetarian."[6] Being vegetarian used to mean that one didn't

---

5   Takata would write the name of the system as Usui Shiki Ryoho, meaning "Usui-Style Therapy". However, writing it Usui Shiki Reiki Ryoho is also correct and specifies this is a therapy that uses Reiki.
6   Just FYI, at the time of this writing, I am not a vegetarian.

eat meat. But in today's world, people commonly say they are "vegetarian" but really mean they just don't eat cows. These "vegetarians" are proclaiming that the fish and chicken they eat must be a vegetable or a mineral or something. I actually had a woman tell me that fish wasn't meat, so I asked her, "Is it a mineral, fruit, or vegetable then?" Over the years, I discovered how the system of Reiki was once defined many years ago and how its meaning has significantly changed in today's world.

Following the transition (death) of many of my Reiki teachers, I feel it is the time to do more of what I can do to educate others about the system of Reiki as Takata taught it. I have traveled, trained, and spoken with many of the Masters who were trained by Takata. These Masters lived through the many changes made to the Reiki system, and I want to share some of what I have learned from them. As the Reiki Elders pass on, people will have to hear the stories secondhand from people like me who had the privilege of hearing it firsthand.

With that said, this book is a resource for people who want to know more about the system of Reiki called Usui Shiki Reiki Ryoho. It is no laughing matter to me that what is taught as "Takata Reiki" in the world has very little to do with the system of Reiki as Takata really taught it. There are hundreds of books and thousands of websites out there today all claiming to be about the Reiki system. So why do they all contain different information? Why is there conflicting data in these books and websites? Let's find out.

# *Chapter* ONE

## *What is Reiki?*
## *What is the Practice of Reiki?*

# CHAPTER
# 01

## *What is Reiki and the Practice of Reiki?*

The word "Reiki" can be translated as "universal life force energy," "spiritual energy," "Cosmic Energy," or "life energy." Hawayo Takata, the woman responsible for bringing the system of Reiki to the United States, used the phrase "Universal Life Energy" to describe Reiki at times. But this in and of itself did not grasp the depth or full meaning of the word "Reiki" for Takata. From Takata's own notes (typos included), which comprise some of what is called the "Grey Book,"[7] she states: "Reiki is a radionic wave like radio. It could be applied locally or as in short wave.[8] A distant treatment could be successfully given. Reiki is not electricity, nor radium or X-ray....Because it is a universal wave, everything that has life benefits when treated."

Sometimes Takata would also refer to Reiki as "God Power."[9] She basically said that all forms of life have this divine energy or God Power in them and refers to Reiki as a blessing from the Divine. "It is a limitless force. It is the source of energy that makes the plants grow...the birds fly."[10] Earlier in the

---

7    This "Grey Book" was given to Takata's 22 Master students and a few other Master students. It was compiled by Takata's daughter, Alice, after Takata's passing. It has a compilation of diary entries and essays written by Takata. Also included in it is the handbook that Hayashi would give out to his own students, a healing guide of hand positions used to treat various illnesses. Alice Takata, ed., "Grey Book," (self-published, 1982).

8    Takata sometimes called absentee or distant treatments "short wave" treatments.

9    In fact, the working title for Takata's autobiography was *Reiki Is God Power*, formerly titled *Look Younger, Feel Stronger, and a Way to Longevity*. Remember this when people start claiming to have created or channeled a newer, better, or more powerful form or type of Reiki. If Reiki is "God power," then what they are saying is they have created some kind of Cosmic or Universal Energy stronger than God power! It would be different if the claims were to have created a different *system* of accessing this same Cosmic Energy. There have always been many systems around the world that access Universal Life Force Energy. Some are easier to learn and use. Some have better and more effective ways to access and deliver this Cosmic Energy than others. Usui Shiki Reiki Ryoho is simply one of these systems that use this Cosmic Energy of the universe. But to claim a system uses an entirely new form of Reiki is questionable.

10   Vera Graham, "Mrs. Takata Opens Minds to 'Reiki,'" *The Times* (San Mateo, CA), May 17, 1975.

book, she states, "I believe there exists one Supreme Being - The Absolute Infinite - a Dynamic Force that governs the world and universe. It is an unseen spiritual power that vibrates and all other powers fade into insignificance beside it. .....every single living being is receiving its blessings daily, awake or asleep......it radiates vibrations of exultant feeling and lifts you into harmony. I shall call it 'Reiki' because I studied [it] under that expression."

The word "Reiki"[11] by itself can be used to describe many different things in the Japanese language. In this book I will interchangeably use the translation of the word Reiki to mean "Universal Life Force Energy," "Cosmic Energy," and "Spiritual Energy." The original system that Mikao Usui created for using Reiki is called Usui Reiki Ryoho (Usui's Universal Life Force Energy Healing Method).[12]

In Usui's system, practitioners primarily use their hands and breath to transfer Reiki to another person, plant, or animal.

Look at the way Takata wrote the word "Reiki".

---

11   Actually, there is no "R" sound in the Japanese language. A more accurate way of pronouncing "Reiki" would be "Leiki" and it is written as such in Takata's diary. Takata, ed., "Grey Book," n.p.
12   Takata states this on an audiotape recorded on August 24, 1979.

Here is a breakdown of what these two Kanji mean.

**Rei** – Strokes, 24. Consists of three parts: Top is rain, middle is things and bottom is shaman. **Rei means "spirit or spiritual."** The Japanese dictionary defines Rei as: *(1) Spirit; the spiritual aspect of the human being as contrasted to the physical. (2) Divine, numinous, charismatic, supernatural, mysterious. (3) The luminosity of the spirit; the luminosity of a God or Sage. (4) Inconceivable spiritual ability; charismatic power; charisma; wonderful; a wonder. (5) A rainmaker, a diviner; a person or being with spiritual or supernatural powers. (6) A shaman. (7) Goodness; good, excellent, efficacious.*

**Ki** – Strokes, 10. Consists of breath with rice (rice in Japan is sometimes used as a synonym for people). **Ki means "energy."** The Japanese dictionary defines Ki as: *(1) Vital energy connected with the breath. Invisible life-force (2) In the view of Zhuxi and other Neo-Confucians, the material force of the Universe. The generative forces of heaven and Earth, by means of which all things are constantly reproduced. (3) Air. (4) Breath, steam.*

*Description of the old form Reiki kanji*[13]: On the earth stands a shaman with his arms raised against the sky. From the heaven the rain comes down with lifesaving energy consisting of three parts: light, love and power/wisdom. The shaman acts as a channel (channeling this energy down to all the people of the Earth). The Reiki teacher is the channel when he or she initiates students, and the practitioner is the shaman when he or she channels this spiritual energy to the people treated.[14]

By practicing Usui Shiki Reiki Ryoho we can use Reiki to benefit our minds and our bodies. Practicing can be a catalyst for spiritual development and improved physical well being.

Usui passed on five precepts as guidelines. These were to be recited each morning and evening to help us obtain this state of living. Usui stated these five precepts were the "secret method to inviting happiness and the miraculous medicine to cure all diseases."

---

13   This form of *kanji* was used prior to World War II. After World War II, Japan adopted a new simplified version of *kanji*, commonly called "new *kanji*" (*shinji*).

14   This section on the *kanji* is taken from my teacher Adonea's First Degree (Shoden) manual and is used with permission.

*Just for today, do not anger*
*Just for today, do not worry*
*Just for today, count your blessings*
*Just for today, do your work honestly* [15]
*Just for today, be kind to all things that have life*

These are known now as the "Five Reiki Precepts."[16] Usui actually borrowed these precepts from a 1914 book entitled *Kenzen no Genri*, or the *Principle of Soundness*, by Dr. Suzuki Bizan.[17] There are many translations of the precepts,[18] but they all are very similar in meaning.

We sometimes allow others to push our buttons. We worry, or even imagine or anticipate how someone may react to something we say or do. Right or wrong, it affects how we act and feel about ourselves.

When I was training as a Master Candidate under Fran Brown, she told us, "It is none of my business what you think of me." I think of that statement often, as this seems to address many reasons why we worry or become angry. A Reiki practitioner's goal is to keep these precepts in our minds and try to live by them in each moment.

In the late 1990's while living in South Carolina, I heard a monk give a lecture that helped me with the fifth Reiki precept. This monk offered two helpful "tricks" one could use that would result in being kind to others. I don't recall the first "trick" as all I needed was the second "trick" to do the job. He said to imagine that all the people you meet are your mother and treat them accordingly. Of course, this only will work for those of us who have wonderful mothers to think of, which thankfully is my own case.

Being in the state of absolute inner peace, called *Anshin Ritsumei* in Japanese, is a lot easier when we give or receive a Reiki treatment. After a Reiki treatment, it is really hard to become angry or to worry. We just feel too good. That is why it is important to have a daily hands-on practice; it helps us to live the Reiki precepts.

I tell my students to focus on the third precept and see how the other

---

15   Another translation of this Reiki Precept, which I like, is, "Just for Today, work diligently".

16   I sometimes will also use the phrases "Reiki Principles" or "Reiki Ideals"; this is something Takata did as well.

17   This first was mentioned by Reiki Master Hiroshi Doi at the Usui Reiki Ryoho International Conference in Toronto, Canada, September 27-29, 2002.

18   Here are the Five Reiki Precepts (Principles) as given by Hawayo Takata from an audiotape of her teaching. "Just for today, thou shall not anger. Just for today, thou shall not worry. Just for today, we shall count our blessing. [Just for today] Do our work honestly. [Just for today] To be kind to all things that have life." Hawayo Takata, *Takata Speaks: Volume 1, Reiki Stories*, Rindge, NH: John Harvey Gray Center for Reiki Healing. The wording used by The Reiki Alliance is: Just for today, do not worry. Just for today, do not anger. Honor your parents, teachers, and elders. Earn your living honestly. Show gratitude to every living thing.

four precepts automatically start becoming easier to live by.

Simply put, the more one practices the system of Reiki, the more time one spends in a different form of Consciousness (capital "C"); a non-duality consciousness. This form of Consciousness is easy to recognize, as these are the moments that you are feeling the best—at peace—with all things as they are. The Reiki precepts are obtainable in this Consciousness. However, like a runner's high, this state of being is temporary, and one tends to degrade back into ordinary "consciousness" where one is no longer at peace.

The solution is to practice more with the Reiki to get back into this state of Consciousness. The trick is staying there. The more you practice and use Reiki, the longer the effects will be.

# *Chapter* TWO

---

**My Reiki Journey**

*Determination or Obsession?*

**The Beginning**

**Making the Leap**

**The Search Begins**

**Traditional Training with many Masters**

# CHAPTER
## 02

*My Reiki Journey*
*(Determination or Obsession?)*

*"You can only find truth with logic*
*if you have already found truth without it."*
~ G.K. Chesterton

On March 28, 2013, Phyllis Furumoto interviewed me for her Reiki Talk Show. She asked me to share my Reiki journey up to that point in time. A recording of that interview can be found at: http://www.reikitalkshow.com/shows/view/318. This interview can be used as a "quick summary" of the material found in this chapter. So, if you would rather listen to me telling my story, rather than read about my story, feel free to do so.

## The Beginning

My Reiki journey began in 1995 in a way that seemed completely by chance. I used a free-purchase reward from a book club I'd recently joined and, on a whim, ordered a book about Reiki. I'd never heard of Reiki, nor was I interested in healing. I didn't read the book when it arrived, but later packed it up, along with my other belongings, when I transferred from The Ohio State University[19] to Bowling Green State University, in the northern part of Ohio. An entire year's worth of dust had now collected on the book—until one day

---

19   Yes, the capitalization of "The" is correct. It is The Ohio State University!

when I was sitting around with nothing to do and the book, which sat on the bookshelf my dad had made when he was a boy, caught my eye. Curious, I opened it and read the introduction. Reiki was fascinating, but I closed the book after only a few pages, wherein I learned that in order to practice, one needs to receive initiations from a Reiki Master. I seriously doubted I'd come across any Reiki Masters in my neck of the woods.

Not one week later, in a coffee shop, a small sign caught my eye. It was advertising a First Degree class. When I called the Reiki Master to inquire, he informed me that he needed at least five students to hold the class and that he needed to have registrants immediately, as he was returning to his home in Maui shortly. So if I wanted Reiki training, I would have to put together a class for him to teach.

Armed with information from the Reiki book, I quickly convinced four friends to join me. We, along with two other students, began class on October 28, 1996.

## *Making the Leap*

We were taught in class to practice Reiki on ourselves every day. I did this faithfully, but quickly became angry because I didn't feel anything and felt I'd been duped. Sticking to routines is often difficult for me. Despite this tendency I continued to practice, feeling that I ought to make the effort because I'd paid for the class. While I still did not feel anything, I noticed changes in my body and began to have very vivid and unusual dreams, one of which was about my Reiki Master. I called him to tell him about it.

The synopsis of my dream was that my Reiki Master was being attacked by several malevolent forces. When I revealed the full details, he interpreted them as a warning; he decided to remain in Bowling Green a bit longer than he had originally planned. He said my dream was a sign that the Kahuna[20] he had upset was still angry with him.

This experience taught me that Reiki allows one to go beyond the five senses to interpret information, as my Reiki Master had, and realizing this opened a whole new world for me. Inspired, I got together with my Reiki classmates and we began group practice. It was shortly after we started holding group practices, also called Reiki shares, that I started feeling the sensations of Reiki.

---

20    A Hawaiian sorcerer.

Six months later, I took Second Degree, continuing my studies with a different teacher, Jone Eagle, since my First Degree teacher was back in Maui by then. Later that same year, I took my Master training[21] and began to teach. Jone had suggested I take the Master training before my upcoming move to Charleston, South Carolina. Jone and I continued to be in contact via e-mail and phone for several years. Whenever I traveled back to Ohio to see family, I always made it a point to drive a few more hours north to visit with Jone.

While living in South Carolina and talking to other practitioners, I discovered that we all had learned the system of Reiki differently. Seeking the truth about how the system of Reiki was originally taught, I decided to start with finding out how Hawayo Takata, the woman who brought the system to the United States, had taught it. I began by tracing back my own Reiki lineage.

## The Search Begins

During my first Reiki class I was, incorrectly, given the lineage of:

Mikao Usui-Chujiro Hayashi-Hawayo Takata-Seiji Takamori-Ranga J. Premaratne-Beth Sanders-Stephanie Douvris-Anthony "Spirit" Thiebaut.[22] I later found out that Seiji Takamori was not a student of Takata. After doing lots of research, including contacting Ranga, I found the original lineage of Beth Sanders.[23] It turns out Beth actually taught Ranga the system of Reiki first. Later, Ranga claimed to have studied with a man named Seiji Takamori[24] and then retrained Beth Sanders. It was because of this discovery, of my incorrect lineage, that I started my Reiki journey into finding out who trained whom. This is what also led to me to start my research into the history of Reiki.

I had also been erroneously taught that none of the Japanese Reiki Masters had survived World War II. Based on this assumption, I concluded that I must find the Masters trained by Hawayo Takata. Because of incomplete and sometimes inaccurate information that had been published, this proved to be a more difficult task than it appeared. One must keep in mind that this was before there were many web pages on the Internet and before Google existed.

In 1999, I got in touch with Fran Brown, one of Takata's Master students.

---

21  My initiation as a Reiki Master was on August 27, 1997.

22  Note: Ranga's would change the spelling of his last name to Premaratna.

23  Mikao Usui-Chujiro Hayashi-Hawayo Takata-Iris Ishikuro-Arthur Robertson-Rick & Emma Ferguson-Margarette L. Shelton-Beth Sanders-Stephanie Douvris-Anthony "Spirit" Thiebaut. Beth Sanders studied with other Reiki Masters as well.

24  Ranga states that Seiji Takamori studied with a man named Venerable Takeuchi; reportedly a student of Chujiro Hayashi. Ranga write, "Initially I was under the misconception that Seiji received training from Takata. This was because of language difficulties." Personal e-mail to the author, May 31, 2000.

She confirmed that the system of Reiki as I'd learned it was not the same system as taught by Takata. I desperately wanted to train with Fran, but she told me that she'd recently had a bad experience with retraining a Master and didn't want a repeat of that experience. This other Master she retrained went back to her old ways of practicing and teaching Reiki. Fran wanted her own Masters to keep the teaching of Takata unaltered. Fran's price of $10,000 was impossible for me financially at this time, as I was working as a graduate assistant in a medical library to put myself through graduate school at the University of South Carolina, where I was pursuing my Master of Library and Information Science degree (M.L.I.S.).

In hindsight, I can now see that my quest to find accurate information on the Reiki system led me into this specific graduate degree program. The M.L.I.S. degree is where I learned and honed the skills of researching and finding valid pieces of information.

I continued my pursuit, and in the same year I was able to contact Reiki Masters Light and Adonea, who had also been researching the system of Reiki. They gave me valuable input about what they had learned, and while I wanted to join them at the first Usui Reiki Ryoho International (URRI) conference in Vancouver, Canada, for training, again, the timing was not right. I had just graduated with my M.L.I.S. degree in August 1999 and had moved to Colorado to begin studying for my degree in acupuncture and Oriental Medicine, which would start a few days later. This would be a four-year, 2,800-hour, accredited four-year Master of Science in Oriental Medicine degree program at Southwest Acupuncture College.

I feel the practice of Reiki also led me to start studying Traditional Chinese Medicine (acupuncture and Chinese herbal medicine). From this training I would receive, I could understand the system of Reiki at a deeper level. For instance, when it states in Reiki Ryoho Hikkei (a handbook used in the Usui Reiki Ryoho Gakkai), "You don't have to take bitter medicine or stand for hot moxa treatment," I understand what Usui is referring to. The same goes for the idea of getting rid of "old blood" by performing Ketsueki Kokan-ho, also called Ketsueki Joka-ho (Blood cleansing technique). This technique is called "The Finishing Treatment". Takata referred to parts of this technique, the "The Nerve Stroke" and the manipulation of the arms and legs, in the "Grey Book". There are plenty of examples, but these few should suffice. I feel that my training in Traditional Chinese Medicine has given me insight into the Reiki teachings and their clinical usefulness.

## Traditional Training with Many Masters

During a break from my Chinese Medicine studies, in March 2000, I drove from Boulder, Colorado, to Lake Montezuma, near Sedona, Arizona, to visit Light and Adonea, and I trained with them for three days. Light and Adonea had taken Reiki training in many Reiki lineages. As I was interested in learning how Takata taught Reiki, they taught me what they had learned from one of their teachers, Brigitte Byrd, in a Barbara Weber Ray lineage. They also passed on to me what they had learned as "traditional Reiki techniques" from Hiroshi Doi (lineage Usui–Taketomi–Koyama–Doi), who is, or was, a member of the Usui Reiki Ryoho Gakkai (the Reiki society Usui founded).

At this point, we had been in almost weekly contact for over a year. Our meeting and training was nothing less than spectacular. It was through them that I first learned a lot of traditional Reiki information and techniques, and for the first time, experienced Reiju—the spiritual blessing ritual.

Two months later, in May 2000, I flew back to Ohio to visit my parents for a few weeks while I was on break between semesters at acupuncture school. From there I then drove from Mansfield, Ohio, to Cambridge, Massachusetts, for two consecutive weekends to take First and Second Degree with John Harvey Gray, another Master student of Takata's and his wife Lourdes. I was very excited to get training with one of Takata's Master students, and I learned a lot in class and by asking detailed questions about Takata and her teachings. John mentioned that not all of Takata's Master students had learned Reiki in exactly the same way. I took this in quietly and continued to listen.

During this training, I was privileged to listen to one of about 20 unpublished tapes of Takata teaching Reiki classes. A highlight of this experience was during the Second Degree class. My Reiki practice partner and I were assigned an old massage table with aluminum legs. As we exchanged treatments on this table, I was happily surprised when John's wife, Lourdes, told us that Takata herself had used this table when she taught classes sponsored by John, and his first wife, Beth in the 1970's.

Light, Adonea, and I kept in contact, and I visited them again in the spring of 2000 with my girlfriend at the time, Heather Bullock. We exchanged Reiju, a Spiritual Blessing process, and Reiki treatments. The Reiki that came through their Reiju was incredible.

By this time, I was continuing to reexamine all the things I had first learned about Reiki history. I was originally told that there were groups out there trying to "control" Reiki. One of these so-called "evil" groups trying to "control" Reiki was called The Reiki Alliance. However, I decided that I really needed to form my own opinions and not carry what might be the prejudices of my past teachers. So, I decided to initiate contact with the Alliance.

I was fortunate that the first member of The Reiki Alliance I met was Reiki Master Kathy Harmony Gaston. From this first meeting came a total reshaping of how I thought about The Reiki Alliance. No longer was I going to believe that The Reiki Alliance was this "evil entity" out there trying to control Reiki and deciding who could teach it. I came to understand The Reiki Alliance as a community of Reiki Masters who held Reiki in high respects and with professional standards. The Alliance wasn't trying to control Reiki; they were trying to preserve it from the onslaught of changes being made to the system.

I revisited my intention of retraining with Fran Brown as a Reiki Master. I had learned much in my training with Light and Adonea and John Harvey Gray, but I was still on my quest to know exactly how Takata taught Reiki at the Master level. I had enough money to do the training with Fran, and I started e-mailing back and forth with her. Fran agreed to train me as a Reiki Master in a weeklong intensive class format; this was something she did later in her career instead of the normal apprenticeship route for those people who were already Reiki Masters but wanted to be retrained as Masters in her lineage. She told me that the next Reiki Master Intensive class was to be held in France, the following week. This was April 2001. However, I would not be able to attend it due to the Chinese medical school I was attending, which had a strict no-absence policy.

Shortly after Fran's return from France, she decided to no longer take on the responsibility of training or retraining Masters. She felt as if she needed to just finish up with the ones which she had already started. I felt absolutely heartbroken that I had missed my opportunity to train with her.

As I continued on my journey, I reached out to Japanese Reiki Master Hyakuten Inamoto (lineage: Usui–Hayashi–Yamaguchi–Inamoto). At this time, he was still in training under his teacher Mrs. ChiyokoYamaguchi. We e-mailed about the possibility of me traveling to Japan to train under Mrs. Yamaguchi as a Reiki Master. However, since I was not Japanese, she would train me and all the other foreigners only up to Second Degree. I considered this offer, but declined.

As luck would have it, for the first time Hyakuten Inamoto was going to start training non-Japanese Masters outside of Japan at the fourth Usui Reiki

Ryoho International (URRI) conference, held in Toronto in the fall of 2002. Hiroshi Doi was going to be training Masters there as well. However, there was one catch to me attending the conference: The weekend of the URRI 2002 conference and the following week of Master training with Hyakuten and Doi senseis were the scheduled dates for my midterm exams. In acupuncture school, the attendance policy was very clear: No absences would be excused.

I didn't want a repeat of my experience with Fran Brown. So I went to the director of the school, Valerie Hobbs, and explained my situation. I told her that Reiki was the catalyst for me even being in Chinese medical school and what a wonderful opportunity this would be for me to continue my Reiki education. I asked her if I could go despite the fact that it was against the rules and I would have to miss midterms. Valerie could see that this meant a lot to me and so asked me a question in return. She asked, "In five years, will you regret not going to this conference?" I exclaimed without hesitation, "Absolutely!" She stated that I could go; however, I would have to take the consequences: I would receive a failing grade on all of my midterm exams and I would have to pay a $150 fee to retake each midterm. The fee was necessary because the professors would have to rewrite the tests for me so that no other student could accuse me of cheating by getting examination questions from other students who had already taken the exams while I was away. I was going to miss five or six midterms, so this was a significant amount of money in addition to the fees for traveling, the URRI conference and the Master training seminars. Despite these consequences, my determination to continue on my Reiki path was clear. So, in the fall of 2002, I attended the URRI conference and retrained with both Hyakuten Inamoto-sensei and Hiroshi Doi-sensei as a Reiki Master.

I was excited to train with Inamoto, because I wanted to learn how he was taught by Mrs. Yamaguchi. However, during the training I discovered that he had altered the training from what he had received. My understanding, now, is that this was the honorable thing to do because his teacher was still alive and teaching (otherwise it would be like stealing your teacher's income). I wanted to study with Doi to reinforce what I had learned from Light and Adonea and to receive initiation into his lineage, as well.

Shortly after my return from training, I received an e-mail invitation from Fran Brown agreeing to once again retrain me as a Reiki Master. I accepted her offer despite some uneasiness. Fran wanted me to teach Reiki only as she taught it, not including some of the Japanese techniques I had learned along the way. After all the other traditional Japanese Reiki techniques I had learned up to this point, I wasn't sure about making the commitment, but I was steadfast in my pursuit to learn exactly how Takata had taught Reiki.

I officially began my retraining with Fran in her home in California in May 2003, where I observed her teaching both a First and Second Degree class.[25] I also was initiated by Fran in First and Second Degree. Heather, now my fiancée, trained and was initiated by Fran in First Degree. I remembered that John Harvey Gray had mentioned that Takata's teaching was not consistent among her students, and now I had firsthand knowledge of that after training with both John and Fran.

Not only was some of the Reiki information taught slightly different from how John Harvey Gray taught it, but also the Reiki initiations and symbols were slightly different. I felt disappointment in not having discovered one true way but that revelation, in itself, was a good Reiki lesson.

During my training with Fran, I found out that she had met my teacher Hyakuten-sensei and his teacher Mrs. Yamaguchi in Japan a few years earlier. Fran questioned me several times why it was that I wanted to train with her as a Reiki Master since I was already a Master student of Hyakuten-sensei. I always replied with the truth that it was because I wanted to learn Reiki exactly how Takata taught it.

In 1999, Hyakuten-sensei had acted as the translator for Fran and Mrs. Yamaguchi as they compared what they had learned from their teachers and their initiation process. They found them to be very similar, and Fran expressed her happiness about this to me. At the end of the training exchange, Mrs. Yamaguchi acknowledged her as being the only one she knew of in the West who was teaching the authentic Hayashi method.[26] Fran mentioned that she wanted her own Master students to meet with Mrs. Yamaguchi and asked if I could again put her in contact with Hyakuten-sensei. I told her that I could, but that it was my understanding that Mrs. Yamaguchi's son, Tadao, did not want Hyakuten to see Mrs. Yamaguchi alone.

Shortly after this training, Fran informed me that she no longer was going to do a weeklong Master intensive training course. Instead, she wanted to go back to training and retraining Masters in an apprenticeship route. This wasn't our original agreement, but I decided it was worth trying to stick it

---

25   The "internet archive" is a valuable resource for researchers as it archives web pages on the internet. Sometimes information is taken off a web page I want to read again for instance, so I use this massive internet archive called "The Way Back Machine". You can find it here: https://archive.org/web/
    If you type in Fran Brown's old web page address containing her bio: http://www.reikifranbrown.com/bio.htm you will see I am listed as a Master Candidate on her website in the latter part of 2003 and early part of 2004.

26   Fran told me this story on many occasions both in person and through e-mail.

out. In truth, I think Fran forgot our agreement.

I graduated in July 2003 with my Master of Science in Oriental Medicine and planned to begin my Chinese medical career doing acupuncture and prescribing Chinese herbs (and, of course, continuing to do Reiki treatments and classes). But before moving to set up my clinic, I sponsored Hyakuten-sensei to come to Boulder, Colorado, in August 2003 to retrain Reiki Masters. This would be his first time teaching in the United States.

This was prearranged before Fran had accepted me as a Master candidate, and I was looking forwarding to seeing Hyakuten again. It would be my second time training with him as a Master. I recall Fran talking about how she would sponsor Takata to come and teach classes as often as she could. In fact, the experience becomes deeper with each additional training by the same teacher. Since I sponsored Hyakuten, I also got to share the days with him when he wasn't training Masters. We had a lot of deep conversations about many aspects of Reiki and we had a lot of fun. Hyakuten also confirmed what Fran had told me about the meeting between him, Mrs. Yamaguchi, Fran Brown, and Tadao. I even have a picture of Fran's that shows all four of them together.

That October, my fiancée Heather and I moved to Saluda, North Carolina, to open up our Traditional Chinese Medicine clinic and our Reiki clinic and school. In November, I flew to France to continue my training with Fran Brown. The training was held in a Tibetan monastery called Kagyu Ling. There, I again watched Fran teach the First and Second Degrees. I also met more of her Master students, we had a Masters' circle, and we discussed some information about the Master level.

Besides Fran, I believe only one of her other Master students knew I was already trained as a Reiki Master. I kept quiet for the most part as I listened to the discussions. Perhaps it was there that I realized how much I knew about the Reiki system from my previous training and experience—something Fran tried to convince me of before we had even started. During my weeklong visit in Kagyu Ling, I contemplated more about that Masters' meeting and the financial difficulty my fiancée and I were having starting up our clinic and school. This led me to question whether this training with Fran was the right thing to do. During one of the Tibetan religious ceremonies (*puja*) I attended there, I considered ending my training with Fran.

It had been apparent from the start of my training that Fran's memory was an issue of concern. We would have the same conversations again and again about how far along we were in my training and with whom I had studied previously. This led me to break the Reiki Principle of not worrying during the many nights I lay awake in bed. I kept thinking to myself, "What if Fran doesn't remember how much money I have already given her? What if she dies before completing my now longer apprenticeship-route training with her (instead of the weeklong Master intensive retraining I had agreed to)?" I did have a receipt from her; but still the mind wanders, and mine was very worried.

Although my training with Fran was exactly what I had wanted in some respects, it was hard to develop a deep relationship with her. I wanted that bond between us, but if someone's memory just won't hold, it is like the relationship is always at square one. Always the same questions: "How far along are we with your training?" and "Who have you studied with?"

I had the money to finish my $10,000 commitment to her, but I would be unable to continually pay traveling costs to get to her Reiki classes, as she wanted each of her Master students to attend at least 10 or more. With her teaching all around the world plus living in California and me living in North Carolina, this just was not going to be possible; and this wasn't our original agreement. I needed to end my training with Fran, and it was one of the most difficult decisions of my Reiki journey. We parted on good terms, but it was an unfortunate end to what I had hoped to be my final answer to the question of what Takata had taught at the Master level. I have very few regrets in regard to my Reiki training. Not getting on the plane in April 2001 and going to France to attend Fran's weeklong Master intensive retraining, regardless of the consequences, is one regret I held until very recently.

In April 2005, I attended Hyakuten-sensei's Master training for the third time, which was free to former students of his—this time in Asheville, North Carolina. We were again able to spend some time together, and some of my students got to meet him when Hyakuten accepted my invitation to join our weekly Reiki share.

It was at a lunch meeting I had with Hyakuten during this training that we sat down with each other and he insisted that I write this book. I realized that some questions concerning the history of Reiki, mostly dating from 1976 to 1986, still loomed in my mind. Wanting to be as thorough as I could, I decided I would have to continue my quest to seek out as many Masters as possible; Masters trained by Takata and masters trained by her Master students. Since so much time had passed, I was concerned that I needed to get information from as close to the source as possible, or risk losing it forever.

Things quieted down a bit for me on the research front for a while as I contemplated whether to continue my research and writing a book on Reiki… or not. I was content to continue with my Reiki practice with the knowledge I'd already gained.

In 2006, we sold our home and moved from North Carolina to Lexington, Kentucky. In 2009, a couple of things happened to inspire me to begin researching again.

On Easter Sunday, April 12, 2009, Fran Brown made her transition.[27] When I heard that Fran had passed, the news really impacted me. Although Fran and I were no longer in frequent contact, I had often thought about her. I was surprised just how strongly her passing affected me. This led to me thinking about the passage of time and deciding that if I was to ever learn what Takata had taught at the Master level, I had better get going.

Later that same year, I had a dream in which many Reiki Masters appeared, including Takata, John Harvey Gray, and a Master who studied under John. I didn't recognize who this last Master was; I just "knew," as we do in dreams, that he was a Master student of John's. In the dream, Takata was walking down a row of people, giving initiations. I waited excitedly for an initiation from Takata as she got closer and closer to me, but she passed me by. The same thing happened with John Harvey Gray. However, the Master who studied under John stopped and gave me the initiation. I chalked the dream up to the powers of intuition that come from Reiki practice.

From what I'd learned from past experiences about the importance of dreams, I interpreted it and understood this dream to be representational of literally what was to be. A week later, Stephen Comee, a Master student of John's, contacted me for the first time. We had a good conversation, but we did not embark on any training. I figured that since we both didn't feel the need to study with each other, perhaps this wasn't the Master student of John's who would be training me in John's lineage, or at least it wasn't the right time.

My first formal teacher during this quest to find out what Takata taught at the Master level was Glenda Johnson. I had met Glenda at the URRI conference in 2002 where I studied with Hiroshi Doi and Hyakuten Inamoto. Glenda was a former member of The Reiki Alliance and had studied in the

---

27  Something strange happened just prior to Fran's transition. I was told a week or two before Fran's transition that she had passed. When I checked up on it with people who I knew were in contact with her, Fran was alive and well. A week or two later, however, Fran had a fall causing internal bleeding and she passed on. In hindsight, I feel this false report of her death was a sign for me to reach out and reconnect with her, but I failed to act in time.

lineage of Mary McFadyen. Upon joining The Reiki Alliance, Glenda had her initiation procedures and information checked by Mary McFadyen to ensure what she had learned in this lineage was correct. I traveled from my home in Kentucky to Kansas City, Missouri, and we did a Master training over a four-day period ending on March 14, 2011.

The way life unfolds at times never ceases to amaze me, especially where "coincidences"[28] come into play. I couldn't help but purchase a 1983, second-edition training manual written by Barbara Weber Ray[29] that I found at an online bookseller. (I already owned the first, third and subsequent editions, but being a diligent Reiki aficionado, I felt my collection would be incomplete without this one.)

When I opened the manual, inside the cover I found a student's First Degree certificate dated May 5, 1984, signed by a woman named Marcia Halligan. I had never heard of this woman in all of my research, but I felt impelled to speak with her. If she already had been teaching Reiki in the early '80s, she must possess some of the information I so desperately sought. Also, since I found this Reiki certificate tucked inside of a Barbara Weber Ray manual, I felt it seemed logical that she probably had trained in this lineage as a Master.

An Internet search yielded a copy of a community newsletter in which a small notice for a Reiki class appeared. Here I found Marcia's contact information.

Marcia began practicing Reiki in 1981 and completed her Reiki Master training with Barbara Weber Ray. Her Master certificate is dated June 26, 1983. This came well before Barbara began teaching The Radiance Technique®, which includes seven levels.

Since Marcia's Master training, she had moved away from the city and entered a low-tech existence in rural Wisconsin. There she continued to practice Reiki, but also was closed off from much of the modern world, including knowledge of the details of the many changes that the system of Reiki had gone through since she learned it.

Through our phone conversations and many e-mails, Marcia became interested in learning what I had discovered. I, of course, also felt interested in learning what she had learned during her 1983 Master training with Barbara Weber Ray. So I drove from our farm in Kentucky to her farm in remote

---

28  I put the word "coincidences" in quotes because I think coincidences are really "signs."
29  One of Takata's Master students.

western Wisconsin for us to exchange Master-level training over the course of several days. I felt thrilled to meet Marcia in person and hear about Reiki in the United States during its early days, such as her attendance at the second-ever[30] Reiki Alliance meeting in 1984, held at a ski resort near Donner's Pass, California. On July 3, 2011, the last day of our training, we exchanged Master initiations and gave each other treatments: a wonderful experience for each of us.

Between what Marcia told me and information about Barbara's training I received from another of Barbara's Master students, John Latz,[31] I discovered a timeline for when Barbara started making certain changes. Reiki at the time of both Marcia's and John's training still consisted of a three-level system.

I was next blessed to come into contact with one of The Reiki Alliance's founding members, Helen Borth, seemingly through serendipity once again, while perusing information on various branches of Reiki. Helen had been trained as a Master by Barbara McCullough, one of Takata's original 22 Master students. Helen was trained as a Master less than two weeks after Takata had died. Her certificate is dated December 21, 1980.

I once again drove from our farm in Kentucky to Wisconsin, this time Milwaukee, where Helen lived. We spent several days going over the Master material, and she trained me as a Master in her lineage.[32] We spent a lot of time talking about the Reiki history—from the late 1970s, when she had taken First Degree from Ethel Lombardi (one of Takata's Master students), to the current state of Reiki in the world. I always find such pleasure in talking with people who were into Reiki at the early stages of it being introduced to mainland America.

After this training, I had yet another dream about Stephen Comee, and again, not a week later, I heard from him. It seemed like an omen or a sign that Reiki was telling me to study the Third Degree in the John Harvey Gray lineage. We decided to exchange Master initiations[33] and our Master-level notes on December 29, 2011.

I felt that at long last I could be confident that the mystery of Takata's

---

30  This is sometimes seen as the first official Reiki Alliance meeting. The 1983 meeting had resulted in the formation of The Reiki Alliance.

31  John had taken his Master training even earlier than Marcia Halligan.

32  My Master certificate from Helen is dated November 11, 2011.

33  Since traditionally there wasn't a Master initiation given in this lineage (see chapter entitled: "Historical Perspective on the 'Master' Initiation"), Stephen used the Master initiation that John Harvey Gray created. Also, since Stephen was currently in Japan, where he has lived since the 1970s, we decided to do the initiations remotely, something that I had learned in my Barbara Weber Ray lineage. Because I had already received the First and Second Degree initiations from John Harvey Gray in person back in May 2000, I felt okay with this.

teachings at the Master level, including the initiations, had been solved. Based on the extensive conversations and training I had with Reiki Elders, original notes generously offered by family members of those who were deceased, and audio recordings of Takata teaching different levels of Reiki classes, I felt at peace with my understanding and knowledge about the Reiki system. I was at last prepared to write this book.

It was during Helen's training and our discussions that followed that I felt I had come full circle, in a way. She reminded me of the very first person who initiated me as a Reiki Master, Jone Eagle—not in the actual training per se, but in her explanation, view and understanding of Reiki.

I jokingly tell my own students that all that training I did was because I was a slow learner. It isn't necessary to study with so many teachers. I wanted to learn traditional Takata Reiki, so it took me a while to find some teachers in the Takata style, as they truly are few and far between. Since I did not get traditional Takata-style Reiki to begin with, it had a rebound effect on me. I went from not having any knowledge of her style to wanting to make sure I knew everything about the way Takata taught Reiki; including all the little variations she taught and especially the different styles of initiations she used.

When I first learned Reiki in 1996, I thought it was a healing technique. And by thinking this way, I wanted to learn all the Reiki techniques I could. Teacher after teacher kept telling me to start "in sourcing" rather than "out-sourcing." In other words, let Reiki teach me, and go within for answers. Light and Adonea, two of my past teachers, kept telling me to get my mind out of the way so that I could actually learn something. This process started to unfold to me after several years of practicing Reiki. For this reason, I can see the value of having many years of practice before being initiated as a Reiki Master. It takes years of practice to develop this type of relationship with Reiki. Takata would say, "Practice, practice, practice," and "Let Reiki teach you." We need to "practice, practice, practice," so that we can get to the point where Reiki does teach us. This is one aspect of Mastery, and Takata stated it so simply.

Meeting Helen Borth was like holding a mirror up to myself in this way. I could see how I first had looked at Reiki and how I view it now. Sometimes we don't know how much we have changed until something gives us a reminder. Fran Brown put it to me this way: "If you don't get the spiritual teachings in Reiki you have missed the boat. Many people were taught Reiki as a technique and when they come here they find it is much deeper than they ever knew."[34] I appreciate all the teachers I had who have helped me along my own Reiki path. I will continue to trust Reiki to guide me and to pass on to others what I have learned.

During the end of June and early July 2012, my wife and I traveled to Romania to teach First and Second Degree Reiki classes. Our sponsors, Mihai Albu and Constantin Dina, were already Reiki Masters but wanted to learn the way that Takata had taught Reiki. During that time period I did a Master intensive training with them.

After I was done teaching, a student of mine named Petko Lukov, who now lives in the United States but who is from Bulgaria, had coordinated his schedule to be back in Bulgaria when I would be finished teaching. Petko then drove into Romania to take us back to his native country and give us a three-day tour of Bulgaria.

Had it not been for my involvement with Reiki, I may never have been to Romania and therefore would not have gone to Bulgaria! This was a wonderfully kind offer from Petko. Because Bulgarian is a Slavic language, not a Latin-based language like Romanian, there was no way for me to really read and figure out any of the signs on the roads or buildings. For example, while in Romania, when I saw a building with a sign that said "Farmacie," I could ascertain that this was probably a pharmacy. The same word, "pharmacy," written in Bulgarian is "Аптека." The time spent in Bulgaria was nothing less than amazing and is somewhere I would like to return to someday.

I was invited to give a lecture at an international Reiki conference held in New York City on September 22, 2012. I lectured on the history of Reiki in America, with a focus on whether the Master initiation was originally part of the Reiki system (as taught by Takata) or not. It was at this conference that I first revealed my research findings that many of Takata's Master students never received a Master initiation and that the majority of them, if not all of them, were never taught how to perform the Master initiation. I discuss this topic more thoroughly in Chapter 9.

From October 30 to November 5, 2012, Marcia Halligan came to stay with us for a week on our farm and co-teach a First Degree Reiki class with me. During our time together, while not in class, we again went over what we each had learned during our Master training: her with her teacher Barbara Weber Ray and me with what I had learned from the various Reiki teachers

---

34  Personal e-mail to the author, March 28, 2001.

with whom I had studied. Our conversations revolved around Reiki, the teaching of the system of Reiki, and Reiki history. We periodically went on walks on the farm to clear our heads, and then we went right back into these wonderful conversations sometimes lasting far into the night.

During my whole Reiki journey I had the privilege of meeting many current and former members of The Reiki Alliance. I was so impressed with their professionalism and sense of "being" that I decided I wanted to learn more about The Reiki Alliance. In the later part of 2012, I decided that this indeed was an organization of which I would like to be a member. After the application process and required interviews, I was asked to meet with Phyllis Furumoto, whom The Reiki Alliance acknowledges as Takata's successor, so that I might get a sense of who she is in person and a sense of the position she holds as Grand Master as acknowledged by The Reiki Alliance.

Phyllis and Rick Bockner, another of Takata's Master students, were hosting a weekend retreat entitled "Takata's Legacy" in Tubac, Arizona, in February 2013. This would be the first time I would get to meet either Phyllis or Rick in person. Before going, I thought I was going just to meet Phyllis and hear more stories about Takata, something I always enjoy listening to. But my experience was actually much deeper than this. Both of these Masters were so open and friendly that I felt we had known each other for a long time. Granted, Rick and I had e-mailed some in the past, but nothing takes the place of meeting face-to-face and interacting. People can really get the sense of each other energetically when they meet face-to-face together, something that is much harder to do via e-mail. I knew I wanted to spend more time with these two Masters again as soon as possible.

I was accepted as a member in The Reiki Alliance in March 2013 and made plans to attend The Reiki Alliance conference to be held in Ontario, Canada, in May 2013.

From March 25 to April 1, 2013, it was my pleasure to have Pamela Miles as a guest in our home. I invited her to come and teach her Communicating Reiki and Medical Reiki seminars in Lexington, Kentucky. This would also give us a chance to spend some time together and get to know each other better. Although we had been in phone and e-mail communication for approximately ten years, we had met in person only one time, when I was up in New York City to present at a Reiki conference during the fall of 2012. Pamela speaks as eloquently as she writes. Her book, *Reiki: A Comprehensive Guide*, is one of the few books I recommend to my own Reiki students who wish to have something to read on this subject.

In May I attended The Reiki Alliance conference held in Ontario, Canada. It was the 30th anniversary of The Reiki Alliance, and four founding members of The Reiki Alliance would be present.[35] It was a week of meeting lots of new Reiki people, putting faces to people's names that I had only heard or had no in-person contact with during my years of researching, and reconnecting with others whom I hadn't seen in a long while.

During this conference it was announced I would be one of two people to compose The Reiki Alliance's historical archival department. I had put my name in for this prior to the conference, upon hearing about the retirement of the current archivist.

I learned things about Takata that I was unaware of at the time from people who knew her. Overall, it was a week of nonstop interaction between Masters from many different countries. Although I had attended other Reiki conferences, never had I been to one in which the commonality of practice was held by such a large and diverse group. I truly was amazed at the caliber and professionalism of the Reiki Masters attending.

Contrary to popular belief, one need not be a member of The Reiki Alliance to attend its annual gathering, albeit most Masters attending are members. I hope other Masters will take advantage of the opportunity to attend one of The Reiki Alliance's annual meetings. I believe that having firsthand experience of a Reiki Alliance conference and getting to know some of its members will go a long way to clear some of the negative prejudices some hold against The Reiki Alliance. As told previously in this chapter, I held unfounded biases against The Reiki Alliance, passed down from one of my teachers to me, until I took the time to find out for myself how I felt about the organization.

Having never been to a Reiki Alliance conference, I didn't have an idea of what to expect. The energy in the group was palpable. The experience of sitting in this group and respectfully sharing our thoughts, experiences, and stories, was wonderful. I knew I had made the right choice in joining The Reiki Alliance.

In July 2013 I heard that Hyakuten would be giving a lecture on Mount Kurama and Reiki in Columbus, Ohio. I asked the sponsor, Jodi Patton, if it would be okay if I came up with some of my students for a lunch visit with

---

35  The founding members present were Rick Bockner, Marta Getty, Paul Mitchell, and Susan Mitchell.

her and Hyakuten. We would then stay for his lecture, which turned out to be amazing. It had been many years since I had seen Hyakuten in person, and it was great to reconnect again.

In September 2013 I traveled to the University of Chicago to research whether or not Mikao Usui had attended there or not. This will be discussed in depth in Chapter 3.

From October to early November 2013, it was my pleasure to have Takata's Master student Rick Bockner stay with my wife and me for three weeks on our farm in Kentucky. This gave Rick and me a chance to really get to know each other better. I set up First and Second Degree Reiki classes for Rick to teach while he was here, and he participated in our weekly Reiki share as well. Rick also taught a special class just on the precepts of Reiki.

It just so happened that Hyakuten Inamoto would be in Atlanta, Georgia, during this time. So I e-mailed him and his sponsor, Dana Lisa Young, to ask if she and Hyakuten would like to meet Rick in person. The answer was a resounding "YES," and so we drove down for a visit and to watch Hyakuten give his lecture on the history of Mount Kurama. We had a great time with a series of conversations punctuated with laughter.

*(Hyakuten Inamoto, Robert Fueston, and Rick Bockner)*

In April 2014, after researching some information about Takata at Duke University, I had a meeting with Mary Goslen, who was first trained as a Reiki Master by Barbara Weber Ray and then trained again in each level by Fran Brown. Our meeting was spectacular. I walked into the door, saw Mary on the left side of the restaurant, walked over to her, and before I could even take my seat at Panera Bread Company in Winston-Salem, our pre-arranged meeting place, we started chatting. For over three hours we didn't stop talking, even to order food or drinks. Finally, needing a bathroom break, we stopped talking temporarily. After deciding to change locations, we headed to another restaurant and continued our conversation.

I expressed earlier my regrets that my training with Fran Brown was cut short. With my newly discovered connection to Mary, I felt that this part of my journey could be completed and I could have a sense of closure to my commitment to Fran. Mary agreed to do the weeklong intensive training that Fran had originally promised me and that Mary herself had received from Fran. What Fran Brown and I had officially begun in 2003, Mary and I would finish in 2014.

Later that same month, I traveled to the Netherlands for the 2014 Reiki Alliance Conference. After the Reiki Alliance conference, I traveled to Romania with Rick Bockner and his wife, Carina. Rick and I lectured at the Romanian-American University together. Rick also taught his Reiki Precepts class and had a Master gathering. I taught a First Degree class, two Second Degree classes, and two Reiki techniques classes while there. It was a very busy and fun time in Romania, thanks to our sponsor, Mihai Albu.

*(Rick Bockner and Robert Fueston)*

In July 2014 I made a trip to Green Valley, Arizona, to meet with Phyllis Furumoto, Paul and Susan Mitchell, and fellow Reiki researcher Justin Stein. We were there to archive the materials left to Phyllis that had belonged to Takata as well as other documents and pictures accumulated after Takata's transition.[36]

*(Robert Fueston, Justin Stein, Susan Mitchell, Phyllis Furumoto, and Paul Mitchell)*

In August 2014, I flew to Cortes Island, British Columbia, to spend a week with Rick Bockner and Carina. Knowing Rick is a skilled woodworker, I asked before going if, while I was there, together we could make an initiation bench for me. The idea came to me out of memories of Fran Brown's initiation bench that she used to initiate her students on while teaching at home. This bench is special to me because of the time Rick and I spent together making it and because it also brings up memories of Fran for me.

In September 2014, I traveled to Winston-Salem, North Carolina, to visit Mary Goslen and complete the Master training I had started with Fran Brown 11 years prior. A sense of utter contentment settled within me of having completed my commitment to Fran and begun a new and wonderful relationship with my teacher, Mary, and a deep sense of completion ensued. It felt similar to the sense of reading the last page of a long but wonderful

---

36  In February 2015, I wrote an article for The Reiki Alliance newsletter stating more of the details. This article was republished in The Reiki Preservation Society's newsletter (June, 2015: Volume 2, Issue1): http://www.thereikipreservationsociety.org/Resources/Newsletters "The Gift of the Takata Sensei Archives," *TRPS Quarterly* 2:1 (June 2015), 5.

book, closing the cover, and taking a deep breath…and then remembering that this is just one book in the series and that there is more to come but it will be a different kind of journey altogether.

My personal journey was inspired by the desire to learn more about the history and practice of Usui Shiki Reiki Ryoho. This book reflects a portion of what I learned along the way.

# *Chapter* THREE

---

## *The Beginning of the Reiki System*

### *Mikao Usui*

### *"Reiho Choso Usui Sensei Kudoku No Hi"*

Memorial of the merits of Usui Sensei the founder of Reiho (Reiki Ryoho)

### *Takata's version of*
### *Reiki History and Dr. Mikao Usui*

Recorded by Mrs. Takata -- August 24, 1979

### *Comparing the Memorial Stone and Hawayo*
### *Takata's Story*

# CHAPTER

# 03

## *The Beginning of the Reiki System: Mikao Usui*

*"History is the version of past events that
people have decided to agree upon."*
~ Napoleon Bonaparte

### Mikao Usui
*August 15, 1865 [37] – March 9, 1926*

---

[37] Justin Stein notes that at the time of Usui's birth, the Western calendar had not yet been adopted in Japan. Thus, Usui's birthdate, the fifteenth day of the eighth month of the first year of the Keiō era (1865-1868), might actually refer to October 4, 1865, not August 15 as is commonly thought. Personal e-mail with author, April 3, 2015.

There have been many different stories about the origins of the Reiki system passed down over the years. I suggest a scholarly or "no-nonsense" approach to the history of Reiki, and that is to have verifiable evidence.

The earliest history of the Reiki system is literally written in stone.[38]

In 1926, Mikao Usui, the founder of the Reiki system, died from a stroke. One year later, in 1927, his senior students erected a very large memorial stone that measures 294 cm (2.94 meters) in height and 125.5 cm (1.255 meters)[39] in width to honor him. Written on this stone is the history of the Reiki system. Reiki Master Hyakuten Inamoto's translation of that memorial stone follows, with my commentary in footnotes.

## "REIHO CHOSO USUI SENSEI KUDOKU NO HI"
### *Memorial of the merits of Usui Sensei,[40] the founder of Reiho (Reiki Ryoho)*

*That which is attained within oneself after having accumulated the fruits of disciplined study and training is called 'Toku' and that which can be offered to others after having spread a path of teaching and salvation is called 'Koh'. Only with high merits and great virtues can one be a great founding teacher. Sagacious and brilliant men of the olden time or the founders of new teachings and religious sects were all like that. Someone like Usui Sensei can be counted among them. Sensei newly founded the method based on Reiki of the universe to improve the mind and body. Having heard of his reputation all over, people crowded around to seek his teachings and treatments. Ah, how popular it is!*

*Sensei, commonly known by the name 'Mikao', with an extra name 'Gyohan' is from Taniai-mura (village) Yamagata-gun (county), Gifu-ken (prefecture). He is descended from Chiba Tsunetane. His father's name was Taneuji, and was commonly called Uzaemon. His mother was from the Kawai family.*

---

38  Takata told another detailed account about the origins of the Reiki system and its founder, Mikao Usui, which can be found at the end of this chapter.

39  115 ¾" (9' 7 ¾") in height and in 49 " ( 4' 1 ") in width. Ms. Makiko and Nahoko Yahata (two sisters who are both Komyo Reiki teachers took these measurements. Height: 294 cm ( 2.94 meters), Width: 125.5 cm ( 1.255 meters)

40  "Sensei" means "One who has gone before". In Japanese culture, the word "Sensei" is a title of respect for someone who has achieved a certain level of mastery in a skill or subject. This in some ways is similar to the American use of the title "Dr." to address persons who have obtained a Ph.D., M.D., D.D.S. or any other type of doctorate degree. We would address a medical doctor not as "Mr. Jones," for instance, but as "Dr. Jones." Since the word "Sensei" is a Japanese term given in Japanese culture, American Masters are not called Sensei by their students. Takata addressed Usui as "Dr. Usui" to convey the respect for him in a way her Western students would understand. It is also possible Usui held a doctorate degree. My research on the use of the title "Dr." by Hayashi and Takata regarding Mikao Usui is ongoing. It is worth noting that Hayashi also referred to "Dr. Usui" on Takata's English-language Dai-Shihan certificate. More information about Takata's four Reiki certificates from Hayashi is found in chapters 5 and 8. According to the memorial stone, Usui was a scholar, and perhaps this explains the reason why Hayashi would refer to him as "Dr. Usui." The stone also mentions that he studied religion and specifies the religion of Christianity, which fits the story that Takata would tell her students about Usui being a minister. It is my opinion that Dr. Usui must have done significant studying in Christianity for it to be mentioned on the memorial stone.

*Sensei was born on August 15 of the first year of Keio (1865 A.D.). From his youth he surpassed his fellows in hard work and endeavor. When he grew up he visited Europe and America, and studied in China. Despite his will to succeed in life, he was stalemated and fell into great difficulties. However, in the face of adversity he strove to train himself even more with the courage never to yield.*

*One day, he climbed Kurama-yama and after 21 days of a severe discipline without eating, he suddenly felt One Great Reiki over his head and attained enlightenment and he obtained Reiki Ryoho[41]. Then, he tried it on himself and experimented on his family members. The efficacy was immediate. Sensei thought that it would be far better to offer it widely to the general public and share its benefits than just to improve the well-being of his own family members. In April of the 11th year of Taisho (1922 A.D.) he settled in Harajuku, Aoyama, Tokyo and set up the Gakkai to teach Reiki Ryoho and give treatments. Even outside of the building it was full of pairs of shoes of the visitors who had come from far and near.*

*In September of the 12th year (1923 A.D.) there was a great earthquake and a conflagration broke out.[42] Everywhere there were groans of pains from the wounded. Sensei, feeling pity for them, went out every morning to go around the town, and he cured and saved an innumerable number of people.[43] This is just a broad outline of his relief activities during such an emergency.*

*Later on, as the 'dojo' became too small, in February of the 14th year (1925 A.D.) the new suburban house was built at Nakano according to divination. Due to his respected and far-reaching reputation many people from local districts wished to invite him. Sensei, accepting the invitations, went to Kure and then to Hiroshima and Saga, and reached Fukuyama. Unexpectedly he became ill and passed away there. It was March 9 of the 15th year of Taisho (1926 A.D.), aged 62.*

*His spouse was Suzuki, and was called Sadako. One boy and one girl were born. The boy was named Fuji and he succeeded to the family. Sensei's*

---

41  Stephen Comee does not use the word "enlightenment" to describe Usui's experience. His translation of this section reads, "Suddenly, he felt a very great spiritual energy above his head..." According to Justin Stein, the word in question (katsuzen) can be used in the context of satori, but it would usually have another word after it to make it clear that it's definitely talking about satori.

42  The Great Kanto Earthquake was one of the most destructive in world history, and its devastation left Tokyo and Yokohama in ruin. Usui went out to help heal the survivors and thus knowledge about him and his system of Reiki spread. Magnitude 7.9 and an estimated 142,800 deaths. (Note: By comparison, the earthquake and following tsunami of 2011 in Japan caused an estimated 30,000 deaths.)
There was extreme destruction in the Tokyo - Yokohama area from the earthquake and subsequent firestorms, which burned about 381,000 of the more than 694,000 houses that were partially or completely destroyed. Although often known as the Great Tokyo Earthquake (or the Great Tokyo Fire), the damage was apparently most severe at Yokohama. U.S. Geological Survey, "Historic Earthquakes," http://earthquake.usgs.gov/earthquakes/world/events/1923_09_01.php last accessed December 1, 2014.

43  Although this relief activity took place in Tokyo, not Kyoto, it is possible that this is the origin of Takata's stories of Usui's work in the "beggar camp."

*personality was gentle and modest and he never behaved ostentatiously. His physique was large and sturdy. He always wore a contented smile. He was stout-hearted, tolerant, and very prudent upon undertaking a task. He was by nature versatile and loved to read books. He engaged himself in history books, medical books, Buddhist scriptures, Christian scriptures and was well versed in psychology, Taoism, even in the art of divination, incantation, and physiognomy. Presumably Sensei's background in the arts and sciences afforded him nourishment for his cultivation and discipline, and it was very obvious that it was this cultivation and discipline that became the key to the creation of Reiho (Reiki Ryoho).*

*On reflection, Reiho puts special emphasis not just on curing diseases but also on enjoying wellbeing in life with correcting the mind and making the body healthy with the use of an innate healing ability.[44] Thus, before teaching, the 'Ikun' (admonition) of the Meiji Emperor should reverently be read and Five Precepts be chanted and kept in mind mornings and evenings.[45]*

*Firstly it reads, 'Today do not anger', secondly it reads, 'Do not worry', thirdly it reads 'Be thankful', fourthly it reads, 'Work with diligence', fifthly it reads, 'be kind to others'.*

*These are truly great teachings for cultivation and discipline that agree with those great teachings of the ancient sages and the wise. Sensei named these teachings 'Secret Method to Invite Happiness' and 'Miraculous Medicine to Cure All Diseases'; notice the outstanding features of the teachings. Furthermore, when it comes to teaching, it should be as easy and common as possible, nothing lofty. Another noted feature is that during sitting in silent meditation with Gassho and reciting the Five Precepts mornings and evenings, the pure and healthy minds can be cultivated and put into practice in one's daily routine. This is the reason why Reiho is easily obtained by anyone.*

*Recently the course of the world has shifted and a great change in thought has taken place. Fortunately with the spread of this Reiho, there will be many that supplement the way of the world and the minds of people. How can it be for just the benefit of curing chronic diseases and longstanding complaints?*

*A little more than 2,000 people became students of Sensei. Those senior disciples living in Tokyo gathered at the dojo and carried on the work (of the*

---

44  Takata also emphasized this point in her teachings.

45  Hayashi would always hang a scroll in the classroom of the Five Precepts when he taught a Reiki class. You can see this in the 1937 photo of Hayashi and Takata teaching together in the Hawaiian Islands, widely reproduced on the Internet but first published in Takata, ed., "Grey Book," n.p. Thanks to Phyllis Furumoto, I had a chance to view the *gokai* (Five Precepts) scroll that Hayashi gave to Takata. This scroll is shown hanging in many pictures of Takata teaching classes earlier in her career.

*late Sensei) and those who lived in local districts also spread the teachings. Although Sensei is gone, Reiho should still be widely propagated in the world for a long time. Ah, how prominent and great Sensei is that he offers the teachings to people out there after having been enlightened within!*

*Of late the fellow disciples consulted with each other about building the stone memorial in a graveyard at Saihoji Temple[46] in Toyotama-gun[47] so as to honor his merits and to make them immortalized and I was asked to write it. As I deeply submit to Sensei's greatness and am happy for the very friendly teacher/disciple relationships among fellow students, I could not decline the request, and I wrote a summary in the hope that people in the future shall be reminded to look up at him in reverence.*

*February, the 2nd year of Showa (1927 A.D.*

*Composed by: Ju-sanmi (subordinate 3rd rank),*

*Kun-santo (the 3rd Order of Merit)*

*Doctor of Literature Okada Masayuki*


*Calligraphy by: Navy Rear Admiral,*

*Ju-yonmi (subordinate 4th rank), Kun-santo (the 3rd Order of Merit),*

*Ko-yonkyu (the distinguished service 4th class)*

*Ushida Juzaburo*


Translated by Hyakuten Inamoto

---

臼井先生の 「戒名」 Usui Sensei's Buddhist name (posthumous)

---

**Reizan-in shūyo tenshin koji**

靈山院秀譽天心居士

---

俗名臼井甕男 Secular name: Usui Mikao

大正十五年三月九日没 Deceased, On March 9th, 15th Year
of Taisho (A.D. 1926)

靈山院 = Reizan-in

秀譽 = Shūyo

天心 = Tenshin

居士 = Koji

Note: A posthumous Buddhist name is customarily given a person upon death by a Buddhist priest of the temple to which the deceased used to belong. Usui Sensei's Buddhist name is typical of Jōdo-shū (Pure Land sect of Japanese Buddhism); again giving weight to the evidence that Usui was a Pure Land Buddhist at the time of his death.[48]

## Takata's version of Reiki history and Dr. Mikao Usui

Hawayo Takata would, on many occasions, give a free public lecture about the history of the Reiki system. For this reason, I feel it appropriate to include below an original transcription of one of these free lectures.[49]

*Recorded: August 24, 1979*[50]

This is the story of Dr. Mikao Usui who is the originator of the Usui Reiki Ryoho. That is in Japanese, which means Usui Reiki system of natural healing. And at this time in the beginning of the story, Dr. Usui was the principal of the Doshisha University in Kyoto, also minister on Sundays, and at the University they had a chapel. So he was a full-fledged Christian minister,

---

48   Information provided by Hyakuten Inamoto.

49   Transcribed by Tammy Worthington for Robert N. Fueston; edited by Debbie Coomer and Robert N. Fueston. A few times we removed phrases like, "and so I said" to make the transcript easier to read. However, we left the bulk of these phrases in the transcript so the reader can get a better understanding of Takata's speech pattern.

50   The best quality copy of the August 1979 tape I received was from Helen Borth.

and my teacher, who was Dr. Hayashi, was his pupil, and also he carried on the work after Dr. Usui's passing. So in other words, Dr. Chujiro Hayashi was his #1 disciple and this is through Dr. Hayashi that I have learned about Dr. Usui. I have never met him and he said that Dr. Usui was a genius, very, very brilliant, intelligent, great philosopher and a great scholar.

One day, on a Sunday, he was at the podium giving Sunday service or lecture and that day he found there were about a half dozen students on the front pew. Usually the students of the University sit in the back. Then he said "Good morning, everybody." He said "I am going to deliver our regular Sunday sermon." Then one of the boys raised their hand. He recognized him, and he said "Yes, what is it?" and this young man said "We who are sitting here are some of the graduate students which are, going to in two months be leaving this school, and we'll be graduating from this University. But we would like to know for our future, whether you have absolute faith in the Bible." And Dr. Usui said "Certainly, I do, and that is why I am a minister, and I accept the Bible as it reads."

So Dr. Usui was surprised to be asked. And then the boy said, "I represent this group, this graduating class and we would like to know more about your faith. Is it because you absolutely have faith in the Bible, that you accept the Bible as written?" And he said, "Yes, because I have faith, and also I have studied the Bible and therefore, I believe." Then the boy said, "Dr. Usui, we are young people in our twenties and we have a very big future. And we would like to clear this once and for all. And if you have so much faith in Christianity, I believe and you believe that Christ was able to heal by laying on hands." And Dr. Usui said, "Yes, I believe." Then the boy said, "We would like to believe as you do, we would like to have that kind of a faith but we ask you, you are our great master and great teacher. We honor you and we respect you. Please, give us one demonstration." So Dr. Usui said, "What kind of a demonstration?" He said, "We'd like to see you heal the blind or heal the lame, or walk on the waters." And Dr. Usui said, "Although I am a good Christian and I have faith and I accept the Bible as it is, and I know Christ did it, but I cannot demonstrate because I did not learn how to do it." So the boys said, "Thank you very much. Now we shall choose our way, and what we believe is we can only say that your belief in the Bible is a blind faith, and we do not want to have blind faith, and then to live all our lives. We want at least to see one demonstration so that we will be able to follow you, and accept and to have faith like you." So Dr. Usui said, "Well, since I cannot demonstrate at this time, let us not argue about it, but some day I would like to prove it to you. And when I find the way, I shall come back and I shall show you, and I can demonstrate, I hope. "And with this, I resign as of now. Immediately I will step down and I will put in my resignation as minister of Doshisha and also principal of this University". And he said, "Tomorrow being Monday, I shall start on a visa. And I shall go to a Christian country to study the Bible, and to study Christianity in a Christian country. And I might find the answer. And when I do, I shall come back. And I shall let you know that I can do what you have requested." And he said good-bye.

And he left the church as of that time. And the next day Dr. Usui started to apply for visa, and he chose America. And when this was all done, he took the boat, and he came and traveled by train, and he entered the University of Chicago.[51] He studied philosophy, but number one, he wanted to study the Christian, Christianity, and also the Bible. And when he went through the studies in America, he found that the Bible and the Christian school that he went to were identical, the teachings were the same. And he could not find in the Christian Bible even in America where Christ had left the formula of the healing.

So being in this University where they had philosophies of the world, he went into other philosophies. He studied Hinduism, Zoroastrianism, and of course Buddhism. When he came into Buddhism he found a passage where it said that Buddha healed by laying on the hands. He healed the blind, tuberculosis, and also leprosy. When he found this out he said "I should further my studies in Buddhism and to find out whether Buddha has left any kind of a formula for the healing art." So Dr. Usui spent seven years in the United States and then he said, "It is time for me to go back to a Buddhist country, and to study Buddhism and find the formula."

And when he arrived in Japan he did not waste any time. He went, he landed in Kyoto, where he lived before, and he went to all the great monasteries, and even today Kyoto is a mecca of temples and it is the seat. At that time Nara was the seat of Buddhism, but Kyoto had the most temples and the biggest monasteries in Japan. And so he decided to visit to every single one. So, he started with the most biggest temple, the Shin, and when he arrived there he met the monks, and he said "does the Buddhist Bible or the Sutras, the Buddhist Sutras, say that Buddha healed? Is it written down in your Sutras that Buddha had healed leprosy, tuberculosis, and the blind by laying on of

---

51 According to another audio recording of Takata recorded on May 7, 1978, by Barbara McCullough, Usui earned his living at this time in Chicago by having learned the French art of ironing dinner shirts. The full transcript of this particular audio recording can be found in: Judy-Carol Stewart, *Reiki Touch: The Essential Handbook*, second edition (Houston: Reiki Touch Institute of Holistic Medicine, 1995).

hands?" And the monks answered, they said, "Yes, it is written in the Sutras." He said, "Have you mastered the art, can you do it?" And the monks said, "Well, in Buddhism, physical is very important, but we consider the church, or ministry, is to minister the people so they have better minds. We want to straighten their minds first so they become more spiritual and then more show more gratitude and learn all the better things of life. And this is a temple or a church, and we monks do not have time for the physical in reaping the spiritual growth, spiritual healing is first." Dr. Usui bowed and said, "Thank you." And he walked away and he went to the ____. Then he went also to the different temples and everyone had the same answer. They said "Yes, it is registered in the Sutras, and therefore we accept and we believe that Buddha was a healer. But, we are trying to heal the mind first, and therefore we do not know anything about healing the body." After days and days and months of search, Dr. Usui was very depressed. But he did not give up. He said, "I have one more place to go." And finally he landed in a Zen temple.

And when he approached the temple, he rang the bell, and a little page-boy came out. And he said, "I would like to speak to the highest monk of this Zen temple." He said, "Please come in. and who are you?" And he said, "I am Mikao Usui and I would like to study Buddhism, and therefore I would like to meet the monk." So the message was delivered, and when the monk came out, he was about a seventy-two year old monk, very lovely face like a child, innocent looking, beautiful face, kindly voice and very gentle. He said, "Come in, and so you are interested in Buddhism." He said, "Yes, but first, I would like to ask you a question. Do the Zen believe in the healing?" He said, "Yes, we do. It is written in the Sutras that the Buddhist, that the Buddha did it, and so in Buddhism we have the healing." "Well, can you heal the physical self?" He said, "Not yet." And so he said, "What do you mean by not yet?" He said, "Oh, we monks are very, very busy, giving our discourses, and lectures and preaching so that the mind can be attuned for the spiritual level. And we want to better the minds first before we touch the physical." And then how are you going to get the physical training?" He said, "That will come. We have not given up although we do not have it yet. And therefore the Zen prayers and our chanting of the sutras are very necessary and our faith, is stronger than ever and we have not lost faith, and someday, during our various meditations, that we shall receive the great light, and then we shall know. Then we know we are ready, but just at this present, we are striving for it, but we know we are not ready. But before our meditation ends and before I go into transition I am sure this will all be enlightened and I will be able to do it." And he said, "Thank you very much." He said, "May I come in and stay here and study all the Sutras that you have? And also I would like to hear your lectures on Buddhism because I was a Christian minister and I have faith in the Christian Bible, and I looked all over and yet I could not find any formula of healing, though I believe that Christ did it, and I still believe it." And so the monk said, "Come in." And he said, "I would like to join your monks, your priests, and then study here."

It took him about three years to go all through the Sutras in the temple.[52] And when meditation hour came, Dr. Usui sat with the other monks in hours and hours of meditation. And then it became very vivid to him that this was not enough, so he told the monk, "Thank you very much for your very good help and for keeping me here, and I shall like to stay on and I would like to further my studies." And the monk said, "You are most welcome, because we believe in what you are searching, we believe too. And the only thing that we are doing besides prayers, we meditate a lot to receive. But, if you want to further your studies, he says, do it, right here in this temple."

So he said, "the Japanese characters that are written in the Sutras, all these characters, originally came from China. We have adopted the Chinese characters as Japanese characters, and so like when you read the Sutras, you cannot understand, but it's just like English people reading Latin, you know, but the characters are read as written." He could do it. So finally he went very deep into the Chinese characters and became a master of the Chinese characters. And after that was completed, he said, "Not enough," he said, "After all, Buddha was a Hindu, and therefore" he said, "I should study the Sanskrit, and if I study the Sanskrit, there may be something in Sanskrit taken note by the Buddha's disciple, because Buddha had many, many disciples, and that's how the scriptures were written."

And so, when he went into studying the Sanskrit, and when he really studied very hard to master it, he found a formula, just as plain as mathematics. Nothing hard, but very simple. Like two and two equals four, three and three equals six, as simple as that. And so he said, "Very well", he says, "I found it. But now, I have to try to interpret this, because it was written 2500 years ago – ancient. I don't know if this will work or not. But I have to go through the test. And going through this test," he said, "I cannot guarantee myself whether I will live through it, or not. But if I don't try the test," he

---

52  Interesting to note that the Usui Reiki Ryoho Gakkai's booklet, Reiki Ryoho No Shiori, also mentions Usui studying at a Zen temple for three years. Afterwards, he went up to Mount Kurama for a 21 day fast and meditation. There are more similarities between Takata's story and the story passed along in the Usui Reiki Ryoho Gakkai. I bought a copy of this booklet in 2012 online at: http://www.dlmarket.jp/products/detail/192787

said, "everything will be lost. We'll go back to zero."

And so, he talked it over with the monk, and the monk said, "Yes, you are a very courageous man. Where are you going to test this, right in this temple?" He said, "No, I would like to go up into the mountains," and this was in Kyoto also. Then he went up to Mount Kurama Yama. And he said, "I will test myself for twenty one days. And if I do not come back on the night of the twenty-first day, on the twenty-second day morning, send out a searching party into the forest to find my body. I may be dead." And so, with that farewell, he left, and he said, "I shall go on three weeks meditation without food – only water." So he took some water up and he found up in the mountains he found a stream that was close to water and therefore he sat under a big pine tree and he started his meditation. But before he sat down, he had no timepiece, no watch, no calendar, and so how was he going to know twenty-one days? So he gathered twenty-one small rocks or stones and then piled it in front of him and then his water jug, and he knew where to get more water if this ran out. And there he started his meditation, and so he said, "This is the first day." And then he threw one rock away - first day. And that's how he counted his days.

And he said, he expected some kind of a phenomena but he didn't know what. He didn't know what to expect. And all this time Dr. Usui, very faithfully, he read the Sutras, chanted, meditated and then he only drank water. And then every day came, then another day. Finally came the morning of the twenty-first, that was early morning. And he said, "The darkest of night is in the earliest of morning, before sunrise is the darkest." That's how he witnessed. There was not even one star, no moon or any kind of a light. He said the sky was just as dark, as dark as it could be. And when he finished his meditation and he said he opened his eyes and looked into the dark sky, and all he was thinking was, "This is my last meditation." And then he saw a flicker of light only large as a candlelight in the dark sky. And then he said, "Oh! Now, this phenomena, he said, very strange, but," he said, "it is happening, and I am not going to even shut my eye, or I shall open my eyes as wide as I can, and to witness what happens to them now."

And the light began to move very fast towards him. Then he said, "Oh, the light! Now I have a chance to shuck the light, or dodge. What shall I do?" Then he said, "Even if the light strikes me, and if I fall, you know, if I – the contact is so severe - that I might drop, or I might burn." He said, "this is the test," he said. "I am not going to run away, I'm going to face it." And when he faced it, he began to brace himself more, you know, and to say that, "Come!"As if to say, 'Come and hit me, I'm ready." And with that, he relaxed and his eyes wide open, he saw the light strike in the center of his forehead, and naturally he said, "I - with the contact," he said.[53] He fell backwards because the force was so great. But then he said, "I died, because I have no sense, no feeling, my eyes were shut and my eyes were open, but I couldn't see." And then he said, "I don't know how long, how many minutes I was down but," he said, "when I look," he said, "that light was gone, but I could see it was beginning to have daylight, and faraway I could hear the roosters crowing. And far away I could see that there were movements, and then I know that there was going to be dawn pretty soon."

Then he happened to look a little on the right side, and then he saw from the right side of his face millions and millions of bubbles all came out, bubbling up, bubbling up, bubbling up, bubbling up, millions and millions and millions of bubbles. And these bubbles all had colors. And they had the colors of the rainbow. And he said they danced in front of him and then went to the left, and then that went, he said, another streak of light. "This time" he said, "the color of another rainbow." He said, "the blue came out, and then went through the right, to the left" and then he said, "the lavender came out," and then he said, "the rose came out, and then the yellow came out," and he said he was counting those colors, and it had the seven colors of the rainbow.

And so Dr. Usui said, "Waaa! This is a phenomena I must not forget." Then last of all, he saw the great white light come from the right, and then like a screen", he said, "stood right in front of him, like a screen. And when he glued his eyes to the screen, he said, what he had studied in the Sanskrit, what he saw and studied in the Sanskrit, he said one by one came out, and then in golden letters, he said they just radiated out in front of him as if to say, "Remember, remember!" And so he said he didn't even blink his eyes but he just studied and studied and he said, "Yes, I remember." He said, "Then this one went to the left, and another came out." And all that what he had studied and learned out of the Sanskrit danced in front of him as if to say, "This is it, this is it. Remember, remember." And so he just glued his eyes, and he said he felt no pain, no hardship, and he said he felt no hunger, no thirst. He said, "I began to feel his/my body would float." And so when all this phenomena had passed on, and he said, "I must close my eyes and for the last meditation, and he did." And he could see all the glowing letters in front of him.

---

53   This transmission of Light received by Usui was the inspiration for the name of this book series.

And so he said, "Now, I can open my eyes and throw away the last stone." That was the last stone, and he said, "I'm going to stand up." And he stood up. When he stood up and he tried his legs and his feet on the ground, and he said, "They are strong. I sat for twenty-one days." But he said, "I feel I can walk back to Kyoto", which was, in Japanese, seventeen miles is almost about twenty-five miles, "but I will reach there before sundown" and he did. And he found that as if his body had had a big dinner last night. And he said, patted his stomach, and he said, "Well, that is the first miracle, I'm not hungry. And I feel very light." And he dusted all the pine cones and the dust and skirt.

Then he picked up his cane and his straw hat and he went down the mountain. And when he went down the mountain and almost to the foot of the mountain. When he stumbled on a little rock and then lifted his toenail, you see. Then the blood began to squirt out, and he felt pain. So he said, like this - just like anybody else would say, "Ah, I hurt myself." And he took his right hand and he held the thumb the toe. And when he felt the toe, he felt some pulsating, "thump, thump, thump, thump" as if there was a heartbeat in here. Then he kept on holding it, then he said the pain began to go away. And then the blood stopped flowing. And so he said, okay, to him, and he held it. And then when all the pulsation was gone, and the pain was gone, then he saw that the blood had all dried up, but the toe had gone back to its normal position, but he could see where all the blood had come out. Then he said, "That is the second miracle."

"Now," he said, "I must look for a snack bar." And when he looked around there was a bench with red blanket and an ashtray, Japanese ashtray is a big box, with pipes in it. In those days they all smoked pipes. And when you see that, in any strange place or any parks, that, that ah, means welcome. Red blanket is a welcome: "Please sit here. There is a snack bar close by."

And so he set his cane and his straw hat and he sat down and then he looked around, he looked around. And in the right hand corner he found that there was a snack bar, and a very old man. He had an apron on, un-shaved, starting the charcoal stove, you know, like the Japanese hibachi. So he walked up to him and he said, "Good morning, old man." And the man said, "Good morning, my dear monk." He said, "You are early." He said, "Yes. I would like to have that box of rice, you know Japanese left over rice they have a bamboo box made you know. And then they put the rice in there and a cover for rice box. If you have any left over rice from last night, I would like to have that rice and as soon as you make your tea, I would like to have that piece of nori that you ate today, I would like to have that nori, and also some salted cabbage, and also dried fish if you have any." (That is a regular Japanese breakfast.) And he said, "I shall wait for you at the bench." And so this old gentleman said, "I would love you to have the rice but you have to wait until I make a soft rice gruel, like mush." He said, "According to your dirty face," you know, that means Dr. Usui's dirty face is the beard, he said, "many people go up this mountain, this is known as a very famous mountain for meditation. And when they come down in seven days, one week of meditation, the beard is much shorter, and then some do two weeks, but according to your dirty face, you've been up there three weeks. And when you do not eat for twenty one days," he said, "I cannot let you have that rice and just hot tea and all those things to go with, because you're going to have acute indigestion, and when you have that, he says, I am no use, I have no medicine, and I cannot help you. And therefore, he says, seventeen miles away in the city of Kyoto, there are doctors. But I cannot reach the doctor. So therefore, he says, you have to wait."

So Dr. Usui said, "Thank you, you are very kind. But I think I shall try it." And so he crawled to the table, on the table and went for the rice box. He carried it, because he didn't want the old man to take it away. And left it by his red bench. And he waited, and in a few minutes the old man gave up already, he said, "Well if he wants to do it his way, fine." So he sent the girl. This was his granddaughter, about sixteen years old, and she brought out the tray with the rice bowl, chopsticks, and hot tea, pot of hot tea and with all the other ingredients to go with the rice. And so she put this on the red bench. And so this girl was crying – tears running down – and noticed that her face was swollen. And she had a big towel here, tied up here like rabbit ear. And so Dr. Usui looked at her and said, "My dear young girl," he said, "why do you cry?" she said, "Oh, my dear monk, three days and three nights I have a toothache so bad that I cannot stop my tears. And I cannot eat. I didn't have any kind of a food for three days and three nights. And it hurts so much I cannot stop my tears. And yet the dentist is so far away, I cannot ask my grandfather to take me seventeen miles to Kyoto. And therefore I have to just suffer and cry. But I can't stop my tears." So Dr. Usui stood-up and began to dig into her cheek and said, "Is this the one? Is this the one?", you know. Then when he came to the right one she said, "Yes, yes, yes." "Oh, all right!" Then he put his hand there. And then the girl began to blink, blink the eyes, and she said, "My dear monk, you just made magic!" He said, "How do you feel now?" She said, "The toothache is gone!" "Is it really? Are you telling me the truth?" "Yes, I do not have to shed tears any more. I can stop crying." And then she took off her rabbit ear and wiped her face. And by the time Dr. Usui put two hands on and then he said, "Now, I think you are well."

And the girl smiled, thanked him, and ran to the grandfather. And she said, "Grandfather, I took off my rabbit ears, the toothache is gone, and he is no ordinary monk, he makes magic!" That's what the girl said. So the grandfather came out, wiping his hands on the apron, and he said, "My dear monk, you did us a great service. You just did magic on my granddaughter, stopped the toothache. We are so grateful, oh we are so grateful, because she was suffering. And for our gratitude," he said, "the food is on the house. And this is all we can offer, because we do not have much, you know." And Dr. Usui put his hands together and said, "Thank you! I accept your gratitude. Thank you very much." And he said, "All right, now, for my food!" And he filled the rice bowl, and then put the hot tea and started shoveling with the chopsticks. And he ate happily, so the people didn't disturb him while he ate. But they were wishing that he wouldn't have any kind of indigestion. So Dr. Usui enjoyed his breakfast this way, and he said, "Now, this is the fourth miracle. The third miracle was the toothache gone." And he said, "I have no indigestion."

"Now, I'm ready to start on my seventeen mile hike and by sundown I shall reach the temple according to schedule." And he did. And when he did, he knocked at the doorbell, and that little pageboy came out. And he said, "Dr. Usui, we are so happy that you are home, because if you did not come home tonight, you know we were going to send a searching party tomorrow morning as you requested." You see, all the little monks in the temple, they are about six to ten years old. They go in when they are six years old to study Buddhism. And they are very, very wicked and very smart, you see, but that's how he tried to tease him. First thing Dr. Usui said, "How is our dear monk?" "Oh, he's suffering from arthritis, backache, and this is a cool evening, so he is hugging the chapel stove, and he is under silk covers." This is what the little pageboy said. "So if you will go and take a bath, and while you do this, we'll lay out your clean clothes and warm up your food. And after you've had your dinner, then you will visit the monk, who will be waiting for you. And he will be very happy to know that you are home and I shall deliver that message. So, go take your bath." And so he did.

And after his dinner, he went to see the monk. And the monk was sure in bed, hugging the chapel stove. He said, "My dear monk, I am back." The first thing he asked was, "How was it, how was your meditation?" "Success."

That is the only word he could use, was success. And the monk said, "Oh, I feel so happy, I feel so happy," he said, "Let me hear about it." And so he said, "Yes, and while I talk to you, I would like to put my hands on top of the silk covers," where he had the silk futon covers on him. And then told him all about what had happened, and from the time he sat for meditation and on the twenty-first morning, and what has happened throughout the day. And then it was late at night already so he said, "Very good, very good, we shall hear more about it, and let me think tonight," the monk said. "And by the way, my pain is all gone. I can sleep now, I can leave the stove alone, my body feels wonderful! I feel that I am very, very full of energy," and so he said, "This is what you call Reiki?" He said, "Yes, Reiki. We'll talk more about it tomorrow morning after our breakfast."

And so Dr. Usui had a good night's sleep, and so the monk, the next morning after breakfast, first thing Dr. Usui said, "What shall I do to experiment with this?" And so they talked over and over and the other monks came in, and they decided that the best place for him to experiment was to try and go into one of the very big slums in Kyoto.

And so they chose one of the largest slums, and in the slum they found all kinds of diseases, even leprosy. And so he went there as a monk, dressed up like a monk, but as a vegetable peddler. So he had one basket of vegetables in the front and one in the back and then he had a pole, and he carried that. And he walked and went into the slum, and all the beggars came out. And he said, "Oh, we are having a different kind of a guest today." And so Dr. Usui said, "Please, I would like to be one of you, I would like to live here." And so, they looked at him and he said, "If you want to stay here, we have a chief. And so we shall call him." So like in any gypsy camp you find a gypsy chief, you know, of the clan. And in this slum there was also a chief. So, when this chief was there, he came and he said, "I understand that you want to live here and become one of us." He said, "Yes." He said, "If that is the case, all right, let me have the vegetables." And he took all the vegetables. And he said, "No need to wear new clothes here. He said bring the initiation clothes." And so they brought the rags, dirty smelly rags. And then took off all his clothes off, and when they undressed him, they found a money belt on him over here, money belt, and also the chief smiled, and he said, "You see, my eyes are really sharp and keen. He said I could see all through those shining clothes, new skirt, new kimono, and a cloak you know. I could see the money belt. And that has to be released." And so he released it, and so the chief took it. Then he said, "All right, bring the clothes." And put on this initiation clothes.

And he said, "All right, the obi" and put the obi around.

Then he said, "Now you have gone through the initiation and you can stay here. But what are you going to do?" He said, "I will not beg for food outside of this compound. I would like you to give me a cottage by myself where you can send patients and I am going to heal." "Very good, that's a wonderful exchange for food. All right, we will feed you three meals a day, and give you a place to stay and where all the sick people visit you. We need it. And we have all kinds: impetigo, we have all kinds of diseases, even tuberculosis and leprosy."And he said, "You're not afraid to touch them?" He said, "No, I am a healer. So, I shall work from sunup to sundown, and therefore I want my meals brought up here". He said "This is a very, very good thing." So this pleased the slum chief very much, and of course they took all the money and everybody divided the vegetables, and so that was fine.

So Dr. Usui started the next morning, he started to do it. But before he started he chose his clients. All the ones that were sick got in a group, and then he chose young people, because he felt if they are young, the cause must be shallow. So he started to work on the cause and effect, cause and effect. And he was right. The older the person and the deeper the disease, he found it took many days and months. And so, when he worked on the shallow cases, in about a week they were all better and ready for new life. So he said, "You go to this address." And this was the temple, the Zen temple. "And ask for this monk, and he will give you a new name and he will give you a job. And you go into the city or anywhere they assign you, and become an honest citizen and forget the slum. Now that we have helped you physically, you are a complete whole."

And so this went on for years. So Dr. Usui had lots and lots of experiences. So, to make a long story short, if you ask me was he successful? Was he a success? Far from it! Because Dr. Usui when he left Kyoto and his ministry, he left in search of how to heal the physical. He thought he was a very good minister, so when he came back and went to all the Buddhist temples, searching, then all the monks said, "Spiritual first, the mind first and physical second. So why should we bother with the human body when we have medicine and doctors."

So Dr. Usui was disappointed, because that was not his aim. His aim was to do something for the body. So he forgot the spiritual side. And then all these people went out of the slum. He was there seven years. One evening at twilight he found himself at the Dojo. So he walked around the compound to see how much accomplishment. Then he found a familiar face. He said, "I don't know your name but your face looks familiar." And he said, "You too, and you too!" "But I don't know your name. Who are you?" He said, "Oh, you should remember. I was one of the first guys that came here and got healed, then you sent us to the temple. And when you sent us to the temple they gave us a new name, and we had a new job, and so we became honorable citizens and then we worked." And so Dr. Usui was disappointed. He received the greatest shock of his life. And he just threw himself on the ground, and there was a mud puddle, but he didn't, he had no choice, he just threw himself down. And he said that he cried and cried like a little child, and he said, "Oh, what did I do? I did not save a soul". So the physical is number two and the spiritual is number one. Therefore, all the churches in Kyoto were right, they were right and I was wrong. And therefore I am going to seal, absolutely seal, no beggars, no more beggars, no more beggars. And it was my fault for making them come back here as beggars." He blamed himself, he said. So while his head was in a mud puddle, he began to think and he said, "I forgot to teach them before they left, gratitude. All the beggars are here because they are people only greedy, greedy. Greed, greed, greed, greed. Want, want, want, – nothing to return, and nothing to show gratitude." So therefore, the five ideals were born at that time.

And the ideals are: Just for today, do not anger; just for today, do not worry. Number three, we shall count our blessings and honor our fathers and mothers, and our teachers and neighbors; and honor our food. We shall not waste any food, because food is also God-given, although the farmers they do cultivate it. But if you do have famine, you do not have food. But we have to show gratitude towards food. And then, number four, make an honest living. We have to work in order to make an honest living, which is number four. And number five is to be kind to everything that has life. These are the five ideals of Reiki. It was born at that instant when Dr. Usui recognized his failure.

And so he said, "If I had taught them the spiritual side of it first, and then healed the body, it would have been effective." But now all these beggars were coming back. He said, "How many years did you work outside?" "A couple years." "How many years did you work?" "Only about a year and a half. But it's easier to fill up my stomach rather than work," he said, "begging is a very easy profession." And he says "I fill up my stomach better than working and hustling by myself." And therefore he said, "Beggars are beggars, no more Reiki. No more healing for them." And that evening Dr. Usui walked out of the compound.

And then he made a pilgrimage all over Japan, you know the main island part from the north to the south on foot. And he chose a big mall, where the people will be there. And he took a torch, and lighted this torch and he would be walking up and down the mall where there were thousands of people. So one young man would come to him, and he said, "My dear monk, if you are looking for light," he said, "You don't need that torch. Today we have a lot of sunshine. This is a beautiful day," he said, "you don't need this torch light," he said, "we can see." He said, "Yes, that is very true, but I am looking and searching for people that have very sad, depressed minds. People are unhappy, I am searching for people that need this light to brighten their hearts and to take away their depression, and strengthen their character and their mind and body. And so if you want to hear this lecture, come to the church."

And so he visited every temple this way, on foot. And into one of his favorite ____, you know in one part of Japan, that's when Chujiro Hayashi, he was a retired Naval reserve, and he was a commander in the Navy. And when he heard Dr. Usui speak this way, he got interested, and so he attended his lecture. And when he attended his lecture, Dr. Usui kind of pointed him out after the lecture, and he said, "I see that you are a man that is a leader." He said, "Yes, I am. I have just served my time as a navy commander in the Imperial Majesty's force. And now, I am a reserve in the navy, so I have earned all that." So he said, "But you are too young to retire. So why do you not join me in this crusade, and then to help people? I think you would be a very good person to do this." And so Dr. Hayashi said, "Well, I will try. If you recommend so, I am interested too." And at that time, Dr. Hayashi was only forty-five. He was only forty-five. And so he walked with Dr. Usui all over. He said that he was with him, I don't know, I forgot how many years, but until Dr. Usui died, went into transition. And when he did, and he said ____ to go, and Dr. Usui announced that it was Dr. Chujiro Hayashi that was going to continue this Usui system in the art of healing.

This is the life story of Dr. Usui, which I have heard from Dr. Hayashi. And during his reign Dr. Hayashi never changed the system. It is even until today, and even my students, and my followers learn this art of healing as the Usui Reiki Ryoho, and in English, the suffix is Japanese, but it is the Usui System in the Art of Healing.

And this Reiki is Japanese word, but in English it is Universal Life Energy. But I use it as Reiki because I learned in Japan, and therefore I still continue to say it in the short word Reiki.

Dr. Usui had this experience at the beggars camp. And when he was down in the mud, the body in whole, that's when his thinking came out and he said, "Ah! I have made a great mistake. All the churches were right, spiritual first. And here, I did not preach the spiritual side, but I was so interested in healing the body that I just thought the best thing was to do the healing to make them well enough to appreciate, so that they could go out into the world as normal people." But he failed. And when he failed, the five ideals were born. And in these five ideals, where did the beggars fail? The beggars have no sense of gratitude. And therefore, he said, "I'll seal it! No more free treatments, no more Reiki, Reiki, Reiki, or classes, because, he said, they will never learn to appreciate."

And which is very true, that Dr. Usui forgot at that moment he was so happy that he could do it. And so he said, "The seven years of experience, I shall charge it to bad experiences, which I could not master. Therefore, he said, no more Reiki free, free. Everything has to be on the upper-upper, so that we will have a good mind, and a good body, good mind and body to make a human being a complete whole."

And this is very, very true. Because in 1936, when I came back from Japan, and Dr. Hayashi had warned me. He had warned me, he said, "Whenever you become a master, never do it free because they will never use it, because it was free. Because it was free, it has no value." But once again, I asked my teacher, "Dr. Hayashi, will you permit and consent that I have one class free. And that is for all the people that have helped me through these years of sorrow and my sickness." I said, "I would like to teach them and give them a free lesson in Reiki so that they could benefit." So Dr. Hayashi said, "Now that you are well, you can return your gratitude by giving them treatment when they need it, but not to say I'll hold a class for you people, and then to use it, and then to benefit yourself because that will never be effective."

Now with that understanding, I said to myself, "Well, I have to try." And so the first people that I gave free lessons were my best friends and relatives. They were my in-laws. All my in-laws had free lessons and then all my neighbors; they had free lessons. And then when my two sisters came, I said, "Wait, wait. I'm not going to teach you yet." So, my sisters were kind of upset, and said, "Well, we heard from all your neighbors and all the in-laws that you taught them something really wonderful." But I said, "I have to see their success first." So I said, "At this moment, I will say no for the moment." Then I waited. One day I was hanging my laundry, then my neighbor came and said, "My daughter didn't go to school today, because she had a little stomachache. And so I brought her. I said, "Why don't you go in and give her a treatment? Why, I said, why did I teach you? Why don't you try? You didn't even try?" She said, "No, why should I? You're the expert that lives next to me. So, it's easier to bring her to you than do it myself because I know she'll get well." And so that was one disappointment. And then on the other side of the town, another one said, "My daughter has runny nose and the teacher said go home because it's contagious, she has the flu. And so I brought my daughter, I want you to give her a treatment." I said, "Didn't I teach you?" She said, "Yes. Why should I, when I have a car and can run to you? You're the expert here, and when you do it I know they are going to get well." And so I said, "You never even tried to use it?" She said, "No, why should I?" You see, no gratitude whatever.

And believe it or not, I hid in my house and I cried. And then I looked towards Japan, and bowed my head to Dr. Hayashi, and also towards Dr. Usui's grave. I said, "Forgive me for being wrong. I did not help any person because they did not accept it gratefully and spiritually because they didn't spend a penny. It is very sad, but I will turn them down hereafter, so that I will make them use it.

Then after three months my sisters came again. And they said, "Now, do you have time?" I said, "Yes, I have time. But do you really want to learn Reiki?" And so my sisters said, "Yes, we heard good things about you, but why is it that all your in-laws know Reiki, and why not your own flesh and blood?" "Because there is a fee." "Oh, there is a fee. How much?" I said, "Three hundred dollars." And so she said, "Well, I don't have that kind of money right now. So I have to go home and ask my husband." I said, "Very good. And you don't have to pay me cash right now, but I said, "You can pay in installments. But I will not go to your house to collect the money. Every payday you come to my house." So, my sister was in a little not so happy happy place.

She went home, she talked over with her husband, and she said her husband said, "Did you ask your sister that you would like to learn Reiki?" And my sister said to her hubby, "Yes." "Well, if you had asked her that you want to learn Reiki, you pay the fee. And ask her, you will pay her by installments. And if she says she is not coming here to collect the money, you take the money to her, which is proper. It is proper everything is proper. And so you better do it and that is my answer." That's what he said. Because he said it was okay, my sister came back and then she said, "Yes, we will pay you installments, $25 a month". I said, "Fine, fine. I'll help you. Just live up to your word, that's all."

And so my two sisters learned, and they paid me installments. I didn't feel very, very happy about this thing, but it was the principle that I had to follow. And then what happened, the first time her daughter had asthma, she said, because she had paid such a big price, she had to use it. "I couldn't take her to the doctor. You know sister, it worked! And I am happy, I learned, and it works. And who ____. And so, I said, "Now you get your lessons?" She said, "Yes, I came to apologize, you know, for not being happy, happy and being radiant over it, until I experienced. But I know why you charged me. I know. Because you wanted me to be good, and a good practitioner. And then I do not have any more medicine bills and doctor bills. I don't have to go the hospital every time she has a cold, or every time she is asthmatic, every time bronchitis or stomachache." She said, "You know, I have three children." And so, she said, "Now I understand why I'm here today. I hang my head down very low, and then I come to thank you, and I appreciate it so much, I'll make good use of it." And she did.

Today she is a very, very successful woman. She has not failed any in her business. She has her own business. And then she's a great healer, yes. And then she said that "Everlasting I have this power, everlasting. It was the cheapest investment rather than buy a car. Couldn't be any cheaper than this," she said. And every time she sees me she says, "I give you Reiki." She gives me treatments all the time, every day if I am with her. And that is the gratitude.

And all today when I have seen these twenty-four people that I have given the free lessons, not one of them are a success. Not even in business or in their health. And therefore, my teachers were right, they are absolutely right.

## Comparing the Memorial Stone and Hawayo Takata's Story

Takata described Usui as seeing a light coming toward him and striking him. This light contained information that it passed on to Usui; this knowledge of Reiki he passed on to his students. Usui had received a transmission of light from the universe. Light carries information in it. We, in our modern times, use light the same way. For example, fiber optic cables use light to transmit data. This is how we both receive and transmit information in our technologically enhanced world. According to Usui's memorial stone, we are told that Usui, while receiving this transmission of Light, was taught Reiki Ryoho (Method for using Cosmic Energy).

Takata's story about Usui seeing millions of bubbles has drawn much criticism in our modern times. I myself was very skeptical about her descriptions of Usui seeing these colorful bubbles.

Then in 2013 while in Columbus, Ohio, I was watching Hyakuten Inamoto give a PowerPoint presentation and lecture on Mount Kurama. I was amazed when some of the photos contained many small colorful "orbs" or "bubbles" in them. I had seen orbs in other digital photographs but I never made the connection in my mind that what Takata was describing as "bubbles" were what are referred to as "orbs" today.

The realization that this part of the Usui story was true hit me like a ton of bricks. Usui, in his altered state of consciousness, was able to visually see these orbs without the use of technology, such as digital photography. Takata told this story before today's technology could allow anyone to view these unexplainable orbs. My mind opened up a little more after making this realization to the possibility that although some of Takata's stories may appear spectacular, that doesn't mean we should dismiss them; especially when we have no evidence to the contrary.

People talk about Takata being a great storyteller, and she was, but I think it would be more accurate to say that she had great stories to tell. The stories she told sound too great to believe for the majority of Reiki practitioners, especially the ones who don't yet have the experiences of seeing what Reiki can do. However, the more that we practice, the longer we practice, and the more we see with our own eyes some of the miraculous events that occur with Reiki, the better we come to understand the likelihood that the stories of Takata are not just *possible* but are *probable*. This is a realization that stems from both my own practice and research, and it is something I have seen in others who follow the teachings of Takata.

-----------------------------------------------------------

Takata mentions on this audio recording that Usui was working in the slums for seven years. However, this seems to have been remembered differently on different occasions. Fran Brown, one of Takata's 22 Masters, writes in her biography of Takata that Usui worked in the slums for three years, while another of Takata's Masters recounted that Usui worked in the slums for two years.[54] Perhaps Takata didn't remember the details of the story correctly — that happens! If these three dates suggest anything, it is that Takata couldn't

---

54 Fran Brown, *Living Reiki, 52;* Barbara Lugenbeel, *Virginia Samdahl: Master Healer* (Norfolk, VA: Grunwald and Radcliff, 1984), 74.

accurately recall exactly how many years Dr. Usui worked in the slums.

The memorial stone simply states, *"One day, he climbed Kurama-yama and after 21 days of a severe discipline without eating, he suddenly felt One Great Reiki over his head and attained enlightenment and he obtained Reiki Ryoho."*

Hiroshi Doi has claimed[55] that the date was in March of 1922, and this has been widely circulated and accepted without third party verification. Doi may have read this information in a book called *Everyone can do Reiki* by Fumio Ogawa, which states Usui went to Mount Kurama in 1922, or he may have been told this by the Gakkai. It is important to note that Ogawa mentions he was a member of the Gakkai in his book. So it would be no surprise then that the same date would be given.

Some people claim that Usui was practicing and teaching Reiki for many years before March of 1922. What I find interesting is an article written in 1928 by a student of Chujiro Hayashi named Shōō Matsui[56]. According to this article, Reiki Ryoho was founded "some decades ago". This would place its origins at least before 1918 (one decade), maybe even 1908 (two decades), but it could have been earlier than that. Since this article was written only two years after Usui's death, and is the older data, it seems more likely to this researcher that it would be more accurate. Weighing the likelihood of accuracy of conflicting data and dates is one such dilemma a researcher faces. If it is true that Usui started his Reiki experience in 1918 or earlier, it is possible that he could have spent seven years in the beggar village as Takata described.

The other reason I question the date of 1922 is that the Memorial Stone does not specify this year for Usui's mountain top experience. In fact, it should be pointed out that this is one of the few times an exact date is not given on the memorial stone. The other events in which the exact year was not given were also earlier events in Usui's life such as his trips abroad. The stone simply reads, *"One day, he climbed Kurama-yama"*. The writers of the stone seem to know the exact dates of later events in Usui's life, like the founding of the Gakkai, when Usui moved his dojo, etc. This makes me think it happened many years before these students met Usui and so they did not know the exact date.

--------------------------------------------------------------

Takata also mentions that Hayashi was Usui's successor. Recently, Reiki

---

55  I first heard this from Hiroshi Doi himself in 2002 while attending the Usui Reiki Ryoho International conference in Toronto, Canada.
56  See Appendix 3 for an original translation of the full article. A scan of the original article can be found at: http://homepage3.nifty.com/faithfull/sekisyu_2.htm.

practitioners have challenged this statement because the next president of Usui's school, the Usui Reiki Ryoho Gakkai, was not Chujiro Hayashi but a person named Juzaburō Ushida. Because of this, arguments have arisen that Hayashi could not have been Usui's successor.

However, there could be another explanation for this fact. As I will discuss in a later chapter, after Takata died, there was a split in the Takata Master students group. Two of Takata's Master students came forward stating that they were Takata's successor. The two Masters were Barbara Weber, who later became Barbara Weber Ray, and Phyllis Lei Furumoto, Takata's granddaughter. This created a big rift in the Reiki community at that time. While Phyllis Furumoto acknowledges that Takata had originally intended and trained Barbara Weber to be her successor, she also states that Takata changed her mind before her death in December 1980.

These two Masters went on to form their own separate Reiki organizations, the American Reiki Association headed by Barbara Weber, and The Reiki Alliance headed by Phyllis Furumoto. Takata's biographer Helen Haberly writes, "This river of Reiki that was a single channel in Takata now flowed in two major streams."[57] A similar occurrence may well have happened after the death of Dr. Usui, and Ushida and Hayashi may have each gone on to lead their own schools as successors.

----------------------------------------------------------

One of the many points in Takata's story about Usui was to emphasize the importance of the spiritual healing that needs to take place and not just the physical. Today, so many Reiki practitioners think Reiki is just about the physical health/body. I've heard Takata criticized for being interested only in healing the body and nothing spiritual, but nothing could be farther from the truth. Her whole life she emphasized treating both the spiritual and the physical. This is one "change" or deletion of the traditional Reiki training she offered, which was modified and dropped by later generations of Reiki masters. Now most of what people know of as "Reiki" has little resemblance to Takata's traditional teachings. Quoting Iris Ishikuro's notes, she writes, "Like a thunderbolt that had hit him, Dr. Usui came to the realization of how right the teachings of the churches[58] were. This is why the churches did not heal

---

57 Haberly, *Reiki* 111.
58 These "churches" Takata mentions she also called "Buddhist monasteries" at other times. She used these words interchangeably. This is likely because in Hawaii, where she grew up, Buddhist temples are called "churches".

the body – but rather tried to heal the people mentally and spiritually – to help them become better citizens. Dr. Usui realized what a great mistake he made. He was only thinking of the physical – that if he cured the aches and pains and made the people of the slums perfect human beings, he thought they would be grateful citizens. This was not so."

Takata emphasized that the spiritual and mental self is number one and the body is number two, but both are needed to create a whole. Takata states on an audio recording, "So we always say, the mental and the spiritual is number one; number two is the physical. And then you put that together and say we are a complete whole. And when you can say that, that means you have applied Reiki and Reiki has worked for you."[59] Regarding this experience, Fran Brown wrote, "It takes a good mind and a good body to make a human being a complete whole."[60]

--------------------------------------------------------

I would like to focus on three more statements Takata made that people today are challenging:

1. Usui was the principal of Doshisha University.

2. Usui was a Christian minister.

3. Usui studied Christianity at the University of Chicago.

Some people speculate that Takata was hoping that the vast majority of Christians here in the United States would accept another Christian, as she claimed Usui was, despite the fact of Usui being Japanese. Therefore, it is possible that Takata took some of the factual history she learned about Usui and changed it slightly when she taught Reiki to her students.

If this is the case, she did this for a good reason. During and after World War II, there was a lot of anti-Japanese sentiment in the United States, where Takata was living and teaching Reiki. The United States was even responsible for putting Japanese Americans in camps during World War II. So perhaps Takata decided to change parts of the Reiki history to suit her current audience. The idea that Reiki would survive may have been more important to her than whether or not the founder's religion, for instance, needed to be changed.

However, as I will point out, Takata's statements may be the truth. Let's take Takata's statements one at a time.

---

59  Takata, *Takata Speaks: Volume 1, Reiki Stories.*
60  Brown, *Living Reiki,* 56.

## 1. Usui was the principal of Doshisha University.

As I cannot read, write, or speak Japanese, I cannot accurately research this statement. However, fellow researcher Naoko Hirano has made an initial inquiry into this and received the answer that Usui was not the principal there.

In a letter dated December 17, 1991, William Rand received a letter from Doshisha University announcing they had no records of a person named Mikao Usui.

I would suggest further research into the matter, offering up the possibility that he was simply a faculty, adjunct faculty member, or a visiting professor (the latter I would guess would be the hardest to actually track down and verify).

For example, in my research of Barbara Weber, she has listed on her resume the date and topic of a lecture she gave at the University of Kentucky. However, the University of Kentucky and their archives department do not have any information regarding this event. Archive departments do not keep everything. Selection of what to keep and what not to keep is based on the judgments of the archivist. In many cases, materials are thrown out by departments before getting to the archivist.

## 2. Usui was a Christian minister.

Taking a scholarly approach, it would seem that Usui was a Pure Land Buddhist at the time of his death, since his gravestone is in a cemetery of the Pure Land sect.[61] However, the story Takata would tell about him having been Christian may have been true as well. According to Usui's memorial stone, Usui studied Christianity, among other religions, and he may have converted for a short period of time. It would seem that Usui would have been a serious student of Christianity for it to be specifically mentioned on the stone pointing out only the highlights of his life.

According to Takata's own story, Usui was unable to find the answer to how Christ had healed by further study into Christianity and the Bible. At that point, Usui gave up his study of Christianity and decided to further investigate Zen Buddhism to learn how to perform hands-on healing. It is interesting to note that a booklet called the *Reiki Ryoho No Shiori* (Guide to Reiki Ryoho) that was published by the Usui Reiki Ryoho Gakkai for its members also states that Usui was a missionary (*fukyōshi*) and a chaplain

---

61   My gratitude to Reiki Master Hyakuten Inamoto for this information.

(*kyōkaishi*) before he studied in a Zen monastery for three years.[62] This word for chaplain refers to a religious professional working in a prison, usually a Buddhist monk/priest. However, as there are some pre-war examples of Christian prison chaplains. This text from the Gakkai does not explicitly state Usui's religion and it remains possible that he had been Christian for at least part of his life.[63]

In Takata's story it seems that Usui left the Christian faith before he died, so therefore he wouldn't be buried as a Christian. Takata never gave any indication that Usui later went back to Christianity. Given the fact that Usui's quest led him to his experience on Mount Kurama was directly related to his study of Buddhism, it would seem logical that he wouldn't stray from Buddhism after his experience on Mount Kurama. At the time of his death, it is safe to state that he was a Pure Land Buddhist.

It is interesting to note that the robes Usui Sensei wore in the photographs we have of him appear to be a *dōgi* 道着, kind of a hybrid between Buddhist robes and martial arts robes.[64]

### 3. Usui studied Christianity at the University of Chicago.

Usui's memorial stone mentions that Usui came to the United States, as well as Europe. Takata was even more specific than this and stated he came to Chicago. Assuming Takata actually knew about Usui traveling to America, and hadn't just made a lucky guess that turned out to be true, it seems likely that her other information about Usui studying at the University of Chicago would also likely be true.

Again, according to the memorial stone, Usui did come to the USA, but did he study at the University of Chicago as Takata claimed?

To attempt an answer to this question took some extensive research. The University was founded on July 1, 1891, and held its first classes on October 1, 1892, with an enrollment of 594 students and a faculty of 120. I contacted the Special Collections Research Center at the University of Chicago Library for help in tracking down students who attended the school from its inception to 1922. You may see our correspondence below.

---

62  *Reiki Ryōhō no Shiori: Kai'in no Tame ni (Reiki Ryōhō Guidebook: For Members)*. Edited by the Shinshin Kaizen Usui Reiki Ryōhō Gakkai. Self-published, 1974. I obtained a copy in 2012 from: *http://www.dlmarket.jp/product_info.php/products_id/192787*

63  Email from Naoko Hirano to Justin Stein dated May 18, 2015. In another email to Stein dated January 24, 2015, Hirano stated that the characters used here for *fukyōshi* were primarily used by Jōdo-shū and Nichiren Buddhists, while Jōdoshin-shū used a different character for the same word, and Christian missionaries would usually be called *senkyōshi*. She also said that the "entering the gate of Zen" expression means that someone sat *zazen* at a Zen temple, but it doesn't necessarily mean they took monastic vows - during this period there were a number of temples that held meditation training for householders (laypeople).

64  Again, thanks to Hyakuten Inamoto.

Hello,

I am currently doing research into the possible attendance of a person named Mikao Usui at the University of Chicago. Mr. Usui would have attended the university there sometime between the university's inception in 1890 and 1922 - that's a 32 year span...I wish I could have narrowed it down a bit more for you. It is most likely that Mr. Usui would have attended between 1912 and 1922... but the earlier years are very possible for his attendance. I would like to verify if Mikao Usui did attend the University of Chicago and was told there would be records kept of student enrollment during these times. Thank you for your help, the findings will be published in an upcoming book I am writing.

Dear Robert Fueston:

Thank you for your interest in Special Collections Research Center at the University of Chicago Library. Your question was forwarded to me for reply. I searched our student records and found no evidence of a student named Mikao Usui enrolled at the University of Chicago in any division.

You may want to contact the Registrar's office for certainty. As you can imagine, if Usui was a student here, the Office of the Registrar is careful about releasing student transcripts to anyone other than the student or his or her next of kin and you will need to explain why you need the transcript for your research. The Registrar's main phone number is 773-702-7891.

Best,

Monica Mercado
Reader Services Assistant
Special Collections Research Center
University of Chicago
1100 E. 57th Street
Chicago, IL 60637

After receiving this e-mail from the Special Collections Research Center, I contacted the University of Chicago's Registrar's office by phone for certainty. I then forwarded my prior correspondence with the Special Collections Research Center. I received several e-mails during the following week, with this one being the conclusion:

Hello Robert,

I searched through our microfilm records from 1892-1962 and did not find any record of a student by the name of Mikao Usui; I also checked Usui Mikao for good measure.

I'm afraid there is no record of this person having attended the University of Chicago.

Best,

Rita

p.s. It just so happens that the microfilm reels I checked contained transcripts from the 1892-1962 time period. They are organized alphabetically; not by year which is why the date range is so big.

Rita Vazquez

Assistant University Registrar
University of Chicago
5801 S. Ellis Ave., Admin 103
Chicago, IL 60637
(p) 773.702.7452
(f) 773.702.3562
registrar.uchicago.edu

At this point I thought that my research might come to an end. However, after speaking with Reiki Master Marta Getty, she told me that her initial teacher, Bethal Phaigh, said that Takata told her that Usui studied at a theological seminary *associated* with the University of Chicago.

I wrote the following e-mail to the University of Chicago:

Hello,

This is a follow up question of sorts to your earlier reply. Can you tell me if the Divinity school at the University of Chicago was perhaps an independent school before the University of Chicago existed. Any history or points in the right direction would be helpful. Even the entry level data usually found on Wikipedia on these matters is lacking a history section for the University of Chicago Divinity School.

There is a seminary here (Lexington, KY) that is affiliated with the University of Kentucky but it is still independent of the university. However, they have a relationship and honor each other's classes - they even offer a dual degree together (Master of Theology/Religious Studies from the seminary and Master of Social Work from U.K.).

I am trying to find out the existence of all theology schools in Chicago from 1890 -1922. I will be asking the public library for their help in locating these (if any existed). Thank you.

Sincerely,

Robert N. Fueston

Upon asking the right question, I received this reply:

Dear Mr. Fueston,

Thank you for your inquiry.

I can confirm that the University of Chicago Divinity School was previously an independent seminary that was called the Baptist Union Theological Seminary. This seminary emerged from the Baptist Theological Union (founded 1863), which sought to provide theological education to students at the first University of Chicago (1856-1886). The Baptist Theological Union created the Baptist Union Theological Seminary in 1867.

The seminary's original buildings near the Old University of Chicago on the South Side were dedicated in 1869. In 1877, however, the seminary was enticed by debts on its property and the offer of free land to move to the Chicago suburb of Morgan Park. When John D. Rockefeller offered money to endow the new University of Chicago (founded in 1890), he did so on the condition that the Baptist Union Theological Seminary would become the Divinity School of the university. The union occurred in 1892, while the Baptist Theological Union continues as a supporting arm of the Divinity School.

For more information, see the finding aid to the Baptist Theological Union and Baptist Union Theological Seminary Records, here http://www.lib.uchicago.edu/e/scrc/findingaids/view.php?eadid=I-CU.SPCL.BTUBUTS. You might also consider consulting the book Harper's University: The Beginnings, by Richard J. Storr (University of Chicago Press, 1966).

Please let me know if you have any additional questions. If you are looking for additional seminaries, I can also help you locate others in the Chicago area, some of which were affiliated with the University at various times.

Regards,

Thomas Whittaker
Reference Assistant
Special Collections Research Center
The University of Chicago

This was a potential breakthrough in my research. First, apparently there was an *old* University of Chicago in existence from 1856-1886. Second, the news about the Baptist Union Theological Seminary and its records being accessible seemed promising.

After reviewing the online finding aid, it was time to make a trip to the new University of Chicago archives department to go through the Baptist Union Theological Seminary records to look for Mikao Usui's name.

Days of searching ensued where I went carefully page by page through handwritten notes, books, and ledgers from the late 1800s to the early 1900s.

I read all about the relationship between the Baptist Union Theological Seminary and the University of Chicago. I pored through most of the materials that I thought would most likely contain Mikao Usui's name.

Apparently, many people came from different European countries to attend this seminary. I recalled that the memorial stone stated that Usui had traveled to both Europe and America, but I do not know if he came to America before or after his European trip.[65]

To top it off, there were a number of obstacles to finding Usui's name in the archive records. First of all, the records of attendance are not complete; there are missing years. To complicate matters more, the alumni directories for the Old University of Chicago (a.k.a. Chicago University) state that they contain only those alumni who received bachelor's degrees. This makes me wonder what other types of degrees were being offered by the old University of Chicago at the time.

Furthermore, some Japanese who came to the United States to study took on Anglicized names. For example, Jo Nijima, founder of Dōshisha University in Kyoto, took on the name Joseph Hardy Neesima while attending Amherst College and Andover Theological Seminary in the United States.

In the end, I did not find Usui's name. There could be many reasons for this. To summarize, some reasons why Usui's name would not be found simply by calling the new University of Chicago and asking are:

1. The new University of Chicago, the one currently in existence, does not contain the student rosters and registrations of students who attended the Old University of Chicago in either its electronic database or its microfilm. These are only found in print sources at the University.

2. The four or five seminaries that were affiliated with the University of Chicago during Usui's lifetime kept their own student rosters. These

---

65  Knowing whether Usui first came to the United States from its east or west coast would help to narrow down Usui's possible entry point for future research into finding his immigration records.

would not be found in the new University of Chicago's records. Only one of these seminaries, the Baptist Union Theological Seminary, has handwritten records that can be found in the new University of Chicago's archive department.

3. There were hundreds of handwritten pages in the student rosters. I was not able to go through all the pages in the time I had allotted to spend in the archives.[66]

To give the readers an understanding of what the rosters that I searched for look like, I am including a few pictures.

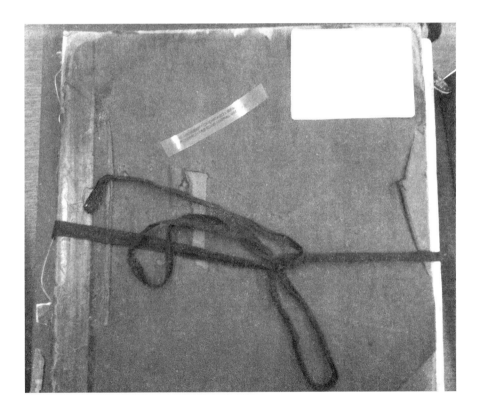

---

66 I normally bring an assistant with me, usually one of my students, but none of my students were available for this trip.

Students of the Baptist Union Theological Seminary, Chicago

*Robert being dramatically funny for the camera while looking for Usui's name at the University of Chicago's archival department. Researching can be both serious and fun!*

The research isn't over, however. As previously mentioned, during my time spent in the archives I discovered that there were actually four or five more seminaries located in Chicago during Usui's time that also had a close affiliation and relationship with the University of Chicago. The relationship was so intimate that these other seminaries could offer their students degrees from "The University of Chicago" although technically they were separate institutions.

One of these seminaries that need to be researched is called the Chicago Theological Seminary. Could Usui have studied at the Chicago Theological Seminary? Even today the Chicago Theological Seminary (CTS) offers in conjunction with the University of Chicago a dual-degree master's program in social work and divinity. This is the same sort of relationship that seminaries during Usui's time offered with the old and new University of Chicago.

I contacted this seminary but was told that due to their current move, all their archives are still in boxes and unavailable at this time.

Evidence also supports the possibility that Usui perhaps studied the subject of Philosophy and not Religion while in Chicago. This also needs to be followed up on.

Based on Usui's memorial stone and Takata's testimony, we know that Usui did come to the United States, but we do not know exactly where at this point. I plan to pick up the threads of this research and perhaps check immigration and emigration records of that time — both in Japan and in the United States. There are records in existence just lying around, waiting to be found somewhere out there.

*Historical point: During the Meiji Period (1868-1912), Japanese society went from a largely agrarian economy to a more industrial one. To support this change, many Japanese scholars were sent abroad to the United States and Europe by the Japanese government to study Western science, technology, and languages. Mikao Usui would have been between the ages of three and forty-seven during the Meiji Era. Logically, then, since scholars were sent out from Japan, these scholars would have been adults. To narrow down one's search, it would seem most likely that Mikao Usui left Japan sometime between 1883 and 1912. But to be more thorough, researching from 1883 to 1922 would be more appropriate. This would be the most likely timeline for future research.*

*It seems that Usui was very well-read, as the memorial stone states: "He was by nature versatile and loved to read books. He engaged himself in history books, medical books, Buddhist scriptures, Christian scriptures and was well versed in psychology, Taoism, even in the art of divination, incantation, and physiognomy."*

*Takata also states that Usui was very well-read and educated. In her story about Usui, she said that he went on to learn Chinese characters and then Sanskrit so that he could study the old Buddhist sutras (books) in their original language. Clearly, Usui was a scholar by any definition of the word and therefore a likely candidate to be sent abroad to study.*

## *Chapter* FOUR

---

### Chujiro Hayashi

# *Chujiro Hayashi*

## Chujiro Hayashi
### *September 15, 1880 - May 11, 1940* [67,68]

---

67  Frank Arjava Petter, Tadao Yamaguchi, and Chujiro Hayashi, *The Hayashi Reiki Manual: Traditional Japanese Healing Techniques from the Founder of the Western Reiki System* (Twin Lakes, WI: Lotus Press, 2004), 13. They cite their source as "'Taishu-Jinjiroku' (general biographical dictionary) published in 1940."

68  May 10, 1940 is the date that Takata gives on many occasions as Hayashi's date of transition.

My research into Chūjirō Hayashi has been limited. I want to focus on just some highlights about his life and what was said and written about him by people who knew him.

When Hayashi met Usui at one of his lectures, he was a retired naval officer. It is unclear exactly what year Hayashi met Usui. Takata has stated that she didn't know what year it was, but she does say on an audio recording that Hayashi met Dr. Usui when he was about 45 years old.[69] Takata's Master student Iris Ishikuro also wrote in her notes that Hayashi was about 45 years old when he met Usui and died when he was 62. If Hayashi was born on September 15, 1880, and died on May 11, 1940, this would make Hayashi 59 years old when he died. However, the Japanese have a different way of counting a person's age. When a baby is born, they are considered one year old already. In addition, on the first New Year's Day you become one year older again. So, since Hayashi was born on September 15, 1880, according to the Japanese he would have been three years old on September 15, 1881. So when Hayashi died in May of 1940, he would have been 61 years old, just four months shy of being 62 years old.

This would seem to imply that Hayashi had been practicing Reiki for 16 years (61-45 = 16. 1940-16=1924). And since he died in 1940, this means he would have met Usui around 1924. But the truth is Iris said he was about 45 years old, so we really cannot determine an exact date strictly using dates given by Takata. However, if Takata was correct about Hayashi being retired when he met Usui, then we can use the date of his retirement to further pinpoint or confirm the date of Hayashi meeting Usui. For example, if Hayashi had retired in 1925, then this would provide more evidence of their meeting in 1925 or 1926. If Hayashi had retired as early as 1923, then their meeting may have occurred anywhere from 1923 to 1926.

Takata would sometimes refer to Hayashi as "Dr. Hayashi," and people have taken this to mean that Hayashi was an allopathic medical doctor, an M.D; this of course is a possibility.[70] There is allegedly some evidence that Hayashi underwent some medical education as part of his naval officer training, yet Naoko Hirano's searches of the Imperial Naval Medical Academy archives have not found Hayashi's name. In an article in the October 2, 1937, issue of the Japanese-language *Hawaii Hochi* announcing Hayashi's imminent arrival in Honolulu, he is called an "ex-naval surgeon and captain" (*zaikyō*

---

69   Hawayo Takata, *Takata Telling the Stories of Dr Hayashi, on CD*, Reikivisions.com, 2003.

70   Yet, interestingly, Takata calls him "Mr. Hayashi," not "Dr." in her diary entry dated May 1936. Takata, ed., "Grey Book," n.p.

*kaigun gun'i taisa*).[71] As this article was written before Hayashi's arrival in the islands, it is likely that Takata provided the information contained therein. It is possible that the reporter confused Dr. Maeda with Dr. Hayashi while writing the article. (I give a personal account of an inaccurate interview being published in Appendix 1.)

Takata refers to Hayashi as a commander in the Navy on one audio recording.[72] However, Shōō Matsui's 1928 article in the *Sunday Mainichi* (Appendix 3) and articles from the *Hawaii Hochi* in the 1930s (Appendix 4) all stated Hayashi was a captain, which is one rank above a commander. As most civilians aren't particularly detail-oriented when it comes to a sailor's military rank, the difference here is understandable. Takata may have thought that Hayashi was in charge of others, making him a "commander," without realizing that a commander is also one of the officer ranks in the Navy.

Furthermore, she said that he was a battleship officer who had the responsibility for giving orders that could result in the killing of thousands of people. This is important, as it demonstrated that Hayashi was what is called a "line officer" in the U.S. military: an officer who exercises general command authority and is eligible for operational command positions. This is in comparison to specialty officers, who are noncombatant officers such as medical doctors, attorneys, and chaplains, for instance. Specialty officers do not assume combat command roles; i.e., they do not give combat orders. It is possible of course that Hayashi had been both a line officer and a specialty officer during his naval career.

Furthermore, in the West, especially during our more modern times, we are a little narrow-minded about exactly who we think of when we hear the word "doctor." We typically think of an allopathic, i.e. "Western," medical doctor and not a person holding a Ph.D., or doctorate, in Philosophy for example. We also must remember that what we think of as Western medicine has only been around about 100 to 150 years. The treatments used before this time frame by western doctors would today be considered quackery, like bloodletting, for example.

Probably during Hayashi's time in Japan things were different than they are today. Today in some states in the United States an acupuncturist is considered a primary health care physician. This was certainly true in China for

---

71   "Reiki Ryōhō's Mr. Hayashi Chūjirō Arrived in Hawaii — Ex-Naval Surgeon and Captain — Will Stay Until December," *The Hawaii Hōchi,* October 2, 1937, available at http://thescienceofsoul.wordpress.com/ last accessed December 25, 2014.

72   Hawayo Takata, *Takata Telling the Stories of Dr Usui,* on CD, Reikivisions.com, 2003.

centuries and may have been true in Japan at this time.

Simply stated, what do you call a person who runs a clinic and treats patients? Answer: a doctor! We know Hayashi was running a clinic and healing people with Reiki. And based on his guidelines for treatment, it is apparent to people who have the sort of training to recognize it that Hayashi was familiar with what is commonly called Traditional Chinese Medicine.[73] In other words, he was an "Eastern medical doctor." His hand placements for Reiki treatments make a lot of sense to an acupuncturist or a person familiar with both meridian and organ theories of Traditional Chinese Medicine.

John Harvey Gray also stated he was told that Hayashi's system of treatment was mostly based on Asian medicine. I can attest to this statement wholeheartedly. I have a Master of Acupuncture and Oriental Medicine degree and am nationally certified in both Acupuncture and Chinese Herbology. This, along with teaching and giving Reiki treatments, is how I earn my livelihood. Reading the booklet Hayashi gave out to his students, it is apparent to me by the body areas that he suggests treating for different illnesses that Hayashi was a doctor, according to this more traditional definition of doctor. Only a person with Chinese medical training would understand the reason why the soles of the feet would affect the tongue or why treating the ovaries would affect the eyes. Time and time again, Hayashi (and later Takata) gave instructions for treating various illnesses as understood in Chinese (Asian) medicine.

In addition, upon reading the Hayashi manual, it is very apparent that Dr. Hayashi had some medical training in allopathic medicine. Most people reading the Hayashi manual would not know the names of the diseases listed in his treatment manual without allopathic medical training. Traditional Chinese Medicine practitioners in the United States, such as myself, are also required to complete many hours of Western medical training in subjects such as biology, anatomy and physiology, Western pathology, pharmacology, etc.

And finally, on Takata's Dai-Shihan certificate, it states, "THEREFORE, I, Dr. Hayashi…"[74]

Since Hayashi's history is intertwined with the history of his most famous Master student, Hawayo Takata, much more about Hayashi can be found in the next chapter.

---

73  There are eight branches of Chinese Medicine: Herbal Medicine, Acupuncture, Exercise (being either Tai Chi Chuan or Qi Gong), Dietary Therapy, Meditation, Feng Shui, Tui Na (Massage), and Astrology.

74  Takata's certificate also mentions "Dr. Usui." I do not believe that Usui was a physician but was a scholar and that this is why he is referred to as "Dr. Usui." Both the memorial stone and Takata told of how well-educated Usui was. In this respect, Usui is referred to as "Dr." because of a doctorate degree, probably bestowed upon him while studying at a college affiliated with the University of Chicago. My research on this topic is ongoing.

# *Chapter* FIVE

## *Hawayo Hiromi Kawamura Takata*

# CHAPTER
# 05

---

## *Hawayo Hiromi Kawamura Takata*

### Hawayo Hiromi Kawamura Takata [75]
*December 24, 1900 - December 11, 1980*

To Iris & family.
Seasons Greetings,
A Happy New Year
and lots of Love.
this is my latest photo.
Gratefully yours
Hawayo Takata

*Original photo sent from Takata to Iris Ishikuro. Photo taken by Gunter Baylow (husband of Ursula Baylow)*

---

75 Although Takata would sign her Reiki certificates Hawayo K. Takata, the "K" standing for her maiden name, Kawamura, she gave her name as Hawayo Hiromi Takata in her interview with Sally Hammond, We Are All Healers (New York: Harper & Row, 1973), 283. The name Hawayo Hiromi Takata was also used during a Senate meeting on Hilo, Hawaii, on the topic "Problems of the Aging."Hawayo Takata, "Statement of Mrs. Hawayo Hiromi Takata, Senior Citizen," in Problems of the Aging: Hearings Before the Subcommittee on Federal and State Activities of the Special Committee on Aging. United States Senate Eighty-Seventh Congress, First Session, Part 12—Hilo, Hawaii, December 1, 1961. Washington: U.S. Government Printing Office, 1962, 1601-1603. Available at http://www.aetw.org/reiki_takata_special_committee.html, last accessed December 1, 2014. Credit to James Deacon for finding this document.

Hawayo Hiromi Kawamura, later known by her married surname "Takata," was born on December 24, 1900, in Hanamaulu, Kauai (one of the Hawaiian Islands). Her parents were Otogoro and Hatsu Tamashima Kawamura, who had immigrated there from Japan.[76] Before she was born, her parents had lost a daughter, named Kawayo after the island of Kauai[77]. They hoped by naming Hawayo after the Big Island of Hawaii, she would grow to be big, strong, and prosperous.

In 1913, at the age of 12, she had to work in the fields of a sugar plantation to help her family.[78] She was physically small, not terribly strong for a 12-year-old, and needed assistance from the other workers to complete her tasks. At the end of the season Takata put forth a request to God that she never have to go back to work in the sugar cane fields. Shortly after this, her prayers were answered.

Hawayo was offered a job as a first-grade substitute teacher. She was given room and board by the principal and was expected to do her own schoolwork at night. For this, she earned a five-dollar gold piece and a silver dollar that she gave to her family.[79]

The next summer, 1914, there was a grand opening of a store in Lihue, Kauai. This was a very big event for the area, and the owner was having a difficult time keeping up with the customers. The owner knew Hawayo and asked her if she could help him in the store for the day. Seeing that Hawayo was a good worker, the owner offered her a permanent job at his store. Hawayo and her parents agreed she could work there on Saturdays. Now Hawayo was working two jobs and going to school!

Takata states that one day an "Elegant Lady"[80] came into the store and was pleased with the service she received from Hawayo and offered her a better-paying job. Hawayo started out as a waitress-pantry girl but eventually rose to be the major-domo of the lady's sugar plantation. This job led Hawayo to meet her future husband, the accountant for the plantation.

---

76  Mary Straub, "Reiki — Japanese Method of Healing Could Spark Public Interest Similar to Chinese Acupuncture," *The Tinley Park Times Herald*, November 13, 1974, p. 13.

77  Patsy Matsuura, "Mrs. Takata and Reiki Power," *Honolulu Advertiser*, February 25, 1974, p. B-2.

78  Hawayo Takata, unpublished autobiography transcript *Reiki is God Power*, page 5 of session 1, recorded December 12, 1979, private collection of Phyllis Furumoto.

79  Hawayo Takata, unpublished autobiography transcript *Reiki is God Power*, page 6 of session 1, recorded December 12, 1979, private collection of Phyllis Furumoto.

80  Thanks to the research of Justin Stein, we have discovered this elegant lady's name was Julia Makee Spalding.

Picture of the "Valley House" where Takata worked, built by Colonel Zephaniah Smith Spalding (1837-1927).[81]

Hawayo married Saichi Takata on March 10, 1917.[82] In the 1920s, Saichi developed lung cancer, and Hawayo accompanied him when he went to Japan to receive treatment from Dr. Maeda.[83]

One day in October 1930, Saichi explained to Hawayo his views on life and death as well as his funeral arrangement wishes. Saichi explained that in reality there is no such thing as death, just transition from one form into another. He also explained that he would be able to be in contact with her for guidance after his physical body had died.[84] On October 7, 1930 Saichi died[85, 86] leaving Takata, at the age of twenty-nine, to raise two small children, Julia[87] and Alice.[88] Takata would often refer to Saichi as her guiding light.[89]

By 1935, Takata was overworked and stressed. She developed several health issues: gallstones, asthma, chronic appendicitis, a benign tumor, and exhaustion. One day, after she complained bitterly in meditation and was feeling very much alone, she heard a voice speak to her. It came as clear as a bell and said, "Get rid of your illness and you will find health, happiness and security." She couldn't believe this to be true until she heard it over and over again. This is one of the many times Takata would experience what today we call clairaudience.

In 1935, her sister died[90] of influenza.[91] Takata needed to inform her parents of her sister's death and get treatment for her own health problems. She

81  Picture from: http://thegardenisland.com/lifestyles/col-spalding-s-valley-house-christmas-celebration/article_525d841c-472f-11e2-8c39-001a4bcf887a.html

82  Fran Brown, *Reiki Takata's Way,* n.p. and Barbi Lazonby, *Reiki: Transforming Your Life, Volume 1: Healing with your Hands,* n.p.

83  Personal conversation with Phyllis Lei Furumoto; Brown, *Living Reiki,* 18.

84  Brown, *Living Reiki,* 18; Haberly, *Reiki,* 16; Barbara Weber Ray and Nonie Greene, *The Official Reiki Handbook,* first edition, (Atlanta: A.I.R.A., 1982), 59.

85  A number of sources, including interviews with Takata, say that Saichi died of a heart attack. Mary Straub, "Reiki — Japanese Method of Healing Could Spark Public Interest Similar to Chinese Acupuncture," *The Tinley Park Times Herald,* November 13, 1974, p. 13; Haberly, *Reiki,* 15; Lazonby, *Reiki,* n.p. However, other sources indicate that he died of lung cancer: Brown, *Living Reiki,* 18; Phyllis Furumoto, personal communication. Furthermore, Rick Bockner recalls Takata telling him that Saichi died of tuberculosis. In the end, it may be that he died of complications from a number of diseases.

86  Hawayo Takata, unpublished autobiography transcript *Reiki is God Power,* page 3 of session 22, recorded December 18, 1979, private collection of Phyllis Furumoto.

87  Who was named after Takata's employer Julia Makee Spalding.

88  Alice would later become the mother of Phyllis Lei Furumoto.

89  Straub, "Reiki — Japanese method of healing."

90  Haberly, *Reiki,* 18.

91  Personal communication with Phyllis Furumoto

also wanted to take her husband's ashes to Ohtani Temple in Kyoto, Japan.[92] In October, Takata secured tickets for fifty dollars on a cattle boat heading to Japan,[93] [94] bringing her sister-in-law and her own two small children. On the ten-day boat trip,[95] she met a monk who was going to be a resident at the Ohtani Temple. He agreed to take Saichi's ashes with him to the temple, with the agreement that Takata would come six months later, in March 1936, for a second funeral for Saichi.[96] In the meantime, Takata would go to the Yamaguchi district, where her parents were vacationing for one year, and tell them about her sister's death.

After visiting her parents for a week and a half, Takata entered Maeda Orthopedic Hospital in Akasaka, Tokyo, near the Imperial Palace.[97] Her weight upon entering the hospital was eighty-six pounds.[98] The doctor told her to rest for three weeks to build up strength. Takata would end up staying and living in this hospital for the next several months.

Later in October, Takata was given a medical evaluation by Dr. T. Maeda, for whom the hospital is named, and who was a good friend of the Takata's. Surgery was scheduled for 7 a.m. the next day to remove a tumor, her appendix, and her gallbladder.

While lying on the operating table as the nurses prepped for surgery, Takata heard a voice inside her saying, "This operation not necessary."[100] After hearing this voice three times, she

*Photograph of Dr. Maeda*[99]

---

92  Brown, *Living Reiki*, 20.

93  Lugenbeel, *Virginia Samdahl*, 76.

94  The rate was a sea deck cabin at the rate of $55 according to an unpublished letter by Joan Kodami; a student from the University of Hawaii. The finished college essay was sent to Takata for final approval. Joan Kodami, "Medicinal Practices," unpublished paper, University of Hawaii, 1977.

95  Brown, *Living Reiki*, 21.

96  Haberly, *Reiki*, 18.

97  This information is found in Iris Ishikuro's notes, although she had a different district written. Akasaka is in Graham, "Mrs. Takata Opens Minds to 'Reiki'." Michiko Gonterman confirmed that Akasaka is indeed the site of the Imperial Palace, which was reportedly near the clinic.

98  Joan Kodani, "Medicinal Practices," unpublished paper, University of Hawaii, 1977. The finished college essay was sent to Takata for final approval.

99  Thanks to Phyllis Furumoto who has granted permission for me to use this photo.

100  Barbara Weber Ray and Nonie Greene would write that this voice was the voice of Saichi, Takata's late husband. *Official Reiki Handbook*, first edition, 59. While Takata herself doesn't specify who's voice it was she heard, she mentions in her autobiography, tape 23, pages 3-4, "After his transition I heard his voice whenever I had to make a crucial decision or if I felt I could not decide...Therefore, what I have said in the book that I have been led to the proper road to find Reiki, it was through his guidance."

asked the voice what she should do and the voice told her to ask the doctor. Takata asked Dr. Maeda if there was another option besides surgery. Dr. Maeda told her that there might be an alternative and asked his sister, Mrs. Shimura, the hospital dietician, to take Takata to Dr. Chujiro Hayashi's Shinanomachi clinic in Tokyo.[101]

Takata learned that Mrs. Shimura had received Reiki treatment some years previously. She had been in a coma dying of dysentery at the Keio University Hospital in Tokyo,[102] and she recovered through receiving Reiki treatments from Dr. Hayashi. She then took Reiki training from Dr. Hayashi and began practicing Reiki on the hospital food to charge and vitalize it.[103]

When Takata arrived at Dr. Hayashi's office, he had two of his practitioners treat her. As the practitioners were performing the treatment, she felt heat and vibrations emitting from the practitioners' hands. This made her very curious as to what could be causing these sensations. The practitioners also seemed to know, by their comments made while performing the treatment, the areas of Takata's body in which she was experiencing problems. Besides the treatments, she received a special diet including sunflower seeds, red beet juice, grapefruit, and almonds, and was told to return for another treatment the following day.[104]

The next day Takata arrived early for her second treatment to inspect the treatment tables. She had concluded there must be a machine that caused the heat and vibrations in the practitioners' hands. But, unable to observe any hidden wires or batteries, she came up with another plan.

During her treatment she suddenly reached up and grabbed the arm of one of the Reiki practitioners. She was expecting to find a wire in his sleeve connected to a machine hidden in the pocket of his kimono. The startled practitioner did not know what she wanted, and offered her a handkerchief. Takata explained to the practitioner that she was looking for the machine that caused the heat and vibrations she felt in her body. The practitioners laughed at her lack of understanding about how Reiki works, which got the attention of Dr. Hayashi, who came over to see about all this laughter in his clinic.

---

101   Graham, "Mrs. Takata Opens Minds to 'Reiki'." Shinanomachi is the name of a neighborhood in present-day Shinjuku Ward, Tokyo. The name of this clinic is found in Brown, *Living Reiki,* 32.

102   Keio University is one of the most prestigious universities in Japan. http://www.hosp.keio.ac.jp/english/annai/kotu/index_en.htm. As a side note, Takata also started treating patients at the Keio University hospital. She mentions this in her May 1936 diary entry. So here we have evidence of at least two Reiki practitioners given rights to treat patients at this particular hospital. Takata, ed., "The Grey Book," n.p.

103   Haberly, *Reiki,* 24.

104   Graham, "Mrs. Takata."

Takata said that Hayashi explained Reiki to her in English. During Hayashi's training as a naval candidate, he was required to take a course in English. During his Navy career he had traveled to Los Angeles, New York, Hawaii, San Francisco, and Australia.[105]

Helen Haberly gives a summary of this conversation, writing:[106]

"Reiki is the Japanese word for Universal Life Energy. In English it sounds like 'Ray-key', and it comes from space, from the universe. The only thing that is different between you and us is that we have the contact with Universal Life Force and you do not. My practitioners all have this contact and they can use it. They are applying it now and are filling your body with Life Energy. This is so big we cannot measure it, so deep we cannot fathom it; therefore, in Japanese we call it Reiki."

She [Takata] thanked him, although she understood little of what he had said. He continued, "Do you have radio in Hawaii? When the radio station broadcasts, there are no lines connected from the station to your house, yet as you turn on the receiver and contact the station, you receive what they are sending. Because we are not radio technicians, we do not know how. The principles are the same with Reiki. This energy goes through space without wire, and we know this great force can be contacted. Once the contact is made, the energy flow is automatic. It is universal, limitless energy. When you have the switch on, the power is unlimited. When you want to stop, you just take your hands away. It is very simple."[107]

Takata was told[108] that because she was not Japanese and would be leaving Japan eventually she couldn't learn the system of Reiki.[109] Americans were pioneers, innovators, and did not value following customs as did the Japanese of this time; therefore the Japanese feared changes would be made to the system. So they did not want to train Takata because she was an out-

105  Hawayo Takata, unpublished autobiography transcript *Reiki is God Power*, page 2 of session 3, recorded December 12, 1979, private collection of Phyllis Furumoto.

106  I am using Haberly's summary instead of the actual unpublished transcript so that readers will be able to look at a published source.

107  Haberly, *Reiki*, 22-23.

108  Sometimes Takata would state that it was Mrs. Shimura who told her this, but at other times it seems that perhaps Dr. Hayashi had said this to her. Haberly, *Reiki*, 24; Takata, *Takata Telling the Stories of Dr. Hayashi*, on CD.

109  Hawayo Takata, unpublished autobiography transcript *Reiki is God Power*, page 7 of session 3, recorded December 12, 1979, private collection of Phyllis Furumoto.

sider, a "Nisei."[110]

It is important to note that the hospital dietician, Mrs. Shimura,[111] had taken the Reiki training and gave Takata a treatment each day. This treatment was in addition to the treatment Takata would receive earlier in the day at the Hayashi clinic.[112] The fact that Hayashi had trained Shimura before Takata shows that Hayashi did not have a problem with training women. The idea that Hayashi wouldn't train Takata because she was a woman is a common misconception. Rather, Takata was told she couldn't be trained because she was not Japanese.[113]

After four days of treatment, Takata experienced an extreme reaction to the treatments. She had excessive diarrhea, eventually causing extreme fatigue to the point where she couldn't stand up and walk but had to crawl to the bathroom. [114, 115] All of Takata's gallstones were flushed out of her system during this time.

After three weeks of receiving Reiki treatments and with her health significantly improving,[116] Takata met with Dr. Maeda and told him of her reaction and told him of her desire to learn Reiki. Dr. Maeda told her that she was recovering very fast and was pleased the treatments were working but he reminded her of the association's rules against training foreigners. In the end, Takata was able to convince Dr. Maeda to help her in her desire to learn. He informed her about the high price of the course and asked how she was going to pay for it. Takata decided she would sell her house and use the money to take the training. With Dr. Maeda's help, Takata convinced Hayashi to train her.

Before officially offering Takata training, Hayashi called a meeting with the directors[117] of "Usui Light Energy Research Association"[118] to discuss the

---

110  A *nisei* is a child of Japanese parentage but born and raised in a foreign country.

111  Haberly, *Reiki,* 20.

112  Haberly, *Reiki,* 23.

113  Haberly, *Reiki,* 24.

114  Hawayo Takata, unpublished autobiography transcript *Reiki is God Power,* page 8 of session 3, recorded December 12, 1979, private collection of Phyllis Furumoto.

115  Brown, *Living Reiki,* 27. According to Fran Brown's book the reaction finally subsided weeks later on December 24, Takata's birthday, and on December 25 she felt much better, like a new person. Brown, *Living Reiki,* 27. However, this date is not accurate and conflicts with the account of Takata talking with Dr. Maeda after her extreme reaction but before her Reiki training. The dates on Takata's certificate show that she took the training before her birthday in December.

116  Although she was significantly better after these three weeks, the complete healing process would take about four months.

117  Takata, *Takata Telling the Stories of Dr. Hayashi,* on CD.

118  Brown, *Living Reiki,* 28. This association is most likely the Usui Reiki Ryoho Gakkai, despite some authors' claims that Hayashi had severed ties with the Gakkai by this time and called his system "Hayashi Reiki Ryōhō." For one, Takata states on a tape that the original name of the system she learned was Usui Reiki Ryoho. All of the newspaper articles we have from the time period, including the 1928 *Sunday Mainichi* articles about Hayashi's student Shōō Matsui and the 1937-1938 *Hawaii Hōchi* articles about Hayashi himself, refer to Usui and "Usui Reiki Ryōhō" or "Usui-style Reiki Ryōhō." The certificates that Takata gave her students were stamped with a seal that reads, "Hanko of Usui System Reiki Study Group Association". And in his farewell address in Honolulu in February 1938, Hayashi said, "I am Chūjirō Hayashi of Usui Reiki Ryōhō." Chūjirō Hayashi, "I Appreciate Everyone's Kindness From the Bottom of My Heart—Mr. Hayashi's Farewell Address," *The Hawaii Hōchi,* February 22, 1938, p. 8 (Appendix 5). It could be that some confusion over the name of the Hayashi Reiki Kenkyūkai ("Research Society") may be to blame. However, this was the name of Hayashi's organization, not the name of the system of Reiki he was teaching. For an example of the alleged rift between Hayashi and the Gakkai, see Frank Arjava Petter, "FAQ," *Reiki Dharma,* http://www.reikidharma.com/en/index_en.html last accessed December 1, 2014.

matter. Hayashi brought with him the scroll, approximately two and a half yards long, that Dr. Maeda had written to him personally requesting Takata be trained. Knowing it would be considered poor manners to turn down the request from such a highly prominent and well respected physician, it was agreed that Takata could become an honorary member and take the Reiki training.[119]

From December 10[120] through 13, Takata took both First and Second Degree training from Dr. Hayashi.[121] Both of Takata's Japanese-language certificates are dated December 13, 1935. This would seem to indicate that the training was over a four-day period. However, the date December 13 may simply have been the day the certificate was filled out, and it could have been dated after completing the First Degree course. As discussed later, the dates written by both Hayashi and Takata on the certificates given to their students were not always the exact dates of the classes.

Hayashi's training courses seemed to have a pretty standard format. A 1928 article by a student of Hayashi named Matsui, found in Appendix 3, states that the training course are five days, 1.5 hours per day. Matsui, being a First Degree student of Hayashi, was referring to the Shoden class only.

Hayashi's farewell address, found in Appendix 4, states that the training courses are usually five or six days long, three hours a day. These classes were held in 1937 and 1938. This was the time frame for the Shoden (First Degree) and Okuden (Second Degree) classes taught consecutively.

In 1938, according to one of Hayashi's First and Second Degree students, Chiyoko Yamaguchi, Hayashi would teach the First and Second Degree classes back to back over a five-day period. The days were longer when teaching the First and Second Degrees together like this.[122]

In January 1936, after four months of daily Reiki treatments,[123] Takata decided she was well enough to practice Reiki on others.[124] This is a significant lesson of Takata's that seems to go unheeded by many Reiki practitioners. That is, one must first take care of oneself with Reiki before beginning to provide treatment for others. Takata taught this concept time and time again in her classes. She mentioned that Reiki doesn't have its full power unless the practitioner has first fully charged his or her own battery (the lower *tanden*,

---

119  Haberly, *Reiki*, 25.

120  Takata's Shinpiden certificate states that she received spiritual bestowments of the first initiation and the highest initiation of Reiki therapy on December 10, 1935. The date December 10, 1935, is also confirmed in Takata's diary, which contains notes from her first class with Hayashi. Takata, ed., "Grey Book," n.p.

121  Takata's Reiki certificates read "Shoden" and "Okuden." Shoden ("first transmission") is what Takata would call First Degree or the "introductory course," and Okuden ("inner transmission") is what Takata would call Second Degree or the "intermediate course."

122  Tadao Yamaguchi, *Light on the Origins of Reiki* (Twin Lakes, WI: Lotus Light, 2007), 28, 30.

123  Takata, *Takata Speaks*. Other times she reportedly said it was eight months of treatments. Ray and Greene, *Official Reiki Handbook*, first edition, 59.

124  Haberly, *Reiki*, 27.

about two inches below the navel).

For example, Helen Haberly's biography of Takata quotes Takata as saying, "[Reiki] must be used. Just as an unused muscle will atrophy, so, too, will Reiki weaken and fade away when it is not exercised."[125]

From a transcript of a talk by Takata recorded in the mid-1970s by the late John Harvey Gray:

*Reverend Beth Gray [who became a Master student of Takata]: "If, for some reason one fails to do Reiki for a period of a month or so, does one lose the power?"*

*Hawayo Takata: "That's a good question. No. Once you have the contact ... through me ... and that is everybody who is here. Reiki stays with you everlasting.*[126] *But, it may, it may not, when you are tired, have the full charge come out at one time. You will become quiet, because your battery down here has run down. So, what do you do to yourself? One, and Two, and Three, and Four [the first four positions of the first Reiki pattern which are the abdominal positions in the Gray lineage]. Your Foundation Treatment [the first four positions on the abdomen] has to be done so that you recharge your own battery. And when that is finished ... and then when you try to treat people, your energy goes up, because you are filled, you are not empty."*[127]

The same idea is also shared in the Te-no-hira Ryochi system taught by a student of Mikao Usui named Toshihiro Eguchi. Reiki was just one of the many systems Eguchi studied....so he was not a dedicated disciple so to speak. A book by one of Eguchi's Master students reads, "We must practice it 30-40 minutes each day to emanate the efficient energy for treatment."[128] As one might expect, there are a lot of similarities between the systems that Hayashi and Eguchi taught, since they share the same teacher, Mikao Usui.

In early March, having been in Japan for six months, Takata needed to go to Ohtani Temple in Kyoto and see the monk from Kona, whom she had met on the boat to Japan, about the services for Saichi.[129] She seems to have also met up with her parents, who had spent a year at their family home in

---

125   Haberly, *Reiki,* 54.

126   Takata finishes her answer to this question with the following: "Reiki is everlasting. There's only one way you can lose and that is, I have said and I have warned you, that no matter how great you become or what an expert in treating and healing, that you cannot teach unless, you go up to the higher degrees. What you have learned is the First Degree. But, with the First Degree it is good enough to give you protection and also you can help yourself and others."

127   Hawayo Takata and Beth Gray, "Questions and Answers with Hawayo Takata," *The John Harvey Gray Center for Reiki Healing Newsletter* (November 2008), http://learnreiki.org/newsletters/2008-11-Reiki-Newsletter.htm last accessed December 1, 2014.

128   Koshi Mitsui, *Te no Hira Ryōchi,* Tokyo: Vortex, 2003 [1930],50.

129   Haberly, *Reiki,* 18, 27.

Yamaguchi Prefecture in the west of Honshu, Japan's main island. Takata writes in her diary that she saw them off for their return trip to the Hawaiian island of Kauai.[130] Immigration records show that her parents sailed out of Kobe (not far from Kyoto), along with Takata's younger daughter, Alice, on the S.S. Empress of Canada on March 9, 1936.[131]

Takata then returned to Tokyo, where she was invited to live with the Hayashis in their home and continue her education in becoming a Reiki practitioner. James Deacon shares the significance of this aspect of Takata's life.

*"Now to 'western' minds, little significance is placed on this fact (- other than perhaps a fleeting thought that the Hayashis were kind to give her a place to stay).*

*And, likewise, even though she spoke about her acceptance into the Hayashi household when recounting information about this time in her life, other than to express her gratitude to the Hayashis, Hawayo Takata herself did not 'make a big ego thing of it'.*

*In Japanese culture, a student being invited to live as a member of their teacher's household (no matter what the nature of the discipline they are studying) has long been seen as something of great significance. It is a great honor - something usually only bestowed on students who display high levels of potential. To be invited to live with their teacher in this way is to become uchideshi.*

*An uchideshi (literally an 'inside student') is a live-in student who receives special training – frequently with a focus on becoming their teacher's successor. An Uchideshi has a far greater degree of contact with their teacher than is possible for other students.*

*Traditionally, only students deemed by the teacher to be highly dedicated to their development within the chosen art would be offered the opportunity to become Uchideshi. It is said that life as an Uchideshi can be a challenging one (for a start, Uchideshi often have to put up with animosity from other students who are jealous of their status[132]), yet life as an Uchideshi can also be a highly rewarding one, as it is believed that only through experiencing daily life with their teacher, can a student truly reach beyond the technicalities of their art*

---

130   Brown, *Living Reiki*, 20.
131   National Archives and Records Administration, Washington, D.C., *Passenger Lists of Vessels Arriving at Honolulu, Hawaii, compiled 02/13/1900 - 12/30/1953*, National Archives Microfilm Publication: *A3422*, Roll: *167*, Record Group Title: *Records of the Immigration and Naturalization Service, 1787 – 2004*, Record Group Number: *RG 85*. Located by Justin Stein through Ancestry.com.
132   And it is to be imagined this might this might be even harder if the uchideshi was a woman, and also a Nisei.

*and learn its inner essence. (Thus, the term Uchideshi can also be understood in the sense of "student of the inner teachings".)*

*And so, to all intent and purposes, Hawayo Takata had become an uchideshi.*

*Not only was she working, day in day out, in the clinic with Hayashi-sensei and the other chosen apprentices, but she was also living in the Hayashi home, 'breathing the same air', in almost constant close proximity to her teacher: observing how he lived his life, how he dealt with various situations, how he interacted with others; and being exposed to endless situational learning opportunities: a comment here, a question there, being asked to find her own solution to a problem or treatment issue; a simple conversation – its content seemingly unimportant at the time - its true significance and value only realized perhaps months or even years later; perhaps being challenged to look at situations from a new perspective - often learning by 'osmosis', a gradual, often unconscious process of assimilation or absorption.*

*To a certain extent, almost every aspect of her daily life would have become part of her training."*[133]

In April, Takata worked in Hayashi's clinic for five hours in the morning. Afternoons, she was sent out to treat clients on home visits that sometimes required two to three hours.[134]

In May of 1936, Takata wrote in her diary that she was learning Shinpiden (Third Degree), which involves learning how to initiate and train others so that they have contact with Reiki and the knowledge of how to apply it.

Takata's Shinpiden (Third Degree/Master) certificate from Hayashi is dated October 1, 1936. However, her Shinpiden certificate states that she studied at Hayashi's institute from December 10, 1935, until May 8, 1936.[135] Takata left Japan on June 2, 1936, arriving in Honolulu on June 10, and does not seem to have returned to Japan until the following summer. Most likely her certificate was dated in October, even though she was already back in Hawaii by then, because that is when Hayashi received her final payment for the Third Degree training (that she had received months earlier).[136] Similar examples of this can be seen on the certificate dates for the Masters that Takata initiated. For example, Bethal Phaigh received her Master initiation from Hawayo Takata

---

133  "Will the real 'Hayashi-Style Reiki Teachings' Please Stand Up?" *James Deacon,* http://www.aetw.org/reiki_real_Hayashi_style_teachings.html Excerpt reprinted with permission.

134  Haberly, *Reiki,* 27-28.

135  Takata's Shinpiden certificate also states that this was a very short period of time for one to normally go through the training. But that Takata was an exceptional student. The certificate also states Takata has learned the initiation process. Takata's Shinpiden certificate is in the personal collection of Phyllis Furumoto.

136  From the stories Takata would sometimes tell, it is probable that the money was most likely acquired by mortgaging her house.

on October 12, 1979, but her Master certificate is dated October 7, 1980. This is because she paid Takata $5,000 up front for her Master training and sent the rest as she made money teaching classes.[137]

*Historical note: Takata told her students that Dr. Hayashi agreed to allow her to take the First Degree class and only after a year of working in his clinic was she allowed taking the Second Degree class.*[138]

*Since Takata's certificates from Hayashi for Shoden and Okuden are dated December 13, 1935, and her Shinpiden certificate is dated October 1, 1936, we know that Takata did not wait a year before completing her Second Degree (Okuden).*

*Why would Takata tell a "revised" version of her own history? Perhaps she wanted her own students to wait between taking the First and Second Degree training.*[139]

*This idea of waiting periods between degrees may immediately instigate a knee-jerk reaction from some people that Takata "changed the system." However, in what way did this change affect Takata herself? Takata must have known that asking people to wait before learning Second Degree would mean that some of the passion First Degree students had to go onto the Second Degree would fizzle out. Thereby, not all who would have taken Second Degree if allowed to take it immediately after First Degree would actually end up doing so. This therefore would not be in Takata's best financial interest.*

*So why did she do this? Maybe she thought it was in her students' best interests, not her own. Students who come to Second Degree with some practice time inevitably get more out of the class than those who have no experience of practicing hands-on treatments prior to the class. In other words, a different caliber of student who would have questions that arise only through practice would be attending. Takata's students would not be working in a clinical setting with their teacher, as she had done.*

*Of course, it is also possible that Hayashi told her that Usui also usually made students wait between the First and Second Degrees but that, either in her case or more generally, Hayashi had disregarded the waiting period. This waiting period is stated in the Reiki Ryoho Hikkei (a manual of sorts containing a question-and-answer section given out by Usui's school, the Usui Reiki*

---

137  Phaigh, *Journey into Consciousness,* 130.

138  My speculation is it was probably at this time that Takata would actually be learning how to teach the Second Degree from Hayashi. Perhaps Takata changed her own story from her learning how to teach the Second Degree into herself learning the Second Degree for the reasons I state in the main text.

139  I doubt Takata's reasons were to avoid a possible severe reaction given that she was receiving both treatments and training because Takata always talked about reactions as being a good thing: not something to be avoided.

Ryoho Gakkai, to its members). In it, the question of receiving Okuden (Second Degree) comes up. Usui responds, "I will teach it to people who have learned Shoden and who are good students, good conduct and enthusiasts."[140] It seems that Hayashi perhaps then had made a change to allow students at times to receive the First and Second Degrees without waiting.

If Hayashi's training with Usui started in 1925, as some evidence suggests, he himself did not have much time between degrees. This may have influenced how he trained others in the system. What is clear from Takata's 1938 certificate is that not many reach the final degree, as it mentions she is, "…one of thirteen fully qualified as a Master of the profession."

Upon returning home, it seems Takata practiced Reiki out of her home for a few months before opening the first Reiki clinic outside of Japan, in Kapaa, in October 1936.[141]

In 1937 Takata went back to Japan for two reasons. The first reason was to talk with her teacher, Hayashi, about her increasing clairvoyant ability, which was troubling her and making it difficult to get sound sleep at night.[142] The second reason, as Takata told the *Hawaii Hochi* in September 1937, was that she returned to Japan that July to receive further "training" (*kōshū*) from Hayashi.[143] This may have been either to learn how to teach the Second Degree, if she didn't know this already, to spend more time with Hayashi and watch him teach additional classes, and/or to learn how to train other Masters (Third Degree/Shinpiden), or something else entirely. Takata had been initiating Reiki practitioners to at least First Degree

---

**Reiki Sanitarium Treatments**

ABSOLUTELY DRUGLESS

Special Treatments for Stomach and Internal Ailments; Nervous Diseases and General Debility

Office Hours: 4:00 to 8:00 p. m.

Office Located at Ota Cottage

Haunla St., Kapaa, Kauai

Special Free Clinics for Children Under Six Months Every Saturday 8:00 to 10 a. m.

**MRS. HAWAYO TAKATA**

PRACTITIONER

*Garden Island Newspaper, October 1936*

---

140 "Explanation of Instruction For the Public," *The Reiki Threshold*, http://www.threshold.ca/reiki/URH_Explanation.html, last accessed December 1, 2014.
141 Brown, *Living Reiki*, 32-33.
142 Hawayo Takata, handwritten notes, p. 3, private collection of Phyllis Furumoto.
143 "Reiki Ryōhō's Hayashi Chūjirō Comes to Hawaii—Accompanied by his Daughter Kiyoe—Arrives Saturday on the Chichibu Maru," *Hawaii Hōchi*, September 30, 1937, 7. See Appendix 5.

on her own in Kauai since 1936. (It seems unlikely she went back to learn how to train others in Second Degree because Takata's Shinpiden certificate is dated October 1, 1936. This makes it likely she already knew how to train others in Second Degree.)

During this 1937 trip to Japan, Takata stated she and Hayashi's wife, Chie Hayashi, were initiated as Masters.[144] Before leaving Japan, Takata invited Hayashi to do a teaching tour in the Hawaiian Islands.

Takata returned to Hawaii on September 24,[145] and Hayashi arrived (accompanied by his daughter Kiyoe) on October 2.[146] Takata was in charge of these classes, and Hayashi would assist as needed. By the end of this time period and training, Hayashi knew Takata was quite capable of instructing others in the First and Second Degrees and performing the initiations. Hayashi formally recognized Takata as a Dai-Shihan, giving her a certificate in English dated February 21, 1938.

The first three of the four certificates Takata received were written in Japanese. The fourth certificate, which I am calling her "Dai-Shihan certificate" or "Master-Teacher certificate," was in English; the latter authorized her to train other Masters or Third Degree students.

After Dr. Hayashi left in February, Takata was asked to serve as a translator for a group of Buddhist monks who were traveling on the mainland.[147] After this job, in April 1938, Takata attended the National College of Drugless Physicians in Chicago, where she studied different body therapies, such as Swedish massage and colonics, earning a certificate in July 1938.[148] Takata returned to Honolulu, where she remained for about a year.

In 1939, she took a trip to Hilo (on the "Big Island" of Hawaii), where she bought a house that served as her clinic and family home for the next decade.[149]

Takata came to Hilo at the request of two school teachers who had expressed interest in learning about Reiki. On a short sightseeing tour, they stopped by a house where one teacher had frequently bought silk stockings. There was a "For Sale" sign in the front yard. When they walked in, the teacher introduced Takata to the shopkeeper, who was hard of hearing. All he could

---

144  Hawayo Takata, unpublished autobiography transcript *Reiki is God Power*, page 6 of session 6, recorded December 14, 1979, private collection of Phyllis Furumoto.
145  "Reiki Ryōhō's Hayashi Chūjirō Comes to Hawaii"
146  Hayashi, "Farewell Address"; Haberly, *Reiki* 31.
147  Haberly, *Reiki*, 32;
148  Hawayo Takata, unpublished autobiography transcript, page 4 of session 6, recorded December 14, 1979, private collection of Phyllis Furumoto.
149  Hawayo Takata, unpublished autobiography transcript, page 7 of session 6, recorded December 14, 1979, private collection of Phyllis Furumoto.

understand was that Takata was from Honolulu and he immediately thought she was there to buy his house. Tears of joy ran down his face, as he couldn't contain his excitement that someone wanted to buy his house.

Instead of Takata correcting him, she inquired further, and all he wanted was $60 a month for ten years. She accepted this offer. Takata immediately had an idea that besides being her home it could also serve as a Reiki clinic. Takata many years later in her teachings would tell students, "Let Reiki guide you." While most people think this might just be regarding hand placements during treatments, it seems Takata applied this to situations both on and off the Reiki table.

On January 1, 1940, about 4 a.m., Takata had a dream of Hayashi dressed in a white kimono. When his kimono touched her face as he walked past her, she woke up. The dream disturbed her. So she wrote to her daughter Julia, who was living with the Hayashis at that time, to inquire if anything unusual was happening. She received a reply that all was normal in the household, but Takata couldn't shake the feeling that something was wrong.[150]

Takata decided to return to Japan, leaving on March 30.[151] Upon arrival on April 3, she immediately went to see her teacher, Dr. Hayashi, at Yokohama. She learned from Mrs. Hayashi that Dr. Hayashi was in Tokyo. Dr. Hayashi told Takata she had arrived a little too early and said he would like her to go to Kyoto to study hydrotherapy. He alerted her to return to their home in Atami quickly when he summoned her via telegram.

Just before Takata left for Kyoto, Mrs. Hayashi told Takata that her husband was debating whether or not to go into transition (to end his life). She explained that Hayashi believed there would be a great war coming and that Japan would be involved. Being in the Naval Reserves, he would be called up for active duty and be responsible for the deaths of many people. Hayashi was a Reiki Master now and tried to save lives and help with their suffering; he could not be called on to harm others.

Takata received a telegram summons on May 9, and rushed to Atami, arriving early the next morning, May 10[152]. At breakfast Hayashi explained to her that shortly after lunch, he would go into transition. He said to her, "I will sit and you shall witness how a Master goes into transition." He explained

---

150  Takata, *Takata Telling the Stories of Dr. Hayashi*.

151  National Archives and Records Administration, Washington, D.C., Passenger Lists of Vessels Departing from Honolulu, Hawaii, compiled 06/1900 - 11/1954, National Archives Microfilm Publication: A3510, Roll: 133, Records of the Immigration and Naturalization Service, 1787 – 2004, Record Group Number: RG 85. These ship manifests were located on Ancestry.com by Justin Stein.

152  As mentioned earlier, Takata gave the date of Hayashi's transition as May 10, 1940, not May 11, 1940.

that after his transition, there would be only seven Reiki Masters left in Japan, with Takata and his wife being two of them.[150]

Hayashi told her that he had written to the Reiki Society and named her as his successor. She was to carry on this work as the Reiki Master of Japan and all over the world. He was leaving her his house and his Reiki clinic. Mrs. Hayashi was given the country home in Shizuoka. Takata asked what he would do after going into transition, and he replied, "I'll be on the other side trying to repair things."

The Reiki supervisors[153], who were probably the other Reiki Masters at that time, started arriving by 10 a.m. At 1 p.m., Hayashi entered the room where his guests were gathered, wearing the same white kimono Takata had seen him wearing in her dream on January 1. As he passed by, his robe brushed against her face as it had also done in her dream. He gave a short speech announcing, step by step, the progression of his transition.

Hayashi transitioned on May 10, between 1 and 1:30 p.m.at his villa in the coastal town of Atami. He was cremated ten days later. In the interim his body was placed in the Reiki clinic in Tokyo, and people came and paid their respects. Although it had been ten days between Hayashi's transition and cremation, his body did not decompose; his smile remained unchanged.

Takata told Mrs. Hayashi that she would not stay in Japan to take over Hayashi's clinic at this time because she still had children to raise and her first duty was to be a mother. Takata left Mrs. Hayashi in charge of the clinic while she was gone. Takata planned on returning in ten years, once her daughters were grown and her parents had made their transition. [154]

Takata stayed in Japan until June 3, leaving from Yokohama on her return trip[151]and she did not return to Japan until 1954. She later told her students that she returned the ownership of the Tokyo clinic and home to Mrs. Hayashi at this time.[155] One reason for this was that the clinic was not being used as a Reiki clinic anymore. After World War II, it was being used primarily by Mrs. Hayashi as a home for refugees displaced because of the war.

Takata wrote about her experiences at this time in Japan in a letter to Doris Duke. Here is the letter, dated November 16, 1954, reproduced with permission.[156]

153   "Reiki supervisors" is a term Takata often used when telling this story.
154   Haberly, *Reiki*, 42; Takata, *Telling Stories of Dr. Hayashi;* Iris Ishikuro, unpublished class notes, 1978.
155   Takata, *Telling Stories of Dr. Hayashi.*
156   Hawayo Takata to Doris Duke dated November 16, 1954, Doris Duke Papers, Doris Duke Charitable Foundation Historical Archives, David M. Rubenstein Rare Book & Manuscript Library, Duke University.

623 Prumehana Apt D- Kapiolani Blvd.

Honolulu. Nov 16/54.

My dear Miss Duke:

How are you? Long time no see, I miss you very much. I made a 4 wks trip to Japan and I'm glad I did. Lots to see and learn it was interesting. The scars of war are still hanging around Hiroshima, others have recovered amazingly well, most in the large industrial cities. The streets are wider and modern facilities are put in, yet the sanitation has a long ways to go before they can come alongside U.S.A. standard. The reason is they know and want to do it, but they are so poor, it is only a dream to them. The women has adapted to dresses, for economical reasons, the young and old have their hair short. No more fancy hairdos unless, for special reason like getting married or a village festival — The peasants and business people both look forward for these spring and autumn festivals, for little relaxation and fun, after putting the hard days, they feel they have earned it, so they go to the limit. It is very crude to see dress and gotas, but I believe in ten years, they will have plus in material things as well as training themselves, especially the legs, where they were hidden with long kimonos, now being expossed, I'm sure they will look like women on 5th ave N.Y. These women work hard, industrious, and have endurance, they work in the farms, build roads and stone walls on side of the hills to prevent landslide, work in the factories, keep shops, take care of the families, so if Japan should ever come up to normal, believe me, they owe it to the women. I guess, it is all over the world men shortage, more so in Japan. The men folks are the supervisors using chores of women and I guess all they know is to make babies — What a life, but you don't find any grumpy lassie, they are always smiling when they work, too happy to have work, the young ones with pretty faces are the luckiest, so they claim, they steal the men and do their darnest to hold them, they make that as their profession, very bold even in public, which they display lots of sex. The women from 30 to 45 are the ones that have children to support, so have home work sewing, pasting labels on match boxes etc., carving e pasting anything they can do at home, are the most sober ones — 58 to sixty and over, are shoe shine girls on the side walks, maids, wash woman e laborer, but their thots run the same, they all want to have a man — then hose they hose —

I went to Hokkaido [3] (north) which is a vast ranch country and lovely mountains and hot spring spas, missed the typhoon by 7 days. A week later, after we rode the Toya Maru, it sank with 1400 people. For a time my friends and relatives in Hawaii were worried about us, so we sent a wire O.K. Our tour ended at Beppu Spa (South) so I took the boat, inland sea trip back to Kobe, Kyoto then Tokyo. Visited my masters home and found the family as best as they could – Mrs Hayashi has retired and doing church work plus treatments – Her only daughter was in Manchuria during the out break of War, lost her 2 boys – her husband was taken by the reds into concentration camp, but after 7 years came home safely – She was put into another camp never dreamed her husband was alive. On the eve of her execution she decided to run away, so cut her hair like a little boy and found some boys clothes, and ran away – all she thot was run south, south and in 3 years she was able to find Tokyo – They're all united and very happy. Even tho the time was short, I tried to make it worth while, so took up Japanese diet, but after a few lessons, instead of a real health diet, it seemed to me more like an economical diet than ever, but it was worth it. Anything to learn and to gain knowledge and wisdom is my motto – Learned of an oil treatment, good for skin ailments and went to lots of onsen Spas to learn the ment of their mineral waters and its uses, so I must say the trip was interesting. The shops are beautiful and very smart, the quality of the articles they manufacture are getting better and better by the month. They are trying to preserve the art and culture as much as possible, even with the changing tide, they call democracy. I went to Kabuki twice and enjoyed it, even here in the ancient dramas, sex is the motive, cleverly done. Capacity crowds attend daily from 3 p.m to 10 p.m and hard to get tickets, you wonder where are the poor? When I first changed my $200.⁰⁰ into Yen, I received 72000 Yen, I felt flushed, until I went shopping — I wanted to buy everything I saw, everything is so beautiful and reasonable. My money ran out like water. The boys in our group certainly that Japan was made for the men, they were yelling their heads off, that it _is a_ Man's country! yes, in a way we agree with them, but when their wives took them shopping, this is where the women had fun — I am glad I saw the both and can stand neutral — In some towns like Hakata, the wives hung on like vines, so none got lost. I am sending you a small bottle of Suzuran perfume to add

4

to the many fine ones you already have. I hope you like it. This is about all I can bring back with my 44 lbs, so this is only a small gift from Japan. For a bigger present, I ordered a special Ekookake (Kimono stand) in fine wood and lacquer, it is being made now, by a fine artist who is very slow to finish it. I had hoped it could be ready for your birthday, I had word it will take more time, as soon it arrives here, I will let Johnny send it to you wherever you wish. May this years birthday be the best in everyway; health in abundance, happiness and the best of luck from a sincere friend. Wherever you are the best of everything and take good care of yourself.

Aloha

Hawayo.

In 1955 Dr. Charles W. Benson and Takata jointly purchased Grayson Farms in La Quinta, California, for $112,500 and renamed it Spring Board Farms. Takata had received a promissory note for $75,000 from Doris Duke for her investment in the property.

*Grayson Farms*
La Quinta
California

*Palm, olive and banana trees spot the verdant turf in front of Springboard Farms' luxurious main house.*

From January 8 to 28, 1956, Takata was invited to visit Doris Duke in New York.[157]

By 1956 there were numerous problems between the two owners, as well as financial problems. This forced Takata to postpone a four- to six-week business trip to Montreal, Canada.[158]

On October 19, 1956, Dr. Benson bought out Takata for $5,000. Takata was simultaneously released from all debts owned by the corporation, including the promissory note given to them by Doris Duke.[159] (On June 13, 1961, Spring Board Farms, Inc., Dr. Benson, made make his final payment to Doris Duke, thereby paying in full the loan she had given him and Takata.)

- In 1957, Takata traveled the world with Doris Duke, who had broken her wrist earlier that year, in exchange for giving her treatments during this time.[160] Later, Doris would take the Reiki training herself.

---

157  Letter from Hawayo Takata to Mr. S. L. Hawkins and Thomas Perkins dated June 24, 1956, Doris Duke Papers, Doris Duke Charitable Foundation Historical Archives, David M. Rubenstein Rare Book & Manuscript Library, Duke University.

158  Letter from Hawayo Takata to Alfred Beck dated September 30, 1956, Doris Duke Papers, Doris Duke Charitable Foundation Historical Archives, David M. Rubenstein Rare Book & Manuscript Library, Duke University. I am currently undertaking research to determine what sort of long business trip this might have been.

159  Box 95, Folder 1 from David M. Rubenstein Rare Book & Manuscript Library at Duke University. I received permission to publish from the Doris Duke Charity Foundation Archives.

160  Matsuura, "Mrs. Takata and Reiki Power."

- In the early 1970s, it was reported, "The last two years she's been traveling all over the world."[161]

- In 1973 Takata taught a class on Orcas Island, Washington.[162]

- In the summer of 1974, Takata traveled to Indonesia to take part in a five-day festival in the art of healing, sponsored by the Indonesian government.[163]

Also in 1974, an airline pilot named Wally Richardson took the First Degree from Takata while he was in Honolulu. Wally decided to then invite Takata to his home in Los Altos, California, (south of San Francisco) to teach classes. Wally contacted Rev. Beth Gray's church, the Trinity Metaphysical Center in nearby Redwood City, California, and asked if anyone there would be interested in taking classes. Rev. Gray was in Takata's first class in the Richardson's' home, and her husband, John Harvey Gray, ended up in the second class. This would lead to Beth sponsoring Takata to teach many classes at her church, and both John and Beth would later become Master students of Takata.[164]

- In the winter of 1975 Takata taught at the University of Hawaii.[165]

- Takata also returned to Japan several times in the 1970s to train students in the First and Second Degrees.[166] In an essay written by Joan Kodani and dated December 5, 1977, it stated she traveled yearly to Japan from 1972-1976.[98]

Takata had been teaching Reiki prolifically since 1936 and planned to retire in 1977 from teaching the First and Second Degrees after training a few Reiki masters: Virginia Samdahl, Ethel Lombardi, and John Harvey Gray.[167]

---

161  Hammond, *We Are All Healers,* 285.
162  Stated by John Harvey Gray in a First Degree class, May 2000.
163  Matsuura, "Mrs. Takata and Reiki Power."
164  This information was verbally told to me in my classes with John and Lourdes Gray. It is also found in their book: John Harvey Gray and Lourdes Gray with Steven McFadden and Elisabeth Clark, *Hand to Hand: The Longest-Practicing Reiki Master Tells His Story* (Xlibris: 2002), 28-29.
165  Graham, "Mrs. Takata Opens Minds to Reiki."
166  Takata, *Telling the Stories of Dr. Hayashi.*
167  Kay Yamashita had been trained prior to these other Masters but is not listed in this letter because she was not expected to teach publicly. I speculate that Iris Ishikuro was also trained at this point in how to teach the First Degree but had not given Takata any money yet for her training, so she is not listed.

John Harvey Gray gave me this retirement letter of Takata.

Seasons Greetings for a Happy Prosperous 1977.
I wish to thank you all for the many kindness given me, with gifts, bouquets, invitations to your lovely homes to share the feasts you so kindly prepared with Love and Reiki Hands.

It is with gratitude and Aloha to you all, that I write this letter to say "Thank You," to let you know that time has come for me to retire this year. I have gained many friends and students during my Reiki Tours, these past years. They were a great Joy, Inspiring receiving knowledge and Wisdom.

Wishing you the Best of Health, Happiness, to have Security and prepare for Longevity, Peace of mind and Success!!!

I remain, most gratefully yours,

Rev. Hawayo Takata

I have created 3 Reiki Masters to carry on this noble work. They are trusting, Capable, kind and with humility serve God and Mankind. They are :—

Master John Gray, 22.7 Highland Terrace, Woodside Calif. - 94062 — phone 415-851-2887 — 851-7404

Master Virginia Samdahl - 419 Winnemac St Park Forest Ill. 60466 - ph. 312-7486639

Master Ethel Lombardi - 93 Spring Creek Rd. Rt # 5 Lockport, Ill- 60441 — ph 815-83882

P.S. Thank You for the beautiful letter. Well see you in May -

On May 29, 1977, Iris Ishikuro threw Takata a retirement party.[168] On the second page there is this dedication:

*Mrs Takata, we are here today to thank you for sharing your Reiki gift with us ......
and to wish you PEACE, JOY, and HAPPINESS in the days to come ......*

*You might think you are getting there in years, but we know you are always young
at heart ........*

*This wonderful seed you have planted within us is only the beginning of a very rich
and fulfiling life ahead of us .......*

*When this wonderful way*
*Of healing the Worlds ills*
*has spread everywhere,*
*The entire world will be changed*
*Into a true paradise .......*

*Once a year, during the month of May; we will have a reunion for all Reiki
members with the purpose in mind of strengthening the Spiritual Bond that we share ..
among ourselves and with you ..... so that we may remain strong and dedicated in our
purpose .......*

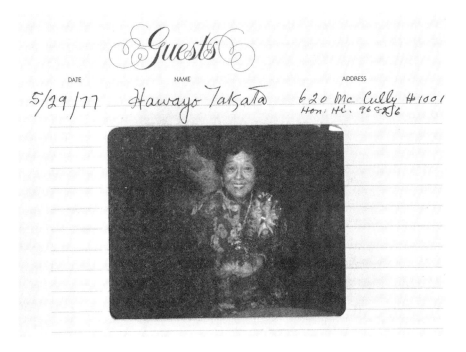

Guests

| DATE | NAME | ADDRESS |
|---|---|---|
| 5/29/77 | Hawayo Takata | 620 Mc Cully #1001 Hon, Hi. 96826 |

---

168   Iris's daughter loaned me the photo album of Iris's retirement party for Takata.

In the previously mentioned 1977 Kodani essay, it stated, "She says she will retire soon, and already has her successor chosen."[98] This essay seems to indicate a single successor had already been chosen rather than multiple successors as Takata's retirement letter implies.

As it turns out, retirement did not suit Takata, and so she continued to teach the system of Reiki until her death. Takata ended up training a total of 22 Masters, with the intention of training at least two more, Marta Getty and Helen Haberly.[169]

In November 1980, Takata suffered a second heart attack in Washington State while traveling between teaching classes. In a letter written shortly thereafter, just days before her death, she mentioned that she planned to return to Japan.[170]

Takata died on December 11, 1980, after training 22 Master students.[171] Takata's chosen biographer,[172] Helen Haberly, writes, *"Although this young woman [Phyllis Furumoto] was trained and empowered to assume the role of Grand Master, Mrs. Takata went into transition without making a formal statement of acknowledgement."*

Takata's 1976 retirement letter and Kodami's 1977 essay, the latter stating she had already chosen her successor, were written prior to Phyllis Furumoto's initiation as a Reiki Master in 1979. In addition, another of Takata's Master students trained in 1979, Barbara Weber, claimed Takata had chosen her as successor. So, it would appear Takata had chosen a few different people to possibly be her successor. This has lead to ongoing confusion since Takata's death.

---

169  Personal correspondence with Marta Getty, 2013. Marta stated because Takata had already agreed to train them as Masters, this task fell to Phyllis Furumoto after Takata died.

170  Letter from Hawayo Takata to Wanja Twan, available for viewing at the 2013 Reiki Alliance Conference.

171  Hawayo Takata's obituary appeared in the *Burlington Hawk-Eye* (Burlington, Iowa) on Thursday, December 11, 1980. Thanks to James Deacon for confirming this.

172  Takata's original chosen biographer was Master student Barbara Weber, with whom she had recorded 12 audiotapes containing her life story. However, the transcription process was being done too slowly, and Helen Haberly was appointed to this task.

# Chapter SIX

---

## The History of the Reiki System: 1980-1993

A Little More History at This Time, and Thoughts…

# The History of the Reiki System: 1980-1993

*"WHAT IS PAST IS PROLOGUE"*
~ line from The Tempest carved on the National Archives Building,
Washington, D.C.

The post-Takata history of Reiki has been a confusing subject due to events that started taking place shortly after Takata's death and have continued till today. Through years of research I have heard a lot of different perspectives about what occurred. It seems that different Reiki groups and people put out varying stories and events at this time.

Takata had trained 22 Master students before she went into transition on December 11, 1980. Shortly after her death, two of her Master students would be recognized as her successor. Reiki groups would form that would shape the history of Reiki practice in the world.[173]

This chapter will discuss two of the three Reiki organizations founded in the early 1980s, The American Reiki Association, Inc. (A.R.A.) and The Reiki Alliance. The other Reiki organization formed at this time was called the American Reiki Master Association.

I want to start this chapter with some lyrics from The Beatles that are worth remembering. As Reiki brothers and Reiki sisters, we should strive to get along when at all possible. At the core of our practices we have the

---

173  The Reiki Alliance and the American Reiki Master Association would form shortly after Takata's death. The American Reiki Association, Inc. formed prior to Takata's death.

commonality of the Reiki Precepts despite our differences. These precepts, if lived by, would eliminate many of the problems that have plagued our shared history. They can help us today as we strive to create harmony between our Reiki organizations, members, and individual practitioners. When we prove incapable of getting along, at the very least, we can refrain from slandering one another. In a utopian Reiki world, "we can work it out".

*"Life is very short, and there's no time*
*For fussing and fighting, my friend*
*I have always thought that it's a crime*
*So I will ask you once again*
*Try to see it my way*
*Only time will tell if I am right or I am wrong*
*While you see it your way*
*There's a chance that we may fall apart before too long*
*We can work it out*
*We can work it out"*

*~The Beatles*[174]

On February 1, 1980, while at the home of Fran Brown, Takata wrote a letter to her granddaughter, Phyllis Furumoto.[175] This letter stated what seemed to have been her intention that Phyllis would be handed Takata's position once she retired.[176] It also mentioned that Barbara Weber was helping Takata with her book and with setting up a patent for Reiki so that no one would be able to abuse it.

The A.R.A. was founded on June 18, 1980, by Takata's Master student Barbara Jean Drum Weber (later Barbara would add the word "Ray" to her last name). At a reception in Atlanta in August 1980, Hawayo Takata welcomed everyone to the new nonprofit organization. "The purpose of the corporation is to provide a membership organization in order to promote, protect and improve the practice of Reiki; to establish professional standards and codes of professional conduct and ethical considerations, as well as to project and

---

174   The Beatles, "We Can Work It Out," by Paul McCartney and John Lennon, in *We Can Work It Out / Day Tripper*, Capitol, 1965.

175   This letter is in Phyllis Furumoto's personal collection.

176   This was just a matter of five or six weeks after December 1979 - the time period in which Barbara Weber would later state she had been secretly trained by Takata in a seven level system of Reiki. Barbara Weber had, in fact, been with Takata in Iowa at that time to record Takata's autobiography. In July 2014, I viewed this letter while working on the Takata Sensei Archives.

enhance the public knowledge and image of Reiki."[177]

On November 9, 1980, Barbara Weber wrote a letter to Helen Borth, stating, "Any teacher can make another person a teacher." In this same letter Weber stated, "If you would like to discuss further the third degree of Reiki and having a class in your area, please reach me again." This seems to imply that Barbara was willing to train Masters before Takata had gone into transition. What is also interesting, given Weber's position later, is her acknowledging at this time that any teacher can make another person a teacher.

However, in a November 2, 1981, letter written to Phyllis Furumoto by Nonie Greene, Barbara Weber's assistant, the statement that "any teacher can make another person a teacher" was retracted. In this letter, Nonie wrote that she had incorrectly transcribed Dr. Weber's words, and that the correct transcription was "Not any teacher can make another person a teacher." She further stated that, due to Dr. Weber's absence from the office because of her travel schedule, Nonie had signed the previous 1980 letter on Dr. Weber's behalf. This would seem to indicate that Dr. Weber was not even aware, at the time, of the incorrect statement that been transmitted in the November 1980 letter.

On December 11, 1980, Takata went into transition.

In February and March of 1981, the A.R.A. sent letters to those Masters who were trained by Takata, stating that if they wanted to become full-fledged Reiki Masters, they would have to retrain with Barbara Weber. Barbara Weber's impression was that she alone had received the full teachings of the Reiki system from Takata, including the knowledge of how to train and initiate another Third Degree Master.

In a phone conversation I had with Takata's Reiki Master student Harry Kuboi, he said he had received a letter from Barbara Weber. The letter stated that if he wanted to be a certified Reiki Master, he would have to train with Weber and pay several thousand dollars. Kuboi saw that as an insult. After all, he had been a Reiki Master since April 18, 1977, before Barbara Weber even took her First Degree class in August 20, 1978.[178] Two other Master students of Takata, Paul Mitchell and Rick Bockner, at the 2013 Reiki Alliance conference related similar stories about the letter and the fee being thousands of dollars.

At first Virginia Samdahl, whom Takata trained as a Master in 1976,

---

177  "American Reiki Association Founded Membership Drive Underway," *The Reiki Review* (Winter 1981, Supplement), 1.

178  Barbara Weber's certificates may be viewed online at: http://www.trtia.org/histpers.html. Notice that Barbara has only three certificates from Takata, the same number as all of Takata's Masters. Later, in the mid 1980s, she would claim she secretly learned seven levels from Takata. However, she has never produced seven certificates from Takata.

was convinced Barbara had indeed received something more than she had. Barbara said she knew how to initiate other Masters, while Samdahl did not (or didn't seem to). Samdahl told one of her students, William Allan Perkins, III,[179] that she didn't know if she knew how to initiate another Master.

Initially, Virginia Samdahl joined Barbara Weber Ray's group, the American Reiki Association, Inc., and decided to take Barbara Weber's Master training course.[180] Samdahl was the only Takata Master student that I know of who took this training with Barbara.[181] She was listed as a contributor in the 1982 first edition of "The Official Reiki Handbook", written by Barbara Weber Ray.

In October 1981, Phyllis Furumoto had a meeting with Barbara Weber in Atlanta, Georgia regarding the claims Barbara was making at this time.

Originally, it would appear that things might have been smoothed out between the two Masters. The Fall 1981 issue of *The Reiki Review*, the A.R.A.'s official newsletter, states, "The ARA is in a process of establishing professional standards for future Reiki Master teachers who will be initiated by Master, Dr. Barbara Weber and certified with the authentic A.R.A. seal as she was instructed by Master Takata prior to her death in Dec., 1980. Master Phyllis Furumoto, Master Takata's granddaughter, also has the authority to initiate Masters and has the other seal of certification."[182]

However, as early as 1982, *The Reiki Review* retracted this statement, saying, "Dr. Barbara Weber Ray is the only known person to have been fully trained in *all* levels of Reiki by Master Hawayo Takata prior to her transition in 1980.[183] Having a special seal is not to be confused with having the correct keys and knowledge for initiating to the Reiki Master level of power / energy frequency."[184]

Barbara writes about this meeting in her third letter sent out to the non-A.I.R.A. Masters on March 7, 1983.[185] Barbara writes, "By her own admission

---

179 William, who went by his middle name "Allan," was a poet from Kentucky. I have copies he gave me of his Reiki certificates. His First Degree certificate was given to him by Virginia Samdahl and is dated February 27, 1983. His Second Degree certificate, given to him by Barbara Weber Ray and one of Barbara's Master students named Marvette Carter, is dated April 17, 1983.

180 These initiation procedures were passed on to me in one of my Virginia Samdahl lineages going through Viola Ebert, Virginia's first Master student. Later, when I took Master training with Marcia Halligan, who did her Master training with Barbara Weber Ray in 1983, I discovered that the initiation methods used were the same, word for word. This discovery, for me, validated that these initiation methods were the ones used by Barbara Weber Ray in the early 1980s.

181 I have a copy of the initiation information that Virginia learned from Barbara.

182 "Purposes of A.R.A.," *The Reiki Review* 1:3 (Fall 1981), 1.

183 Barbara Weber had actually taken her initial First Degree training with Virginia Samdahl. However, Barbara does have a certificate from Takata for the First Degree, which presumably was "retro dated."

184 "Clarification," *The Reiki Review* 2:4 (Fall 1982), 3.

185 This letter refers to the other two letters of a similar nature sent in February 1981 and March 1981. Note that the earlier two letters were sent just a few months after Takata had died in December 1980. In the third letter, the price of the training offered by Barbara Weber Ray was $500. This was much less than the thousands of dollars I heard three Master students of Takata's tell me regarding the price of Barbara Weber's training. However, the discrepancy in price of the training may be simply due to a price change between the first two letters and the third. Letter from the A.I.R.A., signed by Dr. Barbara Weber Ray, Nonie C. Greene, Virginia W. Samdahl, and Barbara St. John, sent to John Latz, March 7, 1983.

to us in Atlanta in October, 1981, Phyllis Furumoto acknowledged she did not have the keys to make a Reiki Master."

I have heard Phyllis, Helen Borth, and Marcia Halligan mention this 1981 meeting as well. The meeting did happen, Phyllis stated essentially that Barbara didn't want to co-create anything with her and that Barbara wanted to be in complete control of the A.R.A. Of course, Barbara Weber told her own students that Phyllis didn't want to share in the role of successor. That leaves us with no defining documentation of what happened at the meeting.

In 1982, the A.R.A. changed its name to the American-International Reiki Association, Inc (A.I.R.A.).[186] Also by 1982, the organization claimed *in print* that Barbara Weber Ray was the only person given the full teachings of Reiki by Takata and therefore was the only person who could fully initiate another Third Degree Reiki Master.[187] It was Barbara's and the A.I.R.A.'s opinion that the other Master students of Takata could only initiate students into the First Degree, some but not all could initiate someone into the Second Degree, and none could initiate a person into the Third Degree. Barbara claimed that this is what Takata had told her in front of two other witnesses.[188]

In 1982, Phyllis Lei Furumoto invited the Master students of Takata, as well as the few other Masters who had been trained since Takata's death, to the island of Hawaii. From April 7 through 14, 15 of Takata's 22 Master students, as well as some of their own students, met in Hawaii to honor Takata.[189] This is a Japanese custom, a way of honoring one's ancestors called "Meinichi," or death anniversary. The ceremony for the death anniversary is called "Hōji."[190]

According to documents I have from the American International Reiki Association (A.I.R.A.), Virginia Samdahl attended the 1982 meeting of Masters in Hawaii, organized by Phyllis Furumoto, as a representative of the A.I.R.A.

These Masters compared what they had learned from Takata and discovered that there were slight variations in the symbols, initiations, hand

---

186  Although the name A.I.R.A. is first seen in print in 1983, it wasn't until January 14, 1985 that this change in name was filed with the United States Patent and Trademark Office.

187  Ray and Greene, *Official Reiki Handbook,* first edition, 5.

188  Those witnesses are listed as: Barbara St. John and Nonie Greene.

189  Personal interviews with Susan Mitchell, Paul Mitchell's wife (Takata's Master students are in bold.): **Dorothy Baba, Rick Bockner, Fran Brown,** Carell Ann Farmer, **Phyllis Furumoto,** Marta Getty, **Beth Gray, John Gray, Ethel Lombardi, Mary McFadyen, Paul Mitchell, Bethal Phaigh, Shinobu Saito, Virginia Samdahl** and her daughter Adair, Bunny Sjogren, **Wanja Twan,** and Barbara West. They all met **Harry Kuboi** and Takata's sister **Kay Yamashita** during that week, meaning15 Takata Masters attended.

190  According to my Japanese student Miho Motono Cunningham, people get together at the house and pray to honor a person who passed away and share fond memories, but some people go to the temple to have a special ceremony. Usually people have "death anniversaries" after 7 days, 49 days, 1 year, 3 years, 7 years, 13 years and 33 years.

positions, etc.[191] Barbara Weber Ray had been saying that since Takata's death. They also learned that some of them had been given a Master initiation by Takata, while others had not.[192] Also, most of the Masters attending had not learned how to initiate another Master. Members at this meeting decided to meet again in a year's time.

The discovery of differences in Takata's teachings led to confusion among those in the group and resulted in a discussion about standardizing Takata's teachings. Although Takata had told some of her Master students that they had permission to train new Masters after her death, the group agreed that only Phyllis Furumoto would initiate other Masters.[193]

Also in 1982, the term "Grand Master" became better known, with its first appearance in book format being in the first edition of *The Reiki Handbook,* written by Larry Arnold and Sandy Nevius: "At this writing there are two grandmasters: Mrs. Phyllis Lei Furumoto-Hartley[194] of British Columbia, the grand-daughter of Hawayo Takata; and Dr. Barbara D. Weber of Georgia."[195] The term "Grand Master" had also been discussed at the April 1982 meeting of Masters in Hawaii.[196]

In the March 7, 1983 letter the A.I.R.A. sent Takata's Master students, it stated they would need to retrain with Barbara Weber Ray if they wanted to be certified as a teacher by the A.I.R.A. The new price of this training was only $500, which was substantially lower than the offer made in the first two letters. This letter also asked that another $1,000 be given to the A.I.R.A. in support of it, making the total cost $1,500. The letter stated that Virginia Samdahl had already gone through this training program from the A.I.R.A.

In early June 1983,[197] some members who had attended the 1982 meeting in Hawaii, as well as a few other Masters, gathered once again—this time at Reiki Master Barbara Brown's home in Lumby, Canada. The meeting's end result would be the formation of The Reiki Alliance.

The Reiki Alliance, headed by Phyllis Furumoto, was formed in part as

---

191   Having personally received initiations and symbols from two of Takata's Master students, I know this is true. I have also been in contact and trained with many students of the original 22 Master students. I can see that the differences in teachings were not restricted to just John Harvey Gray and Fran Brown. But again, for the most part, the discrepancies are slight.

192   This is discussed at length in the chapter titled, "Historical Perspectives on the Master Initiation."

193   Not all of Takata's 22 Master students went along with this idea and trained Masters themselves. Barbara Lincoln McCullough trained Helen Borth as a Master in December 1980, shortly after Takata died, and David Jarrell on August 5, 1981.

194   Phyllis Furumoto-Hartley's last name was misspelled as Furomoto-Hartley.

195   Larry Arnold and Sandi Nevius, *The Reiki Handbook* (Harrisburg, PA: PSI Press, 1982), 15.

196   The term Grand Master was in fact used in a conversation between Takata and one of her students as heard on an unpublished cassette tape.

197   June 6-10, 1983. Anneli Twan, *Early Days of Reiki: Memories of Hawayo Takata* (Hope, BC: Morning Star Productions, 2005), 32.

a response to Barbara Weber Ray's organization, The American Reiki Association, Inc.[198] Members who joined The Reiki Alliance were showing their support for Phyllis as Takata's successor, as opposed to Barbara Weber Ray.[199]

Another purpose of The Reiki Alliance was for members to support each other as Reiki teachers. Founding members, according to The Reiki Alliance's web site, included: Barbara Brown, Barbara West, Bethal Phaigh, Bunny Sjogren, Carell Farmer, George Araki, Helen Borth, Helen Haberly, Marta Getty, Paul Mitchell, Phyllis Furumoto, Rick Bockner, Shinobu Saito, Ursula Baylow, Virginia Samdahl, and Wanja Twan.[200] Ten of these founding members were Master students of Takata's, and the others were students of these students. There were some Masters who were in attendance at this meeting but decided not to sign the founding statement and join The Reiki Alliance, and so are not listed.[201]

It was at this meeting that this group of Masters acknowledged Phyllis as "a Grand Master in the direct spiritual lineage of Mikao Usui, Chujiro Hayashi, and Hawayo Takata,"[202] recognizing Furumoto as the successor to her grandmother, Takata.

Virginia Samdahl, who was a member of the A.I.R.A. at this time, joined The Reiki Alliance as well. I was told by Fran Brown that Samdahl wanted to be the peacemaker between the two groups.

Virginia left Barbara's group, the A.I.R.A., later this same month after Barbara started making changes to the system of Reiki as she had learned it from Takata. Virginia stated several reasons, according to her resignation letter written on June 30, 1983, announcing her decision to leave the A.I.R.A. A few of the reasons mentioned were:

1. Samdahl didn't agree with the new physics being taught in the Reiki classes.
2. Improper usage of the symbols
3. Dropping of the "Reiki Finishing" technique taught by Takata

---

198  Twan, *Early Days of Reiki,* 32.

199  Based on my conversations with the Master students of Takata, it seems that the Masters in this group genuinely felt that Phyllis was Takata's successor. Of course, critics might suggest that most Masters favored Phyllis because Barbara Weber Ray was asking for payment for retraining.

200  "Our Organization," *Reiki Alliance,* http://www.reikialliance.com/the-reiki-alliance/founding-statement last accessed December 1, 2014.

201  For example, John Harvey Gray and Viola Ebert, Virginia Samdahl's first Master student, were also at this meeting. Anneli Twan says a total of 21 people were present for the founding of The Reiki Alliance, 13 of whom were Master students of Takata's. As mentioned before, not all people present decided to join. Twan, *Early Days of Reiki,* 31.

202  At the 1985 Reiki Alliance meeting, this phrase would change to "the Grand Master..." *The History of The Reiki Alliance,* Paul Mitchell, DVD, 1991. This phrase is found in the "Blue Book." Paul Mitchell, *Reiki,* (a.k.a., *The "Blue Book"*), revised edition, (Coeur d'Alene, ID: Reiki Alliance, 2012 [1985]). This "Blue Book" was distributed to Reiki Alliance members and contained excerpts from the earlier "Grey Book." In 1993, the Reiki Alliance would reverse its decision, and replace the phrase, "the Grand Master" with the phrase "a Grand Master".

4.    The A.I.R.A.'s business practices

Virginia Samdahl's name is listed in the first, 1982 edition of *The Official Reiki Handbook* under the heading, "CONTRIBUTORS. A SPECIAL WORD OF THANKS AND GRATITUDE." By the second edition, published in 1983, Virginia's name was removed from this list and other names were added.[203]

By 1984, Barbara Weber Ray was explicitly stating that the Reiki system had seven levels.[204] Note that this was a year before Mieko Mitsui, a Master student of Barbara Weber Ray, traveled to Japan. It is commonly and erroneously reported that it was after Mitsui's research trip to Japan and her discovery of the existence of the Usui Reiki Ryoho Gakkai (the school ostensibly founded by Usui) that Barbara added more levels to the system of Reiki she taught.[205]

A 1984 *Yoga Journal* article that features an interview with Barbara Weber refers to Reiki as a three-level system.[206] However, since Rick Bockner was another source for this article, we do not know where the author learned this piece of information.

In 1985, Mitsui wrote an article entitled, "REIKI TRIP TO JAPAN" for *The Reiki Journal*.[207] She wrote about her 1984 trip to Japan to research more into the origins and history of the system of Reiki. Arriving in Tokyo on July 7, she would end up lecturing several times in Tokyo and Kitakyushu and give Reiki classes in Himeji and Kyoto. While there she wrote an article for the *Twilight Zone* magazine. A nice picture of her and some of her students is also found in this article.[208]

In May 1985, Mitsui traveled back to Japan for more research. Later that year, she published another article, entitled, "Tracing the History: A Japanese Book on Reiki."[209] During this trip she met an elderly gentleman who told her about a book from the Usui Reiki Ryoho Gakkai written by a mathematician at the Meiji University in Tokyo. She was told some information about Usui and that there were seven degrees. The basic philosophy of Reiki is, "that the

---

203   Interestingly enough, no names were added or dropped between the second edition, copyright 1983, and the third edition, revised printing in 1984. Barbara Weber Ray and Yesnie Greene, *The Official Reiki Handbook*, second edition (Atlanta: A.I.R.A., 1983); Barbara Weber Ray and Yesnie Carrington, *The Official Reiki Handbook*, third edition (St. Petersburg, FL: A.I.R.A., 1984).

204   *The Official Reiki Handbook*, third edition, 8, 73. This was the first time the system of Reiki was explicitly stated as having seven levels. From the 1982 first edition of *The Official Reiki Handbook*, Barbara Weber Ray had said that there were levels beyond the third degree, but this was the first time the specific number of levels appeared in print.

205   For example, see Bronwen and Frans Stie.ne, "Levels of Reiki," International House of Reiki, published August 23, 2002, http://www.ihreiki.com/blog/article/levels_of_reiki, last accessed December 1, 2014.

206   Susan Jacobs, "Reiki: Hands-On Healing," *Yoga Journal*, May/June 1984, 40-43.

207   Mieko Mitsui, "Reiki Trip to Japan," *The Reiki Journal* 5:1 (March-May 1985), 10.

208   Mitsui, "Reiki Trip to Japan," 11.

209   *The Reiki Journal* 5:3 (October-December 1985), 9.

universe is ourselves…the act of carrying Light."

Interestingly enough, the article mentioned a second book written about a man named Usui but does not mention his first name. The name of this second book is roughly translated as, "The Mastery of Healing with the Hands." The article ended by stating that Mitsui would return to Japan in October [1985] to continue her research into the book from the Usui Reiki Gakkai.

If we are to take the information in the articles and when the information was received as true, then it seems like Barbara Weber Ray first stated there were seven levels to the Reiki system before receiving this information in 1985 about the Gakkai having seven levels. However, it could be said that Mitsui learned about this in her 1984 trip to Japan and that the 1985 article was written with the 1984 material to "confirm" what Barbara Weber Ray was saying was true. One can't prove this either way, but I just offer it as a possibility here.

If memory serves me correctly, I think I saw a picture of the memorial stone printed in *The Reiki Journal*, or its later incarnation as *The Radiance Journal*, sometime during the 1980s. However, at this time, I am lacking many issues from these journals. If you have available copies, please contact this author.

In 1987, Barbara Weber Ray's group, the A.I.R.A., started teaching what they called The Radiance Technique®. This was done to distinguish, differentiate and control what they were teaching (stating it was the unaltered system of Reiki) from things commonly being taught as "Reiki". They saw what others were teaching as a polluted form of the actual system of Reiki. In other words, they claimed that if Reiki was taught by anyone other than a member of their own group, it wasn't really Reiki.

In 1988, Phyllis made an announcement at The Reiki Alliance meeting (held from May 8-15 in Friedrichsdorf, Germany), that those Masters with enough experience could start to initiate Masters if they felt called to do so.

On December 29, 1988, the A.I.R.A. changed its name again, to The Radiance Technique Association International, Inc.[210] (To complete the history of this organization: On November 17, 1997 the organization changed its name to The Radiance Technique & Radiant Peace Association International, Inc. and on March 10, 1999, it changed its name to The Radiance Technique

---

210    This change was officially recorded with the United States Patent and Trademark Office on December 11, 1991.

International Association, Inc. [211])

In 1992 Fran Brown published her book, *Living Reiki: Takata's Teachings*. She wrote about the existence of the memorial stone to Usui in Tokyo, stating, "There was a large tombstone on which is an engraving about his work for mankind."[212]

In 1993 the Office of the Grand Master was founded by Takata's Master students Phyllis Furumoto and Paul Mitchell.[213]

## A Little More History at This Time, and Thoughts…

I have spoken with people who were initiated as Masters by Barbara Weber Ray in the early 1980s.[214] They all have stated that in the beginning of the A.R.A. and later the A.I.R.A., Barbara taught Reiki as a three-degree system. However, as early as 1982, Barbara had stated in writing in the first edition of *The Official Reiki Handbook* that there were more than three levels. The simplest explanation of this is that Barbara was referring to the knowledge of how to initiate another Master as a Fourth Degree and she may have already been thinking about adding other levels. This topic is explored more thoroughly later in "Chapter 9: Historical Perspectives on the Master Initiation."

It seems that originally Barbara Weber Ray was training people according to the way Takata had taught Reiki. However, by the mid 1980s, it appears that significant changes started being made. I am told by former members of this organization that it was the members who pushed Barbara Weber into making some of these changes. For example, the division of the Third Degree into two parts, 3a and 3b, was at the request of the Masters who belonged to the organization. They felt there needed to be a step between the Second Degree and the Third Degree teaching level.

Another example would be that at some point the three Second Degree Reiki symbols and names were no longer given in the Second Degree class.[215] Instead, the names and how to draw these three symbols were divided up into many different levels of Barbara's new seven-degree system. I have audio recordings of Takata teaching Reiki classes at various levels. In a Second

---

211   Date recorded with the United States Patent and Trademark Office (http://www.uspto.gov).

212   Brown, *Living Reiki*, 53.

213   "FAQ," *Usui Shiki Ryoho*, http://www.usuishikiryohoreiki.com/ogm/faq/ last accessed December 1, 2014.

214   I have spoken with Marcia Halligan, John Latz, and Les Kertay, all of whom were trained as Masters by Barbara Weber Ray. I also had a lot of contact with William Allan Perkins, who had taken First Degree with Virginia Samdahl and Second Degree with Barbara Weber Ray in 1983.

215   I understand and could explain why and how this can be done honorably but will refrain from yet another tangent.

Degree class recording, Takata gives the names and how to draw one of the Second Degree symbols.

Changes should at least be noted as changes. Otherwise, the original teachings that Takata specifically, and sometimes uniquely, gave to each of her Master students are lost. The specific differences taught by Takata to her Master students are what define a lineage. Some of these differences are passed along in these lineages, while others have been eliminated by solidarity and standardization.

This is not to state that any changes in the presentation or explanation of the system of Reiki are "wrong." For example, some of Takata's Master students added more time in their First Degree classes to allow for students to have the opportunity for hands-on practice. While Takata usually taught First Degree over four days in two-hour segments, some of her Master students began teaching the First Degree over four days in three-hour segments. Allowing time for hands-on practice is something they thought would be a good addition to the First Degree class; I concur.

All Masters have a different way of expressing the system. We simply should not mimic another's understanding and presentation of the system. Rather, we must come from a deep place of our own inner understanding and knowing of the system—and then try to express it the best way we can.[216]

It seems Takata was the glue that held intact the system of Reiki she practiced, Usui Shiki Reiki Ryoho.[217] Shortly after Takata's death, disagreements and divisions arose between some of the Masters she had trained. Many of these divisions still remain.

---

216 For example, the Office of the Grand Master, comprising Phyllis Lei Furumoto and Paul Mitchell, has created what they call the four aspects and nine elements to help define and express their understanding of Usui Shiki Ryoho.

217 Takata referred to her system as Usui Shiki Ryoho. However, the term Usui Shiki Reiki Ryoho precisely specifies this is a system that involves Reiki.

# *Chapter* SEVEN

---

## *The Practitioner Levels:*

### *First Degree/Shoden: Beginning Teachings*

### *Second Degree/Okuden: Highest Teachings*

# CHAPTER
# 07

## *The Practitioner Levels:*
### *First Degree/Shoden and Okuden/Second Degree*

### *First Degree/Shoden: Beginning Teachings*

*"With the first contact or initiation, the hands radiate vibrations
when applied to the ailing part."*[218]
~ Hawayo Takata

Reiki is the Japanese word for Universal Life Force Energy. The system of Reiki, consisting of three degrees, activates and teaches how to apply Universal Life Force Energy to improve one's Mind, Body, and Spirit.

Each of the three degrees of Reiki serves a specific function. Central to the First Degree class are the Five Reiki Precepts, which were discussed in Chapter 1, "What Is Reiki and the Practice of Reiki?" To reiterate, they are:

*Just for today, do not anger*
*Just for today, do not worry*
*Just for today, count your blessings*
*Just for today, do your work honestly*
*Just for today, be kind to all things that have life*

---

218  Takata, ed., "Grey Book," n.p.

On July 31, 2014 Phyllis Furumoto and I sat down together in Arizona to record another episode for her Reiki Talk Show. Because the Reiki Precepts are a core component to the system, this is the topic I was drawn to speak about. The interview can be found here: http://www.reikitalkshow.com/shows/view/377

Another core feature of the First Degree is students learning to use their hands to heal themselves and other people. This involves developing the skill to sense with your hands where the causes of the problems are in the client's body. Beginning practitioners may not yet be able to sense imbalances under their hands. Therefore, students learn 12 standard hand positions that cover and treat all the major organs of the body. This is to ensure that the cause of the problems are found and treated. With practice, the students become more sensitive to the vibrations in their hands and then can determine how long to stay on any particular position; whether just a minute, an hour, or longer. Before students have the sensitivity to feel the various energy vibrations though, it is recommended they stay in each position for 7-10 minutes to ensure an effective treatment. The First Degree class also teaches recommended hand positions for specific illnesses. First Degree includes the Reiki system's history as well as knowledge about one's own particular Reiki lineage.[219] This degree of Reiki can bring about growth and learning. It is whole and complete in itself. Some people may feel the calling to Second Degree while others will be content with First Degree.

Students receive the connection with and the ability to use Reiki through the time-honored practice of initiation by a Master. Takata states in the "Grey Book," "Initiation is a sacred ceremony where the contact is made. With the first contact or initiation, the hands radiate vibrations when applied to the ailing part."

The initiations are an important part of Reiki training, as the initiations do something energetically to our bodies. The initiations put our bodies in direct contact with this universal life energy, Reiki, in a different way than before so we can utilize it for healing purposes. We get "tuned into" or "connected" to the Reiki by means of the initiations. Takata stated the Reiki initiations raise a person's antenna so that they can pick up this energy we call "Reiki".

An analogy that could be used is that of radio signals, where our bodies are constantly bombarded with the signals all the time, but we are unaware of them and cannot hear them. We need to adjust the antenna on our radio

---

219   See Chapter 14 "Lineage" for more information.

receiver to properly tune into these radio signals so we can enjoy the programming being broadcast. Likewise, Reiki is everywhere—like the radio waves—and in all living things. But in order to utilize it—like hearing the radio programming—we need our antenna adjusted via the initiations.

In a First Degree class[220] Takata describes that Reiki comes in your antenna on the top of head and fills up your "solar plexus". (Takata would call the area around and below the navel the "solar plexus." She would also refer to it as the "battery". In the "Grey Book" she would state, "It [Reiki] lies in the bottom of your stomach[221] about 2 inches below the navel." This area is the lower *tanden*. Takata didn't like to use Japanese words, like *tanden*, when teaching English-speaking audiences, as it tends to create confusion.) From there the Reiki travels up and comes out the practitioner's hands, which she called "electrodes."[222] She stated that the more a person practices Reiki, the more it fills up his or her battery. As a result, more Reiki would come out of the practitioner's hands while giving a treatment. Going on, she stated that for the first few days after receiving the Reiki initiations, maybe only a quarter of the energy coming into your antenna would actually come out of your hands; the other three quarters would be stored in your battery. In other words, practitioners are beneficially receiving Reiki while they are giving a treatment too.

Takata went on to say that with more practice, the practitioner's battery becomes more charged, and therefore more Reiki will come out of the practitioner's hands when giving treatments. She concluded by saying that she had been practicing Reiki for 45 years and therefore a lot of Reiki came out of her hands during a treatment. She encouraged her students by saying that any person who practices for that long would also have the same strong Reiki flow coming out of their hands that she did. Takata emphasized the importance of daily self-treatment.

This is not to say that therapeutically there would be any difference in the treatment given by a practitioner of many years versus a new practitioner. They are both using Reiki; it is the same "stuff." But while giving the treatment, it would simply take more time for the transfer of Reiki to happen with a new practitioner than an experienced practitioner.

Before Takata had learned the system of Reiki, she asked Dr. Hayashi

---

220  Unpublished audio recording of a First Degree class of Takata teaching Reiki, 1980.

221  In western anatomy, the stomach is not located below the navel. Here again we have a cultural use of the word "stomach". This area is also called the lower *dantian* and specifically is acupuncture point Ren 6 (氣海 Qi Hai or "Sea of Qi").

222  Takata also stated that Hayashi had referred to the hands as electrodes in the article by Graham, "Mrs. Takata Opens Minds to 'Reiki.'" Iris Ishikuro also described the hands as electrodes in her teaching notes.

why the Reiki practitioners' hands got hot when she was being treated as a patient in his clinic. Hayashi said that it was because they all had "contact with the universal life force and you do not."[223]

In the First Degree class, there are four initiations. Each initiation has its own purpose. The first initiation makes the initial contact between the initiate and the Universal Life Force Energy–Reiki. The second and third initiations strengthen that connection and "power up" the initiate's system. The fourth initiation seals in the contact with the divine energy of Reiki so that the initiate will not lose it, even if he or she does not practice for long periods of time.

This first initiation activates/energizes an energy channel that is already present in the body of each person; however, in most people this energy channel is inactive. In other words, the wiring is there but there is no current running through it; the switch is off. The activation of this channel can be attained by many other means besides the Reiki initiation; for example certain Qi Qong practices. The Reiki initiation is simply a guaranteed "short cut" to activate this energy channel. Reiki Master Mihai Albu made the comment to me that the system of Reiki is simply, "Lazy person's Qi Qong" and there is truth in that statement. Instead of the typical years of Qi Qong practice it takes to normally activate this channel by having a disciplined Qi Qong practiced, the Reiki initiations are quick way of activating this channel.

When living in Colorado I occasionally taught the system of Reiki at a Martial Arts school that taught Qi Qong and Kung Fu. The instructor, who also took the Reiki class, commented that after receiving the Reiki initiations it was like having immediately advanced his practice by years; similar comments were made to him by his students who had also received the Reiki initiations.

Transcript of tape: (Note: Iris Ishikuro's notes use the same type of words such as antenna, electrodes, battery, etc., to describe the initiations and energy flow through the body.)

**Student:** *How do you go about putting up your antenna?*

**Takata:** *Oh, that's my business. All your antenna's are up, okay?* (this was after the students had received an initiation). *…You all have antenna and you all have this receiving set, right. This is called the solar plexus [tan-den]. Now we heard so much about solar plexus. And the doctors says that when he operates that person there is no organ called solar plexus. But it is just like the north pole and the south pole. All imaginary. But when you say, "We are going to the north pole" you understand what it means. you*

---

223 Haberly, *Reiki*, 22.

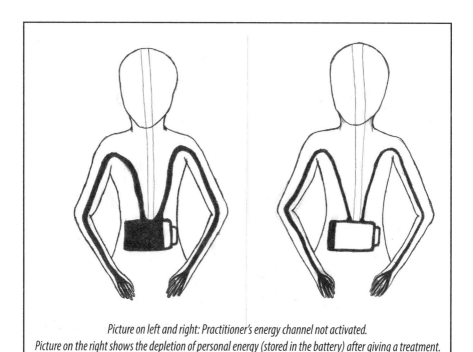

Picture on left and right: Practitioner's energy channel not activated.
Picture on the right shows the depletion of personal energy (stored in the battery) after giving a treatment.
*Original drawings by Kim Rapier.

*say, "We are going to the south pole" you know what it means. You understand? So same thing, we all have a solar plexus. This is the receiving set you see; and the antenna is up. Now if you sit up this is your highest spot in the whole body, so this is the antenna. When you stand up like me this is also my antenna; this is the highest spot in my body, you see. So, when you switch on and the energy comes out, antenna ohhhhhh, fill up your solar plexus, and out she comes – these are the electrodes [hands]. So the first one, two days, you do not give this patient very much. But when you work like 45 years like me I got much to give because my solar plexus or the receiving set is always full. Full. Full of energy. …*

*And so I am little different from other because I did it only 45 years. So when you people do 45 years, you do the same as me.*

**Student:** *So when you say receiving set, does that mean energy is coming in to you?*

**Takata:** *Into you. That's why you do not deplete. Now other systems…*

*Now he* [the new Reiki student] *is going to find the difference when he has the energy flowing and receiving and then letting it out; but he gets it first. So anything good that you do, you get bonus first. That's God power.*

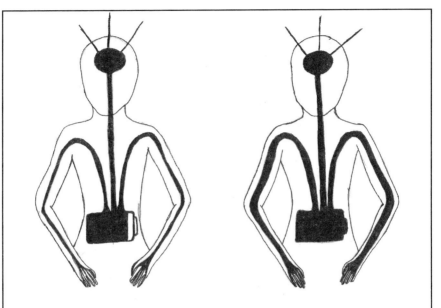

*Picture on left and right: Practitioner's energy channel activated by Reiki initiation.*
*Picture on the right shows the charging of personal energy (stored in the battery) after giving a treatment.*
*Original drawings by Kim Rapier.

*Ok? Isn't it wonderful!*

**Student:** *So does the energy comes in through the top here?*

**Takata:** *Yep* [antenna]

**Student:** *and stores here* [tanden]

**Takata:** *And then the more you are filled here you have more to come out. So the first few days, no, you take most, ¾, only ¼ come out. But when this is filled up, plenty come out. You see?*

Student: *But does it keep coming and replenish you every day?*

**Takata:** *That's it. That is what I am trying to tell you. As long as you have that antenna. Alright, how to lose it…*[224]

---

224   Takata stated that an initiate could lose the ability to do Reiki. This could come about by not holding the system with integrity. Specifically, she mentioned that initiates would lose the power of Reiki if they tried to teach the system to others without first having been properly trained by a Reiki Master. People tend to scoff at the idea of someone losing their ability to practice or use Reiki. How can a person be said to be practicing and teaching the Reiki system, which includes the precept of doing your work honestly, if they are not? A Master is the living system of Reiki; one cannot be dishonest and yet be said to be teaching or practicing Reiki. Takata's chief biographer writes, "There is an inherent wisdom in Reiki which will not let it be misused, and it will disappear of its own accord if there is any abuse." Haberly, *Reiki*, 54. Although this is not a popular idea, that doesn't necessarily make it untrue. Reiki Master Fumio Ogawa (1906-1998), a member of the Usui Reiki Ryōhō Gakkai, also wrote that Reiki can stop emanating from someone if they take wrong actions. "Everybody Can Do Reiki" (self-published), 51. This idea is also expressed in the Usui Reiki Ryoho Gakkai's booklet, Reiki Ryoho No Shiori.

In each of my classes, a lot of time is spent practicing the hand positions and experiencing Reiki. I want the students to be comfortable with the hand positions by the time they leave the class so that they have a sense of confidence. I want them to go away with a sense of wonderment about Reiki, which can come about only by practicing. Whether it is treating yourself or another, remember Takata's words, "Hands on, Reiki on."

In your practice, let Reiki guide you; don't try to guide Reiki. "Let go and let Reiki flow" is my common expression. The flow of Reiki is a one-way street. There is a specific process done in the initiations that prevents the practitioner from picking up something from the client and vice versa.[225] If you have received the Reiki initiations and just let Reiki flow without your own intentions, there is nothing to fear. But if you let your ego get involved and try to tell Reiki what to do, you are doing something other than the practice of Reiki.

Reiki is the Divine Creator's power. We can utilize the energy and see it work without our egos being involved. *When ego goes, Reiki flows.* Our ego wants to take credit and point to our self as the reason for Reiki's success when a client gets better. The truth is, Reiki will work without our egos at all. All we need to do is show up and put our hands on the client and let Reiki do its thing.

It is akin to using a watering can to water plants. The water in the watering can is the Reiki energy. Tipping the can a little is akin to placing our hands on another person's body. When we tip the watering can, we do not need to use intention for the water to come out of the can's spout; it simply comes out, no intention is needed.

When applying Reiki, practitioners use this Cosmic Energy, not their own personal energy. Takata mentions on an audiotape that, without the Reiki initiations, a person uses the energy they were born with; and this is dangerous. This will deplete the practitioner and, if they treat enough people, the practitioner will die from using and giving away their own life force energy.[220]

The "little bit of energy you were born with" Takata mentions is called 精 Jing in Traditional Chinese Medicine (TCM). Jing is one of the 三寶 Three Treasures in TCM. Takata is specifically mentioning prenatal Jing. Simply put, this is Jing you receive from your parents at conception.

This is one of many examples of how the Reiki system is derived from

---

225   This idea is similar to a "check valve" used in plumbing.

Traditional Chinese Medicine. It is also another example that unless a person knows TCM, he or she wouldn't really understand the significance of what Takata was saying. There is a big difference in wording between saying, "using your own energy" and "using the energy you were born with" in TCM. In fact, this shows that Takata herself did understand some core concepts in TCM, which she probably learned from her teacher. Rick Bockner has also stated that Takata knew facial diagnosis, which is one method of diagnosis used in TCM. See Chapter 4 for more details.

The practice is so simple that it is deceptively simple for some. Students ask, "You mean I don't have to think of anything during a treatment? I don't have to DO anything?" I tell them, "No, if you are doing something or thinking something in particular, then you are not practicing the Reiki system. Hands on, Reiki on." Just relax your mind and the Reiki will flow automatically. "Not doing" is the hard part of the practice for a lot of students.

Takata's diary inscription from December 10, 1935, states that practitioners should sit comfortably, close their eyes, put their hands in *gasshō*, concentrate their thoughts, and relax. This is to let the true energy, Reiki, stored in our *tanden* come out of our hands. This part of the diary was written during her Reiki training with her teacher Hayashi.[226] "Concentrate one's thoughts" is referring to bringing one's awareness to the present moment; in other words, not having your thoughts running wild and scattered all over the place. She mentions that it is important that recipients also purify their thoughts and have a desire to get well. She emphasizes having an attitude of gratitude; Usui did this too. While giving a treatment, we keep our minds quiet and place our hands on the body. This is all that is required of Reiki practitioners.

As we practice more, our energy level and awareness change. While providing a treatment, students will notice sensations in their hands indicating that particular body area's need for Reiki. The stronger the sensations in the practitioner's hand, the greater the need is for Reiki in that area. Greater sensitivity to the myriad of sensations will come with practice.

Through practice we gain new understandings and knowledge about Reiki and strengthen our relationship with Reiki, the Cosmic Life Force. By practicing hands-on treatments, we can see how effective Reiki treatments can be. The practice of Reiki can bring one to a place of wholeness and radiant health.

---

226   As described earlier, Takata's First and Second Degree certificates from Hayashi are both dated December 13, 1935.

Many students ask if they can also use Reiki on inanimate objects. Since everything that exists is comprised of this cosmic energy, the answer is yes. It is the "stuff" that we are all made of.

Takata told the story about how the dietician in the hospital where she was treated, Mrs. Shimura, would use Reiki to charge the hospital food for the patients.[227] And on a DVD entitled "The History of Reiki in Canada," Wanja Twan talks about how Takata charged Wanja's Master certificate with Reiki before giving it to her. People comment to Wanja that they feel a warm spot in her house when they walk by where the certificate is hanging. Wanja laughs and tells them it is the certificate hanging on the wall that is radiating the heat, thanks to Takata and the power of Reiki.

There is always ample opportunity to be practicing the main points of Reiki, which are the five precepts and the hands-on treatments. Life in general will give us opportunities that will challenge our holding of the precepts. And since practitioners are always carrying their hands around with them wherever they go, there is usually a chance to be practicing hands-on Reiki.

When we feel ourselves being challenged by the precepts, it can serve as our reminder to do the hands-on practice. Practitioners keep the Reiki precepts in their minds and live by them. Doing Reiki treatments on yourself helps you live by the precepts. If you have ever had a Reiki treatment before, then you know it is easy to live the precepts after that treatment for a while. You feel so good and relaxed that it would be hard to get upset or to worry. You feel so good that you are grateful and treat others kindly. Using Reiki allows us to be at peace with all things as they are. This is why Usui stated that his system of Usui Reiki Ryoho is the secret art to inviting happiness and the miraculous medicine for all diseases. The hands-on treatments will help one live the precepts as well as obtain optimal health.

Usui didn't give us the five precepts and say, "Good luck with those!" He gave us a way, the hands-on practice, to help us obtain living the precepts. The five precepts and the hands-on treatment are two sides of the same coin. They mutually support and engender each other. When we become angry or worried, the hands-on practice helps us with the precepts. When we are following the precepts of showing ourselves gratitude and kindness, we express this by giving ourselves hands-on treatments as a thank-you to our body, mind, and spirit. Doing our work honestly is shown by both the hands-on practice and living the precepts. Since we identify ourselves as being

---

227  Haberly, *Reiki,* 24.

practitioners of this system and its tenets are to live the precepts and do the hands-on practice, doing so *is* doing our work honestly.

The concept of an energy exchange is important. Sometimes new Reiki practitioners have a hard time asking for something in return. Some feel that since Reiki is the energy of the universe, they shouldn't charge for it. I tell my students that they aren't charging for Reiki; they are charging for their time. Only people who have gratitude and are sincere will be willing to give something in exchange for a treatment.

To get a clearer picture of how our own minds work and apply value onto things, I would like to end this chapter with a story about a sociological experiment. I read about this experiment while working on my bachelor's degree in sociology.

The experimenter pretended to be selling compost and set up three compost piles, each with a different price. The researcher was interested in seeing which of the piles would sell more compost and to find out the reason for it.

The end result was the pile that sold the most compost was the one in the middle of the price range. The buyers' rationale was that they didn't want the "cheapest" stuff because it was probably inferior in some way. And since most people didn't identify as "professional" gardeners, buyers didn't think they needed the most expensive compost. So what fit their needs best, they determined, was the mid-range pile of compost.

Now, remember, all this assessment and assigning value to the compost came from the buyers themselves. It was the buyers who immediately placed more value and quality on the different compost piles based on the prices set by the "seller", i.e., the researcher. This is the same thing that people do every day while shopping for a television in an appliance store or food in the grocery store. Based on nothing else but the price, we immediately think that something has more quality and worth. As it turns out, in this experiment the three compost piles contained the *exact* same compost; there was no difference but the price.

The truth is, sometimes giving something away for free or cheaply doesn't help a person. They will think it has no value, because that is what they have decided based on the little or no amount they had to give to get it. One purpose in Takata's story about Usui working in the slums was to make this point. She herself found out that when she didn't charge for Reiki training, people didn't value it and therefore didn't practice. Hayashi had warned her about this, but she didn't listen and wanted to "help" these people; her "help" went unappreciated.

Without practicing, one will not see the results that come only through practice. Buying exercise equipment isn't enough: one has to use it to see results. Similarly, one cannot just take a Reiki class and expect to see results without practicing.

By not setting a reasonable price for treatments or classes, we are cheating our students out of the opportunity to honestly try the practice. We may be thinking we are doing them a favor, doing charity work, or helping them in some way. But in my experience this is usually not the case because immediately the person doesn't think much of Reiki—not because it may not be helpful if done regularly, but because it had a "cheap" price. Takata stated repeatedly that to give Reiki away for free was to cheapen Reiki.

This topic is explored further in Chapter 10, "Fees for Training."

### Second Degree/Okuden: Highest Teachings

*"When the student becomes well acquainted with the above treatments and experience, with proof and testimonials, he is now ready for the "Oku Den", or deeper knowledge."*[218] above

~Hawayo Takata

The Second Degree class is for students who feel or have the calling to go further into the practice. A span of time between taking the First and Second Degree classes allows students time to practice and gain experience.

The Second Degree class constitutes a complete system for utilizing Reiki for healing. In the Second Degree Reiki class, students learn how to perform an absentee treatment: that is, how to treat people who are not physically present.[228] It also includes a technique to work with mental/emotional problems and challenges. This technique works by implanting messages that the recipient chooses into his or her subconscious mind. Also included is a way of strengthening the Reiki flow during a treatment. One initiation (energy activation) is given.

The First and Second Degree Reiki seminars constitute the complete

---

228  Just as a note of interest to some historians like myself, I was told by John Harvey Gray that Takata did her distant treatments early in the morning, 5 a.m., while standing up.

system for the practitioner's level. First and Second Degree graduates have the knowledge and capability to effectively treat themselves and others. Knowledge itself, however, isn't enough to bring about the positive changes one may seek. Experience is needed, which only comes through practice. When utilized, the system of Reiki can bring about a harmonious state of being in one's entire self: mind, body, and spirit. "Practice, practice, practice" and "let Reiki teach you."

Many students ask if, besides sending absentee Reiki treatments to people, they can also send Reiki to situations. In short, the answer is yes.

I heard a story about Takata sending Reiki to a situation. The story was told to me by Marta Getty, who spent some time with Takata in October of 1980 and heard this story directly from her. Marta was kind enough to write it out for inclusion in this book.

*"At the beginning of my Reiki practice in 1980, before becoming a Reiki Master, I had a week with Mrs. Hawayo Takata. She was the Lineage Bearer of Usui Shiki Ryoho then. During the week I asked her many questions. She answered them all. One was about doing distant treatments on situations. She told me a story that I have never forgotten.*

*She had been to an outdoor summer Health fair doing Reiki treatments. Across from her was a young couple that sold pottery. She had enjoyed them very much. At the end of the fair when Mrs. Takata was closing her booth, she saw them packing the pottery away. They were tired and not enjoying packing up the remaining pieces.*

*Mrs. Takata asked them if they would like her to try to find a buyer for all the pottery, and maybe someone else to do the packing. At this point in the story I was wondering about what I had been taught to not ask for specific outcomes.*

*The couple said yes, grateful that she would try to do this for them. Mrs. Takata sent a distant treatment asking 'if this is the best thing for this young couple who are tired and who have worked hard this weekend, would you please find someone to buy all the pottery and to pack it up.'*

*She did the treatment for a few minutes, and then went on dismantling her Reiki space. A little while later she saw another couple walking along the path. They went up to the pottery booth and asked if the people would be willing to sell them all the pottery because they liked it very much, and could sell it in their pottery shop. They would even be happy to pack it up to take with them. The young couple profusely thanked Mrs. Takata for the Reiki after the pottery was gone.*

*I was impressed that this kind of treatment was possible. She said one can't make Reiki do anything so she always asked for only the best for the people involved and if it were not the best, it would have a different outcome. This expanded my understanding of Reiki and its unimaginable number of possibilities."*

Another example that Barbara Brown gave was when Takata would lose something, she would ask Reiki to help the situation. "When Takata lost things she would say, 'Reiki Reiki, take care of this for me please' and then leave it. Wonderful things happened..."[229]

However, it is clear that other Masters do not hold with this idea of sending Reiki to situations. I remember when I was training as a Master candidate under Fran Brown, she told me the following story. Fran said that she was at a Reiki Alliance meeting and one Master, Mary McFadyen, said to the group that they should start this meeting by sending Reiki to the day. Fran leaned over to Paul Mitchell and asked him, "When we send Reiki to the day, do we start on the head or the abdomen?" I laughed, because that was one way of looking at it. It was clear Fran didn't hold with the idea of sending Reiki to the day or to an event, but my own experience says otherwise.

Strictly speaking, I don't think Takata *taught* people to send Reiki to situations or inanimate objects, but she *talked* about doing these very things.

---

229 Twan, *Early Days of Reiki: Memories of Hawayo Takata,* 26-27.

# *Chapter* EIGHT

---

## *The Teaching Levels*
### *Third Degree/Shinpiden: Reiki Master/Teacher*
### *Comparing Takata's Shinpiden and Dai-Shihan Certificates*

## *What Is a Reiki Master?*
### *Preparation and Timing for the Teaching Degrees*
### *The Inward Journey and Process of Master Consciousness*
### *My Own Understanding*
### *Questions for Reiki Master Candidates*

# CHAPTER
# 08

## The Teaching Levels

### Third Degree/Shinpiden: Reiki Master/Teacher

*"Masters are the facilitators of knowledge."*
~Anthony "Spirit" Thiebaut

Third Degree, or the Master level, is the most commonly misunderstood level in the Reiki system. Traditionally, Third Degree is for those who wish to teach the system of Reiki to others. Takata taught the Third Degree (called Shinpiden) in three aspects. [230] However, when Takata trained Masters in North America, she did not use the Japanese words (written in parentheses below) for Master Training or for the different aspects of the Master training:

- First aspect (Shihan-kaku): the student learns how to teach the First Degree course.

- Second aspect (Shihan): the student learns how to teach the Second Degree course.

---

230 This viewpoint regarding the aspects of Shinpiden is also expressed by Tadao Yamaguchi, whose mother took the First and Second Degrees from Hayashi. Tadao states that Hayashi referred to Shinpiden as having multiple parts, the first part being called Shihan-kaku and the second part being called Shihan. He states Shihan-kakus can train others in the First Degree/Shoden class and that Shihans can train others in both the First Degree/Shoden and the Second Degree/Okuden classes. *Light on the Origins of Reiki*, 28-29. Tadao goes on to state just like the second aspect of Shinpiden, the third aspect of Shinpiden was also originally called Shihan. However, this was later changed to Dai-Shihan to avoid confusion. *Light on the Origins of Reiki*, 67, footnote 9 (found on page 188). Tadao's mother, Chiyoko Yamaguchi, had taken the First and Second Degrees with Hayashi a few years after Takata was already a Dai-Shihan, and we are told Tadao's great-uncle was a Dai-Shihan. Chiyoko learned how to perform Reiju from her uncle, Wasaburo Sugano, who was a Dai-Shihan student of Hayashi. According to the Usui Reiki Ryoho Gakkai's booklet, Reiki Ryoho No Shiori written in the 1970's, it also states that Shinpiden contains three aspects, Shihan-kaku, Shihan, and Dai-Shihan.

- Third aspect (also originally called Shihan but later changed to Dai-Shihan): the student is given permission to train others in Shinpiden.

At first, Takata would have a waiting period between teaching Master students the first and second aspects. However, Takata later dropped this waiting period between teaching these two aspects when teaching her students. After receiving training in the first two aspects of Shinpiden and upon receiving full payment of the course fee, Takata would issue the student a Third Degree (Shinpiden) certificate. The issuing of a Third Degree certificate by the teacher after the student's completion of the first two aspects of Shinpiden and payment of training fee appears to be in alignment with how Hayashi had taught Takata.

The word Shinpiden means "mystery teachings". The word Shihan-kaku means "Assistant teacher". The word Shihan means "teacher" but is more thought of as meaning "good example." In other words, a Shihan sets a good example by his or her behavior and actions. "Dai-Shihan" means, "Big teacher" and in contemporary times is used to distinguish between the Shihans who were allowed to train First and Second degree students and those who were granted permission to train others in the Third Degree.

| 神秘傳[231] Shinpiden – mystery teachings (oral tradition, handed down). To transmit God's secret method. *Shinpi* means, "mystery, mysterious, God's secret, supernatural, marvelous, wondrous, miraculous, mysterious, mystical," and *den* means, "To transmit, to relay, to send, to pass (on to). To hand down, to perpetuate." | 師範 Shihan - Instructor, teacher, model. *Shi* means, "expert, teacher, master, army, war," and *han* means, "pattern, example, model." |

Confusion and disagreement about these aspects of Shinpiden have arisen because of a lack of clarity and understanding between Takata and some of her students. The initial misunderstanding about the Third Degree originally stems from the different training methods Takata used when training her Master students. By speaking with some of Takata's Master students and their Master students, I was able to gain an understanding about the different

---

231   This is the prewar *kanji* – the modern version would be 神秘伝

ways Takata conducted her Master training and what she taught. This topic is explored further in the following chapter.

In Takata's case, she learned Shinpiden in 1936. Her certificate is dated October 1, 1936 and has the kanji for the word "Shinpiden" written at the top. Additionally, Takata received a Dai-Shihan certificate dated February 21, 1938.

Unlike her own training by Hayashi, though, when Takata trained her own Master students the distinction between the second and third aspects of Shinpiden was not clearly made with an additional certificate.[232]

Takata would use on her certificates the terms "introductory course" for First Degree, "intermediate course" for Second Degree, and "advanced course" for Third Degree.[233] Sometimes Takata would handwrite the words "3rd Degree" and "Master" on the advanced course certificate.

Following Hayashi's example, I use two different Master certificates. The first certificate I give has the term Shinpiden on it. The second Master certificate has the term Dai-Shihan written on it. I do this to avoid the confusion that seemed to stem from Takata giving out just one certificate for the Third Degree and apparently no one receiving an additional certificate (specifying them as a Dai-Shihan).

## Comparing Takata's Shinpiden and Dai-Shihan Certificates

Takata's Shinpiden certificate dated October 1, 1936[234] from Hayashi is written in Japanese. A translation in English by Justin Stein is below:

Note: It contains the Japanese phrase "shinpiden reiju-hō"; this is referring to the initiation processes that are learned at this level of training.[235]

### Takata Hawayo

*The above person received the reiju ("spirit conferral") for the shoden ("first transmission") and okuden ("inner transmission") of Reiki Therapy on*

---

232  This is true even of Barbara Weber Ray, who claimed that she alone was made a Dai-Shihan or "Fourth Degree". Barbara never presented a fourth certificate from Takata and only had three certificates identical to those received by the other Master students of Takata.

233  I have photographs of some of Takata's Master students' certificates for the First, Second, and Third Degrees. You may find photographs of Barbara Weber Ray's certificates from Takata for the First, Second, and Third Degrees here: http://www.trtia.org/histpers.html

234  All four of Takata's certificates are in the personal collection of Phyllis Furumoto.

235  At the time of this writing, Phyllis Furumoto does not want Takata's Shoden, Okuden, or Shinpiden certificates published. These are available for viewing at some of Furumoto's workshops.

*December 10, 1935. From that time until May 8, 1936, she diligently studied how to treat various diseases at this institute under my direct instruction. While this is not a long period of time, due to natural talent and earnest sincerity, she diagnoses quickly, reliably gives effective treatments, and has the "spiritual ability" (reinō) to cure every type of illness, of course, with this therapy. I recognize this person as the most suitable for the initiation/instruction (denju) of this therapy and give her the reiju of the shinpiden reiju-hō ("secret transmission spirit conferral method").*

*October 1, 1936*

*Master of Hayashi Reiki Research Center    Hayashi Chūjirō*

A copy of Takata's fourth certificate (Dai-Shihan certificate) is on the next page.

Upon examination, one will note that the first paragraph on Takata's Dai-Shihan certificate from Hayashi is written in the past tense and is referring to the abilities she has already demonstrated as a Shoden, Okuden, and Shinpiden student. It is speaking about her past experiences treating others with Reiki and "conferring the power of Reiki on others"; in other words, training and initiating students. This is made even clearer in Hayashi's farewell address where he states, "Then, two years ago in July, she returned to Kauai, where she started healing and teaching; her students numbered more than fifty."[236]

Also, Takata's Dai-Shihan certificate states, "I [Chujiro Hayashi] do hereby confer upon Mrs. Hawayo Takata the full power and authority to practice the Reiki system and to impart to others the secret knowledge and the gift of healing under this system." It is important that Hayashi used the words "full power and authority" and "impart to others the secret knowledge" in this certificate. As opposed to just being able to teach the First and Second Degrees, these words describe Takata's new position to train Masters, including the ability to teach others how to perform the initiations. To "impart to others the secret knowledge" is referring to teaching others the initiation processes.

The Dai-Shihan certificate goes on to say that Takata is "authorized to confer similar powers on others and one of the thirteen fully qualified as a Master of the profession." Again, this is stating she is now able to train other Masters. Hayashi used the term "fully qualified" to refer to the level of Dai-Shihan.

---

236    Hayashi, "Farewell Address." See Appendix 4.

C E R T I F I C A T E

_THIS IS TO CERTIFY_ that Mrs. Hawayo Takata, an American citizen born in the Territory of Hawaii, after a course of study and training in the Usui system of Reiki healing undertaken under my personal supervision during a visit to Japan in 1935 and subsequently, has passed all the tests and proved worthy and capable of administering the treatment and of conferring the power of Reiki on others.

THEREFORE I, Dr. Chujiro Hayashi, by virtue of my authority as a Master of the Usui Reiki system of drugless healing, do hereby confer upon Mrs. Hawayo Takata the full power and authority to practice the Reiki system and to impart to others the secret knowledge and the gift of healing under this system.

MRS. HAWAYO TAKATA is hereby certified by me as a practitioner and Master of Dr. Usui's Reiki system of healing, at this time the only person in the United States authorized to confer similar powers on others and one of the thirteen fully qualified as a Master of the profession.

Signed by me this 21st day of February, 1938, in the city and county of Honolulu, territory of Hawaii.

Witness to his signature:

(SIGNED) *Chujiro Hayashi*

---

*TERRITORY OF HAWAII,*
*City and County of Honolulu.* } *ss.*

On this 21st day of February , A. D. 1938 , *before me personally appeared* * * * * * * * * * * *(DR.) CHUJIRO HAYASHI* * * * * * * * * * * * * * * * * * *to me known to be the person..... described in and who executed the foregoing instrument and acknowledged that WHO executed the same as HIS free act and deed.

*Notary Public, First Judicial Circuit,*
*Territory of Hawaii.*

ADVERTISER 220869

### What Is a Reiki Master?

*Reiki Mastership: Time, Money, and Training (Oh My!)*

There are as many ideas of what Reiki Mastership requires as there are Reiki Masters. Not to mention, many Reiki systems are being taught and practiced today.[237] How does one go about selecting a Master? Let's first define what I mean by "Reiki Master."

A Reiki Master is a person—a human being just like everyone else. He or she knows this as well, and doesn't present him or herself as being better than anyone else. A Reiki Master is a person who has received all of the necessary initiations for each degree in the system, the Reiki symbols (including the knowledge of their usage), and the training and knowledge that go along with each degree he or she is teaching.

A Reiki Master is a person who has dedicated an enormous part of his or her life to using, being in relationship with, and ultimately living Reiki.

A Reiki Master is someone who uses Reiki daily, strives to live by the Reiki precepts, has learned and continues to practice the system that he or she was taught, allows him or herself to be guided by Reiki, and lives and breathes Reiki.

I believe a Reiki practitioner needs seasoning to fully grasp the concepts at the Master level. Without plenty of experience, the major points will be missed. One of the best ways to express this idea comes from a quote in *Dharma Paths*, by Ven. Khenpo Karthar Rinpoche. This is a book on Buddhism and not Reiki, but the concept of having enough experience and openness to realize the higher teachings of any given system is described very well. The quote is:

*"This level of teaching is secret, not because there is some kind of partiality or exclusiveness, but because a given practitioner may not have sufficient openness and intelligence to receive it. For example, because human beings have language, we can communicate with each other more completely than animals. Because we have greater intelligence, we can understand and learn from each other more effectively than animals. We have not somehow hidden our language and intelligence from the animals, but no matter how much we might want to communicate our concepts to them, they are unable to comprehend them. Just as our concepts are incomprehensible to the animals, the vajrayana is self-secret to some people."*[238]

---

237  Unfortunately, some people are keen on creating fictional Reiki lineages. Use your discernment and do your homework on a potential teacher and his or her lineage.
238  Ven. Khenpo Karthar Rinpoche, *Dharma Paths* (Ithaca, NY: Snow Lion, 1992), 258.

"Self-secret" is the key phrase. Just as one must have a solid foundation in addition and subtraction before being able to do multiplication and division, one must have a solid foundation in First Degree and Second Degree, with adequate experience, to fully appreciate the teachings at the Master level. We could try to teach children multiplication and division before addition and subtraction, but they would not be able to understand the concepts. *Right timing is needed.*

Another example of how right timing and self-secret is an important part of the Reiki system can be given. Let's say you tell me about your favorite novel and how good you think the story is. So, you ask me to take the time to read it. Do you suppose that if I ask you to just tell me what happens in the last chapter of the novel that I would have the same appreciation for this novel as you hold? Reading the last page of a book will not give you the complete understanding of the book's meaning the same way as if you had read and reread it many times. Similarly, learning the Master level will offer very little to you if you don't come to it with enough practice or experience.

Some people might think there will be something like a prize at the end of a Master class, like the toy given in the bottom of a cereal box. I think the apprenticeship route gives a student a better overview of what being a Master is about. It allows time for the student to realize that it is a process of developing and unfolding, and not something that can be bestowed upon you by taking a one- or two-day class.

## Preparation and Timing for the Teaching Degrees

Over the years, I have been asked by complete strangers the following questions and here is my standard reply:

**Stranger:** "I want to take First Degree, Second Degree, and Third Degree."
**Robert:** So you haven't taken the First Degree yet?
**Stranger:** No.
**Robert:** So why do you want to become a teacher in a system you haven't practiced yet and don't know about?

*Sometimes the conversation goes like this…*

**Stranger:** I want to be a Reiki Master.
**Robert:** Do you practice Reiki daily?
**Stranger:** No.
**Robert:** Then why do you want to be a Master in a system you don't practice yourself?

It is important to understand that no one can make you a Master. Taking a class does not make you a master of anything. Years of training and practice are required for the path of mastery.

Even after Reiki Master candidate apprenticeship training, one is always learning more about Reiki and opening more to Reiki. You are always a student of Reiki. Mastery is, therefore, not something you can get to in one day or by taking a class; it is a process of living the Five Reiki Precepts and doing the practices of the system each day. It is a continuing process at every moment.

This is why I favor an apprenticeship route for training new Masters. The apprenticeship route is normally at least a year or two. Then there is time for the apprentice to start becoming a Master by his or her own efforts and dedication. As I stated earlier, no one can make you a Master. If no one can make you a Master, then how much truer is it that you cannot become a Master by reading a book or watching a video? Mastery is something that the student achieves by his or her own initiative, understanding, motivation, and practice. The Master doing the training acts as a guide and imparts the sacred knowledge to the student.

If you are contemplating Reiki Mastery, first think about what your motivations and intentions are for this level of training. Is it simply to learn the rest of the system? Is it because you want to teach and pass on the Reiki system to others? Get clear with yourself about your desires for continuing on this path. A list of questions for the potential Master candidate is listed at the end of this chapter.

Mastery is a way of life, not a title or credential for your ego. If your own practice is not firmly grounded, then upon what are you building? Time and experience are needed. Reiki training is like a pyramid. Out of all the people who take the First Degree—which is the base, foundation, and largest part of the pyramid and which is also all most people will ever need—some will go on to take Second Degree. Third Degree is a calling.

This process of deciding and the training can take years, with many twists and turns. Trust in the Reiki precepts on this journey, for you will be tested. Your logical mind and your desire for this level of training will be in direct conflict sometimes. The path you may end up walking down is one that you may not have foreseen. Trust Reiki and trust your inner self. Listen to your teacher; sometimes he or she will say something that you might not want to hear, but listen anyway. A good teacher will have your best interest at heart and will try to guide you along the path. This is not an overnight process, so have patience with it.

Maintaining the integrity of the Reiki system is a key component of mastership. What you teach will define what is thought of as the system of Reiki for a long time to come—possibly even after you are long gone. Holding the teachings as something sacred and not to be changed lightly is part of keeping the integrity of the system intact. We allow our practice of the form to change us; we don't change the form to suit us.

Not everyone has the inner calling to become a Reiki Master. But traditionally, for even those who did, this wasn't enough. The initiating Reiki Master must also have had the calling to train you as well. Takata trained thousands of Reiki students but only 22 as Masters. Usui and Hayashi also trained thousands of students but only approximately 20[239] and 13[240], respectively, as Masters. Clearly, by their example, these three great Masters were interested in training only those whom they felt would become good teachers.

I feel that teachers who offer the First, Second and Third Degrees all in one weekend have a different understanding about Reiki than those who take a longer and more thorough approach. Knowledge is different from understanding and from the wisdom that comes through time and practice. It is my experience that it takes a new Third Degree student time to season. The practice of the system will lead one to understanding all that is offered in the Reiki system. This is not possible to get in one weekend. How can someone be a Reiki Master who may never have given or received a single Reiki treatment?

How can one become a Master if there is no challenge to it? If you are the same before and after your apprenticeship training as a Master, what have you really learned? How have you grown? Today we have people becoming "Masters" in a single day or even via the Internet, with no experience, challenges, or commitments to meet. I feel this is not the best way for new Masters to be trained. I believe we would all agree that, given a choice, we would like to learn the system of Reiki from a person who has had thorough training and years of hands-on practice experience.

Having the ability to hold and understand seemingly contradictory statements is also part of Mastery. When one has gained Mastery, there are no hard and fast rules; this is replaced with flexibility and spontaneity. This is when our understanding of the form is truly reached and spontaneously

---

239  Yamaguchi, *Light on the Origins of Reiki*, 67.
240  Takata's Dai-Shihan certificate, reproduced above, stated that she was "one of the thirteen fully qualified as a Master of the profession."

replaced with formlessness. When we as Masters become the living teachings, not rigidly binding ourselves onto one part or another or merely parroting the words of the Masters before us, we have "gotten it." Until such a time, we practice the form, as this is the path that leads to formlessness.

I had a great acupuncture teacher in school named Whit Reaves. He would frequently end an absolute statement with a phrase like "except when it's not." For example, he would say things such as, "When there is a patient who is exhibiting fatigue, loose stools, and a yellow complexion, the diagnosis is always Spleen Qi Deficiency…except when it's not." Or he would say, "If you needle the point Small Intestine Six, it will always take away pain along the superior border of the scapula…except when it doesn't."

Years ago, I listened to Jack Kornfield, an American Buddhist teacher, retelling a story. The story went something like this: Imagine that you are blindfolded and walking down a road toward me. I can see that you are slowly veering left and are about to fall into the ditch on the side of the road. So I call out to you, "Go more to the right."After another minute, you are now about to go into the ditch on the right side of the road, so I yell to you, "Go more to the left!"At this point you might think I am crazy and telling you contradictory information just to play with you. But sometimes teachers see what the students cannot, and give advice to help the students avoid pitfalls, or ditches, along their path.

*Right timing and experience are important.* The world doesn't need more "Reiki Masters"; it needs more Reiki practitioners who are willing to live the precepts and offer help by providing treatments for those in need.

## The Inward Journey and Process of Master Consciousness

*Mastership as a state of Consciousness (with a big "C")*
*Ordinary mind = consciousness (with a little "c")*

Words were never meant to take the place of reality; in fact, words get in the way. We can't accurately portray the truth with words; however, we can use words to give glimpses of the truth. If you have never tasted a pawpaw fruit, a fruit native to the state of Kentucky, I could tell you it tastes like a combination of a mango and banana custard. This helps you get an idea of what I am talking about, but it doesn't give you the actual experience or the reality of what a pawpaw tastes like. The best way to understand anything is through direct experience.

This also applies in Reiki, where there is value in oral tradition. Oral tradition is important, but again, words will get you only so far. With oral tradition, you have a meeting of the teacher and the student(s). More than simply words are conveyed in a Reiki class. What I talk about, or how I may answer a question, is always dictated by who is asking and who is present. I let the Reiki answer for me. When I teach a class, I let the Reiki flow through me and the words come out of my mouth without my brain getting involved too much.

Many times when I teach, a sentence I use may have several different messages layered into the same sentence. In other words, there are sometimes three or more ways one can interpret what I am saying, and I hope the keen student is catching all the meanings I am intending to convey. A funny example of this is one I remember from the movie *The Hobbit*, where Frodo says to Gandalf, "Good morning," and Gandalf rattles off many different ways he could interpret that and says he would like to know which one Frodo meant. Because people will interpret the same sentence in different ways, this can also lead to misunderstandings. This is another good reason to attend multiple classes given by the teacher.

The practice of Reiki is a hands-on, direct experience that goes beyond words. The initiations are an important process during the class. This is where the students experience direct contact with the energy. Words can get one only so far, and direct experience of Reiki (Spiritual Energy) is a unique feature of this system. Takata stated many times, "Let Reiki teach you!" The more we practice, the more Reiki will teach us.

Takata instructed her Master students not to create another Reiki Master until she went into transition or gave her approval. When Takata died in December 1980, the first group of teaching Masters she trained had been trained as Masters for approximately four years. Takata knew that it takes time and experience for a Master to be ready for the responsibility of training another Master. Ten years of teaching the First and Second Degree classes seems reasonable before contemplating training another Master.

## My Own Understanding

Dai-Shihan, the third aspect of the Third Degree (Shinpiden), seems to originally be understood as the recognition that the person had the potential and authority to train other Masters. This would come as an acknowledgment from that person's teacher that this student has (or will have) the necessary experience and the right character, mindset, and ability to uphold the Reiki precepts, and the teacher's confidence in that student to train other Masters. I feel this is what Takata meant when she said, "they need my blessing" to train another person as a Master.

## Questions for Reiki Master Candidates

I was given these questions as preparation for my own training as a Reiki Master.[241] I have found these to be useful in helping my own potential Master Candidates examine their motives and readiness for this level of training.

By answering these questions, you will gain a sense of clarity regarding your own understanding of Reiki. As your experiences grow and change, you might want to amend your answers. During the Master training, some questions and their answers will become clarified. These are just a starting point.

**In relation to your study of Reiki:**

1.  What is my intended outcome?
2.  How will I know when I have achieved it?
3.  What is Mastery?
4.  What does the word "Reiki" mean?
5.  What is the practice of Reiki?
6.  What is the spiritual practice of Reiki?
7.  What are the benefits of the practice of Reiki?
8.  In what ways is Reiki healing?
9.  Why do you want to become a Reiki Master?
10. What is necessary to be a Reiki Master?
11. What has been the most important experience for you with Reiki?

---

241   I was unable to find the original author of these questions.

12. Do you have any criteria for students of Reiki?

13. What would you avoid teaching?

14. What (if any) have been your disappointments with Reiki?

15. Do you have any goals with Reiki for yourself? As an organization?

16. What is the role of secrecy in Reiki?

17. What is an oral tradition?

18. What do you hope the system of Reiki will be like 10 years from now? Fifty years from now?

19. What concerns (if any) do you have about the corruption of the Reiki system?

20. What do you feel about new Reiki symbols? More initiations? Additional levels of Reiki?

21. What would you do if new symbols came to you? To your students?

22. Whom will you teach?

23. Why have you chosen this time to become a teacher?

24. How do you want your Master training conducted /organized/ structured?

25. What do you expect of the Master who trains you, now and in the future?

26. How do you feel about the term "Master"?

27. What would you charge for Reiki training, and why?

28. How would you respond to those who ask you to make them Reiki Masters? What would you charge and why?

29. What have you liked in the Reiki classes you have attended and what would you like to see handled differently?

30. What are the components of the First and Second Degree Reiki class?

31. If you were to write a job description for a Reiki Master, what would it include?

32. What is your greatest fear (if any) about becoming a Master? How would you resolve it?

33. What questions have been the most difficult for you to answer, and why?

34. Are you ready?

# Chapter NINE

## Historical Perspectives on Master Training and the Master Initiation

*The First Group of Takata's Master Students*
*The Second Group of Takata's Master Students*

×××××××××××××××××××××××××××××××××××××××××××××××××××××××××××××××××××××××××

## *Historical Perspectives on*
## *Master Training and the Master Initiation*

*Pippin: "And whose side are you on?"*
*Treebeard: "Side? I am on nobody's side.*
*Because nobody is on my side..."*[242]

In 2012, in New York City, I gave a lecture about the possible invention of the "Master initiation" by Takata. Since delivering that lecture in 2012, I've discovered more information in the course of my ongoing research.

In fact, this has been one of the deciding factors for me to publish this information. I realize the majority of people practicing in the Takata tradition will be biased in favor that the Master initiation is original to the system of Reiki. No one wants to hear that one of the Reiki Masters in their lineage may have simply made up the Master initiation and/or instructions, and I know people tend to discredit what they don't want to believe, regardless of what the truth may actually be. However, because most of the Masters Takata trained never received or learned the Master initiation, and today most people receive a Master initiation during their Third Degree training, it seems possible this may be what happened. This will no doubt be the most controversial and heated topic in this book. I hope it will lead to a respectful dialogue between Reiki Masters and groups.

Because I was not looking for any evidence of the possible invention of

---

242  *The Two Towers* by J.R.R. Tolkien.

the Master initiation, it took me a while to even realize and understand some of the information I had been given over the years. There had always been discrepancies regarding certain aspects of the history of the Reiki system. However, I was unaware that these discrepancies were all interrelated with the topics discussed in this chapter. In other words, I had the information as one would have random pieces of a puzzle—except I didn't know they were pieces to the *same* puzzle.

My research is based on documents, audio recordings, testimonies, and logical deductions about the history of the Master initiation. The history of the Master initiation in the Reiki system discussed in this chapter gradually came to light, piece by piece and story by story, from different Master students of Takata's and their students (along with accompanying documents). There are some Masters trained by Takata who are still alive and can be asked, as I have done, regarding the history of the Master initiation.

My initial search that led me on this quest was to find the reason why an early Takata Master student, Virginia Samdahl, had decided to join Barbara Weber Ray's organization, the American Reiki Association (A.R.A.). I finally discovered that, according to my research, the early Master students and a few of the latter Master students of Takata's did not receive a Master initiation from her during their training, and Takata may have only taught a few of the students she did initiate how to perform the Master initiation. Knowing this, Virginia's decision about joining the A.R.A. made more sense, as she wanted to both receive this Master initiation and learn the procedure that Barbara Weber Ray claimed she knew. But then the question arose for me: If, in fact, Barbara Weber Ray had learned these things from Takata, then which of Takata's other Master students also received the Master initiation and learned its procedure?

The following chart should be used as a reference for this chapter. The first group of Masters was trained before Takata's retirement and the second group of Masters was trained after Takata came out of retirement. Dividing the Master students into these groups also makes sense for another reason: Students in the first group did not receive a Master initiation, while some in the second group did.

| Chronological Order of Takata's Master Student's Training | |
|---|---|
| **First Group** | **Second Group** |
| *Kay Yamashita** | *Ursula Baylow**[243] |
| *Virginia W. Samdahl** | Fran Brown* |
| *Ethel Lombardi** | Phyllis Lei Furumoto |
| *John Harvey Gray** | Barbara Weber*** |
| *Iris Ishikuro** | Bethal Phaigh.* |
| *Harry Masami Kuboi** | Barbara Brown* |
| *Barbara Lincoln McCullough** | Wanja Twan** |
| *Dorothy Baba** | *Beth Gray** |
| | *Paul Mitchell* |
| | *George Araki** |
| | *Shinobu* Saito* [244] |
| | Patricia Bowling** |
| | Mary Alexandra McFadyen* |
| | Rick Bockner |
| *Deceased<br>Names appearing in *italics* did not receive a Master initiation | **No longer teaching<br>***Status unknown |

## The First Group of Takata's Master Students

It was when I first started talking with John Harvey Gray's Master student, Stephen Comee, that I discovered Takata's early Master students did not receive a "Master initiation". John Harvey Gray, whose Master certificate from Takata is dated October 6, 1976, told his Master students that to his knowledge there was no such thing as a "Master initiation" and that Takata had made one up later on in her teachings.

---

243 Takata secretly trained Ursula as a Master immediately after Ursula's Second Degree training in 1978. Takata asked Ursula not to tell anyone she was trained as a Master. Then, in 1979, when Takata visited Ursula again, she received her Master certificate, dated June 11, 1979. It is possible that originally, in 1978, Ursula did not receive a Master initiation, but then in 1979 she did. However, the possibility of this seems highly unlikely based on other research I have performed.

244 It is unknown at the time of writing this book if Shinobu Saito received a Master initiation from Takata. I have reasons to believe she may not have been given a Master initiation. Therefore, only half of her name is printed in italics.

In 2011, when I did Master training with Helen Borth, a founding member of The Reiki Alliance, she told me she had not received a Master initiation from her teacher, Barbara McCullough. It was Helen's belief there originally was no such a thing as a "Master initiation". Barbara McCullough was an early Master student of Takata's who was trained on June 25, 1977, and did not receive a "Master initiation" from Takata.[245] Helen Borth was trained as a Master by Barbara McCullough on December 21, 1980, just 10 days after Takata's death.

I decided then to verify this information with the only other living first-generation Master student of Takata's with whom I had been in contact previously: Harry Kuboi. Harry Kuboi was trained as a Master by Takata on April 18, 1977. When I spoke with him he stated he had not received a Master initiation from Takata and it was his belief there was no such a thing as a "Master initiation". He also told me he heard Takata later started doing "Master initiations".

After John Harvey Gray made his transition, I realized that Harry Kuboi was the only Master student from the first generation of Takata's Master students who was still alive and who could be contacted by third parties to verify this information. I also knew that if Harry went into transition before my book was published, this might lead to doubts regarding my claims of what he had said. This is why I took protective measures and specifically asked a few other people to call Harry and ask him the same question I had asked: whether or not there was such a thing as a Master initiation. They did, and confirmed with Harry that, to his knowledge, there originally was not a Master initiation. Two people who confirmed this information with Harry Kuboi are Mihai Albu and Stephen Comee. I also posted, with Harry's permission, his phone number on my website. During my 2012 New York lecture on the

---

245  McCullough stated in a letter written to Barbara Weber Ray on May 25, 1983, and also in her Reiki flyers that she was "initiated" as a Master by Takata. A
     physical initiation is highly speculative due to the fact that McCullough's first Master student, Helen Borth, whom she trained 10 days after Takata's transition,
     told me that she did not receive a physical Master initiation from McCullough. Helen stated that a "Master initiation" isn't part of her lineage.
         Interestingly enough, Helen Borth told me that Phyllis Furumoto came to her house in February 1982 and asked her if Barbara McCullough ever initiated
     her as a Master. Since the answer was "no," Phyllis initiated her and gave her a Master certificate. Phyllis didn't ask for any monetary compensation; Helen
     had already paid Barbara McCullough for her training. I have copies of Helen's certificates from both Barbara McCullough and Phyllis Furumoto.
         Another Master student of Barbara McCullough, David Jarell, was also initiated by Phyllis after his training with Barbara McCullough. So it is apparent to
     me that Phyllis knew some of the Master students of Takata's had not received a Master initiation.
         It seems likely that McCullough didn't initiate Borth as a Master because McCullough didn't know about a "Master initiation" at this time (because she
     had never received one from Takata). Once McCullough learned of a "Master initiation", she started giving one to her later Master students and started
     stating she had received one from Takata.
         McCullough states the reason for having Furumoto initiate her Master students in a letter she wrote to Furumoto and carbon copied to Baba, Lombardi,
     Saito, and Borth, on November 28, 1982. The reason she gives is that she wanted Phyllis to recognize the Masters she had trained. In short, McCullough
     stated this because Barbara Weber had threatened a lawsuit against her saying that she had, "legalized the Reiki keys and process as her "trade secrets".
     McCullough thought that by Furumoto giving her students the fourth "symbol" and initiation, Weber would leave her alone. That being the case, and while
     McCullough was still alive, Borth had been training students prior to receiving this "Master initiation" from Furumoto.

history of the Master initiation, I told the audience they could call Harry and ask him this question themselves. As it turned out, Harry Kuboi did make his transition before this book was published.

When Takata trained her early Master students, she would start by teaching them the name of the fourth "symbol"[246] and how to teach and perform the initiations of the First Degree (i.e.: first aspect or "Shihan-kaku"). At a later date, usually months later, her Master students would receive training in how to train and initiate students into the Second Degree (i.e.: second aspect or "Shihan"). No Master initiation was given to these students. For example, John Harvey Gray writes that he learned the First Degree initiations from Takata and then Takata told him she would teach him the Second Degree initiation when she came back in three months.[247]

Based on how the early Master students—the "first generation" of Takata Master students—were trained, it seemed clear that a Third Degree student had the knowledge of how to train others in the First and Second Degrees. And because no Third Degree or "Master" initiation was given by Takata, these early Master students understood that this was all there was to the Third Degree training.

Takata told her Master students they were not to train another Master at this point.[248] It seems most of these Master students believed they had the knowledge and ability to train another Master because they had learned the initiation procedures for the First and Second Degrees. These students believed that they were not yet allowed to train another Master simply because they lacked the proper experience in teaching the First and Second Degree classes, not because there was more training or an initiation beyond what they had already learned.

## The Second Group of Takata's Master Students

Based on how some of the "second generation" of Takata's Master students were trained, some would understand the definition of the Third Degree

---

246 "Symbol" is used in quotes intentionally.

247 Gray and Gray, *Hand to Hand*, 178

248 Barbara McCullough writes in a letter to Phyllis Furumoto dated September, 1981 that Takata told a few Master students they could train other Masters after her death. However, Barbara Weber Ray refutes this in a letter dated March 7, 1983. In this letter Barbara writes that Takata had told her in front of two other witnesses[188]: "And she [Takata] stated that some believed they could make a third degree (teacher) none of them had the set of keys for doing this. Again, Mrs. Takata did not share her rationale for her actions." My research does show that not all of Takata's Master students had the name and/or the written form for the "Master symbol" which would be one of the "keys" Barbara is referring to in this letter.

(Shinpiden) differently than the first generation of Takata's Master students did. First, some of the second generation received a physical "Master initiation" from Takata. Second, these students learned how to perform the First and Second Degree initiations without any waiting times between learning the procedures.

According to Paul Mitchell, both he and George Araki did not receive a Master initiation during their Master training with Takata. Shinobu Saito may not have received a Master initiation either. My research shows that Beth Gray also did not receive a Master initiation from Takata.

Based on my research, the only two who may have been instructed in the Master initiation procedure were Barbara Weber and Fran Brown. Fran Brown was allowed to tape record her Master training with Takata. I was told by Mary Goslen that during her Master training with Fran Brown, Fran read word for word the transcripts of these recordings and the transcripts do contain the initiation procedures for each degree – including the Master initiation. Whether or not Barbara Weber received the Master initiation instructions from Takata has not yet been verified at the time of this writing (although it seems very likely based on my preliminary research). I have also been told by Phyllis Furumoto that she was allowed to watch Takata as Takata initiated some of her Master students.

In an interview done November 2005 by Oliver Klatt, Mary McFadyen leads the reader to believe she learned how to do the Master initiation. However, Mary was trained as a Master in September 1980. It would be highly unlikely that Mary was taught how to perform the Master initiation when most all the other Master students of Takata's I have talked to were not. It also seems unlikely that Mary would be taught the Master Initiation because Takata didn't know Mary very well. They would only get to spend two days with each other: the day they met and the day Mary was initiated as a Master. Mary McFadyen's actual Master training was to take place at a later date, but Takata went into transition before they had a chance to meet again.

## The Confusion Begins

Based on the two different ways Takata trained her first group of Master students and her second group of Master students, there evolved two different ideas regarding the training of Masters. And the confusion continued from there.

Starting in February 1981 (immediately after Takata's death), Barbara Weber Ray sent a series of letters to Takata's other Master students. In these letters, Barbara claimed that she alone, as Takata's successor, knew how to initiate another Master.

At the time of this writing, I cannot prove one way or another Barbara Weber Ray's claim that she learned Takata's Third Degree initiation procedure. It is possible there never was any evidence created that could be used later as proof of this. For example, how many of Takata's Master students can prove they learned the First and Second Degree initiations from Takata? Unless they were given notes or allowed to tape record Takata teaching this to them, there has never been any proof created. This doesn't mean an event didn't happen, it simply means we only have statements made by individuals as to what happened.

Barbara Weber Ray's earlier style of teaching Reiki was that there were four degrees in the Reiki system. Part of the Third Degree class description is written as:

*Third Degree Reiki – is the Master/Teacher level of Reiki which includes another special energy activation beyond the First and Second Degree levels. Third Degree also includes complete instruction in the process of doing the First and Second Degree activations and complete training in teaching a Reiki Seminar.*[249]

From this, we can see that Barbara's Third Degree students would receive the Master initiation and the instructions on how to perform the First and Second Degree initiations.[250] This is what she was claiming the other Master students of Takata had received (in fact, some received less than this, because some also didn't receive the Master initiation). The description of classes goes on to say "the levels of Reiki beyond the Third Degree contain also the knowledge of how to initiate a full Reiki Master." However, it seems that in most other writings of this time, there was only one level, not levels, reported to be beyond the Third Degree: namely a "Fourth Degree".

I have a letter dated July 25, 1983, signed by Master Dr. H. Wesley Balk, member of the Board of Directors for The American International *Reiki* Association (the A.I.R.A., previously the A.R.A.), written in response to Virginia Samdahl's A.I.R.A. resignation letter. This letter is written on official A.I.R.A.

---

249    Ray and Greene, *The Official Reiki Handbook,* first edition, 4.

250    The "Master symbol" was also given in writing in these seminars. I have confirmed this with two Masters, John Latz and Marcia Halligan, who had taken their Third Degree Master training with Barbara Weber Ray through the A.I.R.A. in 1983.

paper with its logo in the background. In Dr. Balk's letter, Barbara Weber Ray is referred to as "a fourth degree Master", meaning that she knew how to perform the Master initiation, giving her the ability to train other Masters (Third Degree students); in other words, a Dai-Shihan. It is important to note that this letter starts out stating, "Dr. Ray asked that I send each of you a copy of this reply…" This should squash any idea that perhaps Dr. Balk made a "mistake" when referring to Barbara as a Fourth Degree Master.

I mention this because shortly after this time, in 1984, Barbara Weber Ray would claim that she was a Seventh Degree Master[251] and she would later base her system of The Radiance Technique™ around this statement. This internal letter from her own organization in 1983 proves that she originally stated she was a "Fourth Degree" Master.

The fact that Takata learned Shinpiden (Third Degree) and was given a certificate dated October 1, 1936, and then was given another certificate dated February 21, 1938 [252], stating she had the authority to train other Masters (Dai-Shihan) makes Barbara's claims about a "Fourth Degree" interesting. However, the way Takata and Barbara Weber defined the Third and Fourth degrees were different. It seems Barbara Weber defined the Third Degree as requiring a Master initiation and Takata may not have defined it in this way. Both seemed to imply, though, that the knowledge to train another person in Third Degree was another step beyond the initial Third Degree training. Whereas Takata may have seen the training of Masters as another aspect of the Third Degree, Barbara Weber saw it as a completely separate degree (see Chapter 8, "The Teaching Levels Third Degree/Shinpiden: Reiki Master/ Teacher," for more discussion on this).

It would appear to the Master students who had received a Master initiation from Takata, that their training—learning only the First and Second Degree initiation procedures, while knowing there was an additional Third Degree initiation procedure they did not know how to do—is all of what the Third Degree contained. This means, by default, that learning the Third Degree initiation procedure would be beyond the initial Third Degree training. This would be considered by some Masters another aspect of the Third Degree (Dai-Shihan) or a separate "Fourth Degree".

251  Ray and Carrington, *The Official Reiki Handbook,* third edition, 8, 65. Barbara claims in this handbook that she received all seven levels from Takata in December 1979.

252  Takata's Shinpiden certificate is written in Japanese, and includes the word "Shinpiden". Takata's Dai-Shihan certificate is written entirely in English and so does not include the word "Dai-Shihan" as that is not an English word. Rather, the entire description written in English on her Dai-Shihan certificate is stating she is given authority to teach all the levels of the Reiki system.

## The Possible Beginning of the Master Initiation

My research indicates that the first person to be initiated in person as a Reiki Master by Takata was Fran Brown on January 15, 1979. I have wondered why Takata started the Master initiation with Fran Brown. Was there perhaps something different with Fran than with any other Master student Takata had trained up until that point in time? The answer is, "yes". Fran was the first Master student Takata would train who had not taken the Second Degree training with her.

Fran took her Second Degree training with John Harvey Gray and so she received her Second Degree initiation from John. Could that have been the catalyst for Takata possibly inventing the Master initiation? Maybe Takata thought on an energetic level there needed to be an initiation done for Fran during her Master training because Fran hadn't received the Second Degree initiation from her.[253] Or perhaps was there another reason Takata had for physically initiating Fran Brown?[254]

## Insights from the Symbols

Lourdes Gray, John Harvey Gray's widow, states, "The First Sacred Key or symbol is used to get more power. With the First Sacred Key, you will be able to raise your Reiki healing energy level to 100% ... same level as a master."[255] This symbol, of course, is learned in the Second Degree training.

This idea is also stated in the earliest English-language book on Reiki, the 1982 first edition of *The Reiki Handbook* by Larry Arnold and Sandy Nevius. It reads, "Second-degree consists of a 100% power transfer..."[256] It is historically important to note that the authors were Reiki students of Virginia Samdahl, the first "Occidental" Master student of Takata's, who was trained in 1976. Virginia checked their book for accuracy, and the hands in the pictures showing the treatment positions are Virginia's.[257]

The words on Takata's Shinpiden certificate, dated October 1, 1936,

---

253  Fran told me that Takata "confirmed" the Second Degree training she had received previously from John. Takata gave Fran a Second Degree certificate dated January 11, 1979, while her Master certificate is dated January 15, 1979. Fran told me that John didn't give out certificates to his students during the time she trained with him.

254  A discussion regarding my research into the "Master symbol" and how its usage in initiations changed over time would be relevant to this discussion. However, I do not feel this research is appropriate in the context of this book.

255  Lourdes Gray, "The Sacred Keys," *The John Harvey Gray Center for Reiki Healing Newsletter*, September 2011, http://hosted.verticalresponse.com/245353/59232afaa5/1410027123/13ce55ae81/ last accessed December 1, 2014.

256  Arnold and Nevius, *Reiki Handbook*, 14.

257  Although Barbara Weber Ray claimed to have written the very first book on the subject of Reiki, her book, *The Reiki Factor*, was published in 1983.

also state that she received spiritual bestowments of the highest initiation of Reiki therapy on December 10, 1935. This seems to imply that the Second degree initiation is the highest initiation students receive.

Another way to look at this is that the Second Degree does bring in 100% Reiki Power. The Third Degree, however, is not about more power; it is about the knowledge of how to activate that power in others. Specifically, it is about how to perform the initiations for each degree.

## Possible Conclusions

Takata had trained her early Reiki Masters how to teach and initiate First and Second degree students without giving them a physical "Master initiation". Assuming that these new teachers could actually effectively initiate students, then it would seem to be evidence that the Master initiation was possibly developed by Takata later in her career.

However, perhaps there was originally a Master initiation procedure all along but Takata wanted to be the only one able to train Masters. So she withheld this information about its existence from her early Master students and the information about how to do the Third Degree initiation procedure from all but a few of her students.

Maybe this is the reason why Takata had warned her early Master students not to try to train another Master. Learning the procedures for the First and Second Degrees was not enough. To effectively pass on the initiations, the Third Degree initiation is required.

Some people might consider that the biggest evidence supporting the invention of the Master initiation by Takata is a handwritten letter from Takata herself announcing her retirement. In it, she listed three Reiki Masters as those she had trained to carry on in her place: Virginia Samdahl, Ethel Lombardi, and John Harvey Gray. These three Masters were all trained in 1976, and none of them had received a Master initiation in person from Takata.[258] Therefore, some may conclude that the three Masters listed in this letter had been fully trained, as the letter seems to imply, which did not include a Master initiation.

However, Takata's letter of retirement was referring only to Takata's retirement from teaching First and Second Degree classes. This is made very clear in Iris Ishikuro's teaching notes stating, "Mrs. Takata is the only person who

---

258   Takata's retirement letter was written before she trained Barbara Weber Ray or Phyllis Furumoto. After Takata's death, some people recognized Weber, or Furumoto, or neither as Takata's successor.

is able to give the 3rd degree class." These notes were written during Takata's retirement. Earlier in these notes, Iris states, "After 41 years of teaching Reiki, she has retired in December, 1977. She now resides in Keosaqua, Iowa, with her daughter and her family."[259] Takata's letter was simply informing students to look to the teachers mentioned in the letter for First and Second Degree training. Takata had planned on continuing to teach Masters (Third Degree). Takata told her Master students to send potential Third Degree students to her for training, which is also stated in Iris's notes.

These notes dictate that Mrs. Takata was the only one "able" to give the Third Degree, and that the Third Degree Masters Takata had trained at that time were "able" to give only the First and Second Degree classes. The word "able" is key. Iris didn't write "not allowed"; she wrote "able." Therefore, this letter cannot be used as proof that the three Masters listed were fully trained.

In audio recordings I listened to that were recorded in 1979 and 1980, Takata stated she received a Master initiation from Hayashi. If a recording exists from 1978 or earlier in which Takata states she received a "Master initiation", before she started giving a physical Master initiation, it could help to confirm whether or not a physical Master initiation is originally part of the Reiki system.[260]

But how and why would Takata have withheld the existence of the Master initiation from her early Master students? One possible answer is by doing the initiation remotely or, as Takata called it, by "short wave" or "remote control." See Appendix 5 for further information regarding remote initiations.

If originally there wasn't a physical Master initiation in the Reiki system, after a time perhaps Takata started to realize the dilemma about training Masters in a culture much different than Japan. Perhaps Takata decided to create a physical Master initiation in the hope of better conveying the understanding of what was being passed on to these students. Maybe she did this to help bridge the gap between Japanese mind and Western mind. It is a possibility that Takata might have created the physical form of a Master initiation to reveal the essence of what she was trying to teach.

One way to look at this is that people shouldn't mistake the ceremony (initiation) for the meaning of it. A diploma (or certificate) represents the knowledge and the essence of what you have gone through and learned.

---

259  As it turned out, retiring from teaching First and Second Degree students didn't suit Takata. Takata was on the road and teaching full-time again in 1978.

260  There is an archive of about 20 tapes that Beth Gray originally recorded during this time period. These tapes were discovered by John Harvey Gray while cleaning out his ex-wife's garage. John's widow, Lourdes Gray now has these tapes. The answer could lie within that collection of tapes.

People can skip the graduation ceremony and it has no effect on the meaning of the diploma. In this light we could say it is possible Takata started giving the ceremony ("Master initiation") to help translate the essence of Reiki into a way the Western mind could understand it. If you don't go to your high school graduation ceremony, you still get the diploma. But going to the ceremony without actually having earned the diploma is meaningless.

This would also explain why several of Takata's later Master students did not receive a physical Master initiation. For example, Paul Mitchell and George Araki, were trained together by Takata. George, being of Japanese descent, had an understanding of Japanese culture. It is plausible then, that this is the reason why Takata chose not to initiate George Araki although she had physically initiated a few Masters prior to this time. Paul Mitchell happened to be trained together with George and so he also did not receive a physical Master initiation. Beth Gray was the wife of John Harvey Gray, an earlier Master student of Takata's. It would seem odd for Takata to physically initiate the wife, Beth, when Takata recognized her as a Master when Takata had not initiated the husband, John, previously.[261]

Perhaps Takata started the Master ceremony or Master initiation because people couldn't understand this; some still wouldn't. They chase after more and more ceremonies but fail to learn anything. We have what are called "diploma mills" here in the United States. These are places online where basically one can buy a diploma from a "college" without doing any work for it.

If Takata created the form to reveal the essence, then what does this say about the many different systems of Reiki today that keep adding more levels, more symbols, and more initiations "beyond" the "Master Symbol" and Master initiation? What if the Master initiation wasn't about increasing one's "power" or "Reiki" but instead about recognizing a transition into a new responsibility and life that was taking place? A ceremony is for marking a space in time in which a change is being recognized.

It seems that if there originally wasn't a Master initiation in the system of Reiki, then Takata at first didn't change from what she had learned from Hayashi when teaching her first group of Masters. But due to her student's lack of understanding about her training, she may have decided to give her later Master students something she hoped they could understand—a "Master

---

261 As noted previously, John Harvey Gray originally trained Beth in the Third Degree (although Takata asked her Master students not to train another Master while she was still alive). In the Takata Sensei archives, there are records documenting this statement. Therefore, I have stated Takata recognized Beth as a Master but did not train her. To keep the peace at the time, the Master students of Takata's who knew the situation considered Beth an honorary Master student of Takata's.

initiation." Perhaps it didn't matter to Takata if it was made up or not, just like it doesn't matter to me how many more acupuncture needles I put in a patient if that is what they really want. I have had patients ask me, after I have inserted all the needles I intend to, "What, that's it? That's all the needles I get?" I reply, grinning, "How many more do you want? And where exactly is it that you would like me to put them? I'll put in as many needles as you want, but these would be 'just for show.'"[262]

In short, perhaps Takata adapted her teachings to meet her students' level of understanding. Good teachers have the ability to adapt their teachings so that their students can understand the essence of their meaning.

Also, Takata's advancing age and her realization that the time remaining to her for teaching was limited may have influenced her decision to initiate her later Master students at this time in their training and to teach students the First and Second Degree initiations together. History shows us that Takata did go into transition before seeing some of these Master students again. I feel these changes may also show us Takata's own learning process as she gained more experience in teaching Masters.

## A Broader Conclusion of Possibilities

Could it be that Takata was simply following tradition with her actions? Maybe Hayashi didn't give a Master initiation to all his Master students. It is possible that Hayashi only gave this level of training and initiation to certain Master students or the complete training only to his successor; just as some of Takata's Master students didn't receive a Master initiation (at least in person), and most of Takata's Master students didn't receive the Master initiation instructions from her.[263]

Going back further in history, the same could be said to be true of Usui. If Hayashi was Usui's successor (according to Takata), then it would be possible that he received extra training from Usui that his other Master students did not. And history does have a way of repeating itself. So, maybe, just as the other Master students of Takata's didn't want to believe Barbara Weber's claim that she had learned more from Takata than they had, perhaps the same

---

262   I tell my patients that the extra needles would be "just for show," but in actuality a needle inserted anywhere would affect something somewhere in the body. The points I am trying to make to my patients, though, are: 1. More is not always better. 2. The acupuncture treatment protocol should be decided by the skilled practitioner, not by the patient.

263   Likewise, not all of Fran Brown's or Barbara Weber Ray's Master students were given the Master initiation instructions.

thing occurred in the Gakkai with Usui's other Master students denying that Hayashi was Usui's successor. We probably will never know for sure.

## A Part of My Own History

I would like to point out that one requirement to join The Reiki Alliance is to have been initiated as a Master; a physical initiation is implied. I voiced my concerns about this during my interview process with The Reiki Alliance. I simply stated that by this rule, the majority of Takata's Master students would be excluded from being able to join The Reiki Alliance. Likewise, any Masters trained in these lineages would also not be allowed to join unless someone along the way had created a Master initiation for their lineage; which is what happened. Masters from both the early and later group either invented a Master initiation procedure for their lineage or used an initiation procedure shared with them by other Masters, because they had not learned one from Takata. The purpose of this requirement for membership into The Reiki Alliance needs some discussion. The Master students of Takata's who are still alive need to be a part of this discussion for anything to be decided and effectively understood.

## Thoughts to Consider

The reader should be aware that if the Master initiation was Takata's creation, then all 22 of her Master students were trained as equals in the ability to pass on the system of Reiki to others. Whether a Master student received the Master initiation or not by Takata would make no difference in that Master's ability. Therefore, this credential could not be used as a reason for establishing some sort of hierarchy among Takata's Master students.

As a researcher, it is my job to question and be open to all plausible explanations to what is passed down as history in the lineages and find evidence to support or deny claims. I am just giving examples of other possibilities in Reiki history. It is up to the readers to decide for themselves, based on the evidence, which version of Reiki history is the truth or closest to it.

A good researcher tries to find faults and weaknesses in his or her own research in order to be able to defend its validity under careful scrutiny. A researcher does not ignore data simply because it doesn't support, or perhaps even contradicts, a point of view the researcher is exploring. To simply report all supporting data while ignoring or silencing the data that seems to shed doubt on the researcher's theories is not research; that is called having an agenda.

One has to decide for himself or herself which is the more likely factual history of our Reiki system, whether or not one agrees with the evidence presented in this chapter. Or, as Napoleon Bonaparte said, "History is the version of past events that people have decided to agree upon."

# *Chapter* TEN

## *Fees for Training*

# CHAPTER
# 10

## *Fees for Training*

*"Money is neither my god nor my devil. It is a form of energy that tends to make us more of who we already are, whether it's greedy or loving."*
~ Dan Millman

*"It is not only the fee that is important.*
*They have to be the choosen [sic] ones."*
~ Hawayo Takata

The fees Takata charged for her classes were not in any way "special" and so did not need to be set in stone. They were somewhere around the equivalency of what she had paid for her training. Over time, the prices for her classes changed according to inflation. Ruth Fujimoto, a 1930s Reiki student of Takata's in Hilo, Hawaii writes in her autobiography, "Mrs. Takata consented to share this mysterious power with our family of four and charged only $50 each, except papa was free because he was 70 years old."[264]

In 1938, when one of Takata's sisters wanted to take the training from Takata she charged her $300.[265] This would seem to indicate that this was for teaching her both the First and the Second Degrees together. Perhaps we can assume, then, that based on the fee she charged the Fujimotos for First

---

264  Ruth Fujimoto, *Chapters of My Life,* large edition (CreateSpace Independent Publishing, 2011), 51. Thank you to Justin Stein for informing me about this resource.
265  Brown, *Living Reiki,* 64.

Degree training that her fee for Second Degree training at this time was $250.

In 1975, Takata charged $100 to teach the First Degree in Illinois. In 1976 she charged $125 for the First Degree ($75 for a spouse) and $400 for the Second Degree.[266] Sometime after this the prices for these two degrees would be $150 and $500. If Takata had lived longer, I am sure the prices of her classes would have kept up with the cost of inflation.

In the same spirit, I feel that the tuition for classes needs to be adjusted to be in accordance with its equivalency in different countries. For example, 68 degrees Fahrenheit is not the same as 68 degrees Celsius. It isn't about the number but its equivalency. To assume it is about the number is to totally miss the point. When asked about the price for the classes, Takata stated, "Not too much, not too little, for some it's free. In a group it's cheaper."[267]

I know Takata taught Reiki in other countries, like Japan, the Philippines, Puerto Rico,[268] and of course Canada. The prices she charged in Canada were the equivalent as she charged in the United States[269]; I wonder if this was true in places like the Philippines. This is one of the many research topics I would like to explore in the future.

I have heard views—sometimes strongly held views—about what the appropriate fee for Master-level training should be. I want to address some of the views I have heard, as well as state my own opinion, on the idea of what to charge for Reiki training at this level. Of course, one cannot discuss what to charge for Reiki Mastership until one comes to an understanding of what Reiki Mastership is or is not.[270]

As far as Reiki Mastership is concerned, ask yourself if there is a "right" or "correct" amount you should pay to get the teachings of the Reiki system and the initiations from someone whom you feel is the right teacher for you. Are you willing to pay a higher amount for the right teacher, or not? If you didn't like the teacher, would you still take the class from him or her if it was free? How much money should you expect to pay to be trained as a Master? The real issue here is with the question, not the answer. The word "should" in the question makes it appear that there is one right answer. Simply put, there is no correct answer.

---

266  Letter from Dr. Paul V. Johnson to William L. Rand dated March 14, 1994. Personal collection.

267  Hammond, *We are all Healers*, 286.

268  Technically, Puerto Rico is a Territory of the United States.

269  For example, during the time Takata was charging $125 for the First Degree in the United States she charged $148 in Canadian dollars. Wanja Twan, *In the Light of a Distant Star: A Spiritual Journey Bringing the Unseen into the Seen*, 25.

270  See more about Master-level training in the chapter entitled, "Third Degree/Shinpiden: Reiki Master/Teacher."

If you recall, as I stated in Chapter 5, at first Hayashi did not want to train Takata because she was not Japanese, she was American; and he was afraid that, because of this, she would change the system of Reiki. This story shows that Hayashi wasn't willing to train Takata just for the money, although there was a hefty fee involved. (And, as it turns out, Hayashi had very good reasons to believe that Americans, the pioneers that we are, would change the system. After Takata died, this is *exactly* what happened.)

The fees that Takata charged were in line with what her teacher Hayashi charged.[271] Takata knew the value of Reiki and wanted her own students to value it too. I have seen advertisements for Reiki classes that sound like a used-car salesman's spiel: "I won't be undersold. I will beat any price!" This doesn't sound right to me when applied to the system of Reiki. Is this a reflection of how much these Masters value the system of Reiki?

Takata also had a good understanding that money is one form of energy. Energy can take the form of money, time, labor, etc. Takata's teacher, Hayashi, allowed some of his students, like Takata, to work in his clinic for a period of time to help offset the cost of training. Again, in this scenario, time and work were offered as the form of exchange for the training. Takata charged $10,000 from 1976 to 1980 for the Master-level training. Today, this $10,000 fee would be the equivalent of almost $40,000.

## If you (the Teacher) don't put value on it, who will?

Takata charged $10,000 for the Master training to instill a sense of respect and appreciation for the value of the Reiki system. I believe Takata thought, by charging this fee, she was making sure the student placed a high value on what they had received. Takata was also placing a high value on her training, her time, and her expertise.

What and how much we spend money on shows what our priorities are. I am not against cable, satellite TV, or even cell phones, but they are luxuries and not necessities. They are not like oxygen, food, water, and shelter which are requirements. So the reality is that one can get rid of some unnecessary expenses like cell phones and stop paying for television that you can get at no cost with an antenna (i.e. rabbit ears), and over a period of several years, generate $10,000. It is all about priorities. This goes for First Degree and Sec-

---

271   In 1938, Hayashi charged Chiyoko Yamaguchi 50 yen, roughly a month's salary for an average worker at the time, to learn First and Second Degree. Yamaguchi, *Light of Reiki,* 30.

ond Degree training fees as well. First Degree training is generally affordable with very little sacrifice or rearranging of priorities for most people. Besides, most people get all that they want or need in the First Degree class. In the First Degree class, you learn how to give treatments and can start your lifelong practice of the Five Reiki Precepts.

I like to call the Master fee "The $10,000 Lesson/Opportunity." Money tends to bring up a lot of issues for people. In the Reiki system, we present challenges, such as a high fee, to allow for the opportunity for personal growth. Part of the student's training is making them look hard at their beliefs about money. The $10,000 fee is to test the ability of the student to generate money, which is part of personal mastery. Another part of personal mastery is the ability to let go of money. Money comes and money goes. Just like your breath, it is natural for it to come and to go. It is a flow of energy.

Here is one Master Candidate's initial struggle regarding this.

**Student:** "There is some resistance to beginning the process and a chunk of it is around the fee."

**Robert:** "Good, I am pushing your boundaries and making you think about your ideas about money."

**Student:** "I can see that you are very flexible, but it's a large sum and my debt issues/fears get triggered when I think of that kind of 'cake'."

**Robert:** "This is the point."

**Student:** "I understand your reasons for charging that amount, but I still feel a little uncomfortable with it. Money and spirituality are odd partners, in my opinion."

**Robert:** "This tells me where you are... being a Master will require you to hold seemingly contradictory ideas and be very much at peace with it—a 'seeing' past contradictions and into how they are the same thing. The reason for the high upfront fee is because this is a lot of money for you. This sets your intention and makes what you are about to start a reality in your mind."

The fee of $10,000 is not to make the Reiki Master "rich." Besides, what is "rich" to one person might be considered "poor" by another, and vice versa; it is relative. Furthermore, if one's intention is to make money and become rich by teaching Masters, it wouldn't be done by charging $10,000 for Master-level training! One would have to charge, say, $1,000 in hopes of becoming rich by teaching Masters. You read that correctly; I did not forget any zeros and it is not a typo. I truly meant $1,000.

By charging a lower fee, one that more people could afford, one would be able to get more Master students, thereby generating much more money than a Master charging $10,000 for Master training. Clearly, charging $10,000 is not the smartest way to become wealthy by teaching Reiki, which is okay, because—ironically, to me—the $10,000 is not all about the money. Ironically, the Masters who were charging $10,000 and then later reduced this amount, might be accused of trying to make more money by doing so by the people who are still charging $10,000. It is all a matter of perspective.

Masters who are charging $10,000, or its equivalent, are doing it partly for the students' benefit. The Master Candidate realizes these benefits over time, and so I won't be discussing them here. Takata allowed her Master students to fulfill the Master fee requirement in a way that worked for them, and I have followed her example. For instance, several of Takata's Master students were allowed to make payments to her. Both Bethal Phaigh and Barbara Brown paid $5,000 initially, either from money they had saved, inherited, or borrowed from a friend. Bethal Phaigh made arrangements to send Takata the money she would make from teaching Reiki classes until the full fee was paid.[272] Barbara Brown, who had the $10,000, was told to pay Takata only half the fee and put the rest into a savings account. Takata asked to be paid money generated from the interest from the savings account.[273] Wanja Twan was able to put together a large First Degree class and a Second Degree class for Takata, and the students' tuition from that class was deducted from Takata's Master fee. Rick Bockner also paid half his Master fee this way.

I personally like the way Bethal Phaigh was allowed to pay. This is a great idea—a student pays a set amount of money to begin the training and is then able to earn the remaining amount by teaching Reiki classes, a way of creating the remaining tuition money in a way that previously wasn't possible. This method also reinforces a main point of the Master class, which is to teach Reiki to others so they can experience the wonderful benefits of Reiki.

To help expose your own feelings about money and what money represents to you, consider this: What if the Reiki Master donated 100 percent of the Mastership fee to charities? How would you feel then about paying the fee? What if 50 percent of the money was donated? How would you feel about that? What if none of the money was donated? How would you feel? I know one Master who charged her Master student the $10,000 fee, and when the training was completed years later, gave the student his $10,000

---

272  Phaigh, *Journey into Consciousness,* 130.
273  Unpublished video of Barbara Brown being interviewed by Wanja Twan.

back. The Master didn't need it, and it was enough that the student had been willing to part with it.

The fee Takata charged was partly to instill in a potential Master student a high value on the system of Reiki. Takata wanted people to value Reiki and, knowing that people greatly value money, wanted to relate Reiki's great worth in terms people could understand. This way isn't right for everyone, but it was Takata's way. Masters are free to decide for themselves the way to best instill the sacredness of the system of Reiki, including the initiations, in their Master students.

In today's world, as opposed to the time when Takata was living, you can now become a "Reiki Master" on the Internet for a few dollars. However, I doubt that these teachers are going to have a serious and time-consuming relationship with their students for years to come. For example, my own Master Candidates typically apprentice with me for one to two years. The student's fee is partly for my time. I couldn't afford to spend the great amount of time and provide the thorough training my Master Candidates receive if they didn't financially support me. It is a win/win situation. Ideally, I would like anyone who is interested in becoming a Reiki Master to be able to do so. But I would be doing the student a disservice if I were to deny the student the trials the Master candidates seem to go through. Their own journey and the experience and insights they gain from such a stringent journey, and accomplishing their goal of becoming a Master, is a part of what makes a Master Candidate into a Master. The students' trials, however, are *their* trials and do not have to include a fee of $10,000; that was just a convenient way to make sure that there was *some* sort of trial for the Master student.

I have paid well over $10,000 for my Reiki training and traveling, and I don't feel like I have overpaid; but that's me. As for the many personal trials…now I can say it was all worth it! Regardless of what people pay for their Reiki Master training, if we are both holding the integrity of the system intact and live by the precepts, I consider us to be equals and part of the same Reiki family. The amount one pays for Master training is not as important as holding the teachings with the reverence they deserve.

The bottom line is that you need to examine your own thoughts and beliefs about the value of your training. How much is it worth to you? Are you willing to put forth the effort, time, and energy required for the type of training you want? If so, then you will need to find a Reiki Master suitable for you. Chapter 13, "Finding a Reiki Master Teacher," will give you a guide for how to start.

# *Chapter* ELEVEN

## *Traditional and Non-traditional Reiki System Practices*

# CHAPTER
# 11

## *Traditional and Non-traditional Reiki System Practices*

*"Art, like morality, consists of drawing the line somewhere."*
~ G.K. Chesterton

Sometimes the definition of *"traditional practice"* can be an emotionally charged topic for Reiki practitioners. Practitioners can become upset to find out that some of what they may have learned, and paid money for, isn't part of Usui Shiki Reiki Ryoho. If what you have works, that's fine. I am not saying that one system is better than another, nor am I the Reiki police. Different does not mean inferior, it simply means different; as in not the same. But let's call things by their proper name so we can all be on the same page. These are some generally agreed-upon names and definitions that we can use for discussion, so there is less confusion.

To discover what was traditionally part of the Reiki teachings took me many years and lots of money, but my method was quite simple. I decided I would have to travel and train with the people who had received these teachings directly from Takata, including her 22 Master students, or one of their Master students. I wanted to find the shortest lineages possible, knowing that would take me back as far as I could go within the living lineage. Then I would politely question the Master if she or he was still teaching Reiki as she or he had learned it. I also trained in some of the shortest non-Takata lineages.[275] I always found a way to go to the source of the information or as close to the source as possible.

Over the years, I have also obtained many tapes of Takata teaching Reiki classes. I have to say that these tapes are important, as they allowed me to hear, firsthand, Takata teaching the different levels of Reiki. I could then cross-reference other bits and pieces I had learned and gathered to see the similarities and differences. Due to all the extensive research I have done into the history of Reiki, some of my students jokingly said that I must be obsessed. It's not true; I just like being as thorough as possible.

Another person in history I know of from my study of Chinese Medicine did this same sort of thing.[276] His name was Huang-fu Mi, and he wrote and compiled *The Systematic Classic of Acupuncture & Moxibustion* (Zhen Jiu Jia Yi Jing) in 282 CE. This massive undertaking took him 26 years to complete. As an acupuncturist, I can say that this book is of great historical value to acupuncturists, even today. *The Systematic Classic of Acupuncture & Moxibustion* preserves some of the earliest teachings on Chinese Medicine and cites its sources. Some of the books that he used as sources have been lost over the centuries. Yet their wisdom and teachings are still available and preserved today, thanks to *The Systematic Classic of Acupuncture & Moxibustion*.

My definition of Traditional Reiki Practice is simple: If Mikao Usui would recognize the system you are practicing, then it is traditional. Usui himself modified his teachings over time—not drastically, but he did tweak them here and there. For example, I learned a very early form of initiation used in the Gakkai from my teacher Hiroshi Doi.[277] Usui modified his initiation process over time. Perhaps this was done because his early students were martial artists with a well-developed *tanden*,[278] while his later students were not. Based on the information I have learned from Hiroshi Doi, whose teachings in part stem from the Usui Reiki Ryoho Gakkai,[279] the book *Everyone can do Reiki* by former Usui Reiki Ryoho Gakkai member Fumio Ogawa, and

275   Mikao Usui-Chujiro Hayashi-Chiyoku Yamaguchi-Hyakuten Inamoto and Mikao Usui-Kan'ichi Taketomi-Kimiko Koyama-Hiroshi Doi.

276   In 1999, I started my formal study of Chinese Medicine at Southwest Acupuncture College in Boulder, Colorado, USA. This program's primary focus was acupuncture and Chinese herbal therapy, but it also included courses in Qi Gong, Tai Chi, Tui Na (Chinese massage), Shiatsu (Japanese acupressure massage), Chinese dietary therapy, and Western anatomy and physiology. In 2003, after four years of full-time study and practice, I graduated with a Master of Science in Oriental Medicine degree.

277   This is different from the initiation or the Reiju process Hiroshi Doi teaches in his Gendai Reiki classes. Those interested can also see another form of an initiation process used by Eguchi, a student of Usui. Mitsui, *Te no Hira Ryōchi,* 10-13.

278   An energy center area located about 2 inches below the navel.

279   This is the school that Usui formed in April 1922 to teach his system of Reiki. This school is still in existence. It is my understanding they have also let Usui's teachings evolve naturally over time.

what I have discovered from Takata[280] and her master students, very little information has changed.

My research and opinion lead me to believe that Hayashi and/or Takata further modified the initiation process for greater effectiveness. Hayashi and Takata spent only four to five days training their students in the First and Second Degrees, and so they may have needed something stronger and/or different for their students, whom they might never see again. This is unlike the frequent gatherings of teachers and students in the Gakkai, where students are expected to practice Hatsurei-ho (discussed in the next chapter) and frequently receive initiations to improve their Reiki ability. Hayashi's and Takata's modifications to the initiation process were a natural evolution, similar to how Usui himself modified his initiation method many times to increase its effectiveness.

Compare this to today…with websites containing videos and books containing pictures all claiming that all you need to do, is to look at, watch, or read them to become a Reiki Master/Teacher. I have seen "Reiki" videos in which the viewer is supposed to stare at a crystal, a process that is supposedly initiating the viewer into Reiki. These Reiki teachings are drastically changed from the original form taught by Usui.

The question is, at what point is it no longer Usui's Reiki system (Usui's style of using and teaching the system of Reiki), and is, instead, someone else's style of Reiki or not Reiki at all - like using personal energy? I think somewhere along the line, with so many changes, Usui himself might not recognize his own system if he were to come back today and view what many are teaching as Usui Reiki. Although one could argue that all things change over time, and use this as an excuse to modify and to change the system of Reiki, the truth is so simple: Reiki as taught by Usui, Hayashi, and Takata works incredibly well! If people drastically change the system, what they have is another system, so the honorable thing to do would be to change the name of the system they are teaching.

Barbara Weber Ray, one of Takata's Master students, decided to make changes to the three degree system she learned from Takata, and now teaches her system of Reiki as The Radiance Technique™. Another master student of Takata's, Ethel Lombardi, stopped teaching Reiki due to the tension, "Reiki politics," and power struggles that ensued after Takata's death in December 1980. Ethel had an inner calling to start teaching a system of energy work

---

280   Information obtained from tapes and CDs of Takata teaching Reiki classes as well as her writings.

she named Mari El. Renaming the system, if it's been changed, helps avoid confusion in the long run. I am not saying other styles don't work; I am just saying that there is honor in changing the name if the system no longer reflects what was received. After all, there are many religions that contain a God as the source of all. Does that mean that all those religions are the same? Certainly not. And the different names of these religions help to distinguish them and clarify to everyone their own certain set of beliefs and practices.

Contrast this with another Reiki Master, Arthur Robertson, who also decided to make significant changes to the system of Reiki. With all the changes Arthur Robertson made, he did the respectful thing and named his system Raku Kei Reiki to distinguish it from the system of Usui Shiki Ryoho that he learned from Iris Ishikuro, another one of Takata's Master students. However, he left the word "Reiki" in the name of his system, which led to confusion, as he would simply teach everything as Reiki to his students. Arthur, by leaving the word "Reiki" in his system, has in part led to the confusion about what is and is not part of the traditional Reiki system. The fact that most of the nontraditional styles of Reiki today originate from his Raku Kei Reiki system attests to this. Many Masters since Arthur Robertson have made significant changes as well. I don't mean to single out Arthur, but just to use him as an example because he was one of the first to make conscious changes to the system, starting in the early 1980s, and his material shows up in so many Reiki variants today.[281],[282]

Today, many Reiki teachers do not *know* if what they are teaching belongs to the traditional system of Reiki as would be recognized by Usui. Many students are told they are learning "The Usui Reiki system" when this may not be the case. Students tend to believe, literally, whatever their Master teaches in the class. The teaching Master may have been misinformed, and then passes on the misinformation, or may have deliberately changed things. Either way, the student is not aware of the changes in the system.

I am speaking from personal experience. My early Reiki training involved many things that I now know are not part of Usui Shiki Reiki Ryoho. Often when someone tells me they practice the Usui System of Reiki, a few sentences later, these same people are talking about chakras, animal spirits, crystals, etc., that are not part of traditional Reiki teaching. Same goes for the people saying they practice "The Traditional Form of Reiki," because their understanding of

---

281  Arthur Robertson and I had many correspondences through phone conversations and e-mails before he died on March 5, 2001.
282  For example, the system of Raku Kei Reiki begot the system Tera Mai Reiki, which begot the system of Karuna Reiki.

traditional form could mean anything and everything. The following table is to help you distinguish between what is commonly considered the traditional system of Reiki as taught by Takata and what is not.

This is not a comprehensive list of what is taught in both systems, but is given here as a general guideline.

| Traditional as taught by Takata | Non-traditional |
|---|---|
| Three degrees | Three degrees to a dozen or more |
| Three symbols in Reiki Second Degree. There is one more "symbol" taught at the Master level. | Some systems include hundreds of symbols. |
| Four initiations for First Degree | One initiation or more for First Degree |
| One initiation for Second Degree[283] | One initiation or more for Second Degree |
| Zero to one initiation at the Master/Teacher level[284] | One initiation or more for Third Degree or higher |
| Reiki Lineage clearly given | Lineage may not be given or known |
| Five Reiki Precepts taught | Microcosmic Orbit[285] |
| Nerve Stroke (also called the Reiki Finish) | Channeled information |
| 12 standard hand positions for a full-body treatment | Psychic Surgery |
| Specific hand placements for specific illnesses and disorders | Healing Attunements |
| | Teachings about crystals |
| | Teachings about chakras |
| | Teachings about meridians |

283   In the Takata lineage, one initiation is done. However, sometimes it is repeated a second time if Second Degree is taught over two days.

284   This one initiation can further be divided and given in two distinct parts and given at different times or it can be done together as one initiation. As this involves lineage specific Third Degree teachings, I will not elaborate further. See the chapter "Historical Perspectives on Master Training and the Master Initiation" earlier in this book.

285   A Qi Qong practice

# Chapter TWELVE

*Similarities Between
Usui's, Hayashi's, and Takata's
Teachings*

# CHAPTER 12

*Similarities Between*
*Usui's, Hayashi's, and Takata's Teachings*

*"The greatest enemy of knowledge is not ignorance,*
*it is the illusion of knowledge."*
~ Stephen Hawking

Through my research, I have found that the way Takata taught the system of Reiki is very close to the original system of Reiki, which Usui created. Indeed, the hanko, a stamp used as an official seal, on the certificates Takata gave to her students, reads 臼井式霊気研究会同盟之印 (Usui-shiki Reiki Kenkyūkai Dōmei no in or "Hanko of the Union of Usui-style Reiki Study Groups").

Before my teacher Adonea's passing on October 2, 2009, she wrote an article outlining how similar the teachings were between Usui, Hayashi, and Takata. I have taken that material, done some editing for better clarity, and added a lot of new material to the original article. Adonea and I had collaborated for many years exchanging the research we had done on the Reiki system, including some of the information contained in the original article.

One very important point to address is that Takata emphasized that the spiritual and mental self is number one and the body is number two, but both are needed to create a whole. One misconception I often hear is that Takata and Hayashi were more into the healing of the physical body and not into the wellness of the mental and spiritual self. But this is not what Takata taught.

Takata states on an audio recording, "So we always say, the mental and the spiritual is number one; number two is the physical. And then you put that together and say we are a complete whole. And when you can say that, that means you have applied Reiki and Reiki has worked for you."[286]

Following is a list of techniques that we know Takata taught, in which I use their Japanese names to emphasize the similarity between what Usui taught and what Takata taught. Takata did not teach the techniques using the Japanese names, because her audience was primarily English-speaking, but she did teach most of the techniques. The full description of how to perform all these techniques is not included here. Rather, this is something that is imparted in traditional Reiki classes.

- *Gasshō:* To place one's hands together, palms touching with fingers and thumbs pointed upward, as a gesture of respect and humility.[287] This is done to help focus and center the mind and to bring the Reiki energy to the hands. It is done before giving a treatment. Students' hands are also in this position during the initiation process.

- *Hanshin Chiryō:* A different way of treating the back, which is different from the way the back is treated with the standard hand positions. This way of treating the back is convenient for people who cannot lie on their stomachs to receive the standard back treatment hand positions (pregnant women who can lie on their side, people with bronchitis who can sit or lean slightly forward in a chair, etc.). The hands are placed on the muscles to either side of spine starting above the scapulas. The fingertips are resting and pointing toward the tops of the shoulders. Hands are moved down until the entire back is treated this way. (Drawing by Adonea.)

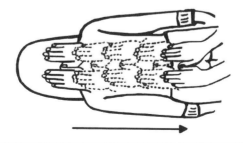

---

286  Hawayo Takata, *Takata Speaks: Volume 1, Reiki Stories.*

287  Takata learned Gasshō from Hayashi. Takata writes in her diary on December 10, 1935, in preparing to give a Reiki treatment, "Close your hands together and wait for the sign." Fran Brown told me that she learned this from Takata.

- *Tanden Chiryō-hō:* A physical detoxification technique as taught in the Usui Reiki Ryoho Gakkai. Takata's version also combined what is taught purely as *Tanden Chiryō-hō* with *Nentatsu-hō.* Takata taught it as the mental/emotional balancing technique. It is interesting to note that Takata chose to emphasize this technique's ability to get rid of negative emotions (emotional detoxification), rather than the physical detoxification that is stressed in the Gakkai.[288] Using this technique as Takata instructed removes mental (stress), emotional (anxiety, anger, etc.), and physical toxins from the body.

- *Heso Chiryō-hō:* As a quick energizer treatment. (Takata called the area two inches around the navel the solar plexus.) Takata called this area the "battery" or "main motor" of the body and said to keep it in "A-one" condition.

- *Nentatsu-hō:* As a mental/emotional reprogramming technique to get rid of bad habits, fears, phobias, etc. This technique works on the subconscious mind and is taught in the Second Degree class. Many Reiki Masters in the West have either dropped this technique or changed it so it no longer resembles the original.[289]

- *E Buki-hō:* A breath empowerment technique taught to her Master students (does not use the microcosmic orbit, and is not the Breath of the Fire Dragon, Blue Kidney Breath, or Violet Breath taught by most Reiki Masters today).[290]

- *Ketsueki Kokan-hō (called Blood Exchange by Hayashi Sensei):* Takata called this the Reiki Finish, Nerve Stroke or the Finishing Treatment. There is a short and long version as taught by Takata. *Ketsueki Kokan-hō* consists of a series of physical manipulation techniques performed at the end of the treatment. Most Reiki Masters do not teach these techniques.[291]

- *Byōsen Reikan-hō:* While doing a treatment, your hands will feel different sensations; treat the cause and the effect will vanish. Takata stated that you would feel different sensations in your hands depending on what was going on with the area of the client being treated. The "Grey Book" reproduces an essay of Takata's called "The Art of

288  Ray and Greene, *The Official Reiki Handbook,* first edition, page 18.
289  This was taught to me by John Harvey Gray and Fran Brown.
290  I learned this technique in most of my Reiki lineages through Takata.
291  I learned this technique from Fran Brown.

Healing," which says, "During the treatment, trust in your hands. Listen to the vibrations or reaction. If there is pain, it registers pain in your fingertips and palm. If the patient has itch, it reacts the same, if deep and chronic, it throbs a deep pain, or if acute, the pain is a shallow tingle." Also in the "Grey Book" is a diary entry written by Takata during her training with Dr. Hayashi, on December 10, 1935, in which she writes, "In all cases, the patient could be diagnosed just by the touch of hand."

**Byōsen** (the diseased or toxic area that gives off a different vibration than healthy tissue) and Hibiki (the sensation felt in the practitioner's hands) were taught by Takata without the Japanese names.

For example, Takata stated, "Everyone diagnoses the same because the vibrations are the same. You [the patient] are the one putting forth these vibrations [Byosen] and we [the practitioners] feel it in our hands [Hibiki]."[292] This was told to Takata by the dietician Mrs. Shimura just after Takata had received a treatment from her. (Earlier that same day Takata had received a treatment in Dr. Hayashi's clinic.) Mrs. Shimura confirmed what the practitioners in Dr. Hayashi's clinic found, i.e., where the problem areas were on Takata. Moving one's hands in a scanning motion over the body was not taught by Takata in the First Degree. She taught students to do a series of hand positions and watch for the Hibiki to sense the Byōsen. This is an easier way for beginners. The way Takata described her Reiki treatments in the Hayashi clinic was that two practitioners worked on her and did a series of hand placements. They weren't "scanning" or moving their hands around looking for spots. The Hayashi Manual seems to also be a how-to guide of hand placements. No need for this guide if we are expected to believe that Hayashi only taught scanning… and yet, there it is.

Based on the articles from 1928 translated in Appendix 3 it also seems that the practitioners used a series of hand positions. The practitioners frequently moved their hands from one position to another until the source of the problem was detected.

It is apparent that Hayashi taught hand positions to his new students; at least until they became sensitive enough to feel Hibiki in order to sense Byōsen. This is what Takata did as well. She taught a standard set of hand positions in her First Degree class. These were beginning students, not advanced students. In fact, Takata wrote on her First Degree certificate the words

---

292  Haberly, *Reiki*, 23.

"introductory course." So both Hayashi and Takata taught their beginning-level students hand placements to guarantee a more effective treatment. Over time the student's sensitivity, ability to sense Hibiki and Byōsen, develop. In Iris Ishikuro's notes it states in all capital letters, "YOU WILL GET VIBRATION OR FEELING ONLY THROUGH PRACTICE."

Helen Haberly, Takata's chosen biographer, writes, "Mrs. Takata taught it is not necessary to know anatomy in order to treat with Reiki, since the hands will respond [hibiki] when they located the source of the problem [byōsen] and the student does not have to analyze what to do. She encouraged the development of this as an intuitive art, not a rigid system, saying, 'Reiki will guide you [Reiji]. Let the Reiki hands find it. They will know what to do.'"[293]

- *Reiji:* To listen to your hands and allow them to guide you to the area that needs treatment. Advanced Reiki students utilize this skill after they have developed sensitivity to feeling energy vibrations. Takata stated, "Listen to your hands!" Ruth Fujimoto, who studied with Takata in Hilo in the late 1930s, gives many accounts of listening to her hands as she was instructed to do by Takata. In one account, her dog got run over by a golf cart and developed a limp a week later. Ruth writes, "I put him on my lap and let my hand go where it felt like going."[294]

- In another story a fellow worker, Lori, fell and hurt her arm. She asked Ruth for a Reiki treatment. Ruth writes, "I put my hands on her arm but my hands moved towards her elbow. Lori said, 'No, it's my arm that's hurting, not my elbow. My arm.' I kept my hand on the elbow, telling her, 'But my hand is going towards your elbow so I'm going to keep it there.' Next day as soon as she came to work she told me that she had gone to the doctor who told her she had hit her elbow."[295]

- *Shūchū or Shūdan Reiki:* A group treatment. With each additional practitioner joining the treatment the effectiveness of the treatment increases. Most Reiki Masters teach this technique.

- *Reiki Mawashi:* Standing in a circle, students in the class hold hands, or keep a little space between the hands, and feel the flow of Reiki. Takata's Master student Virigina Samdahl taught this technique in a

---

293  Haberly, *Reiki,* 56.
294  Fujimoto, *Chapters of My Life,* 54.
295  Fujimoto, *Chapters of My Life,* 55

1979 First Degree class attended by Mary Goslen. Another version of this technique Takata used was performed after students received an initiation. Takata would have her students place chairs one in front of the other. Students would then place their hands onto the shoulders of the student in front of them.

- *Renzoku Reiki:* A Reiki Marathon in which practitioners take turns and treat a person who has great need of Reiki treatments (terminally ill, post-surgical patient, etc.) for many hours simultaneously or even around the clock. This takes many willing Reiki practitioners. I've heard audio recordings on which Takata mentions this style of treatment for serious cases like cancer. Normally Takata would train the patient's family so they could also help with the Reiki treatments.

- *Reiki Teate:* Hands-on treatment. Most Reiki Masters teach this.

- *Enkaku Chiryō-hō: A*bsentee or distance Reiki treatment. Most Reiki Masters teach a version of this.

*Other similarities:*

Usui and Hayashi said to always start with the head; in the "Grey Book," Takata says, "Kindly and gently apply the hands starting from the head downward."

On February 21, 1938, Takata received a certificate from Hayashi-sensei calling the system she learned by several names, including "Usui System of Reiki Healing," "Usui Reiki system of drugless healing" and "Dr. Usui's Reiki System of Healing."

Takata named her system Usui Shiki Ryoho, which means "Usui Style Healing Method," because she had slightly modified the system that was given to her and wanted to distinguish it from what she had originally learned, called Usui Reiki Ryoho (Usui Spiritual Energy Healing Method). On an audiotape I have of her teaching a class, Takata mentions that the name of the system Usui taught is Usui Reiki Ryoho.[296]

On her certificates, however, she wrote "Usui Shiki Ryoho," which translates as "Usui Style Healing Method." As mentioned previously, the hanko Takata stamped her certificates with translates to "Hanko of the Union of Usui-style Reiki Study Groups."

---

296  The original tape was made by Barbara Weber (Ray). Copies were given to some of her students, and eventually those outside of Barbara's group received a copy, including my teacher Fran Brown.

*Hanko used by Takata*

I must emphasize that the adjustments Takata had made to the system she learned were very slight. In fact, I would argue that they were not changes per se as much as an improved way of teaching the original system. John Harvey Gray mentions that Takata changed parts of the system to make it easier to learn for Westerners. Specifically, she is responsible for the somewhat standard twelve hand positions of Reiki.[297] Ironically, she would sometimes teach a different set of the twelve hand positions at times, but nonetheless, she did this to simplify the teachings. As far as I am concerned, this was a brilliant idea.

Hayashi gave his students a handbook listing illnesses based upon a medical diagnosis. The practitioner would then do a group of specific hand positions on the body that were thought to treat that particular ailment. Takata's copy of this handbook, given to her by Hayashi, was reprinted in the "Grey Book."[298] This required the student to either memorize the entire handbook as to where to place one's hands for any given condition or look up each set of hand placements when a client came in with a medical diagnosis. Advanced students of Hayashi were expected to be able to detect for themselves where the areas of need were in the client's body and to treat the areas accordingly. At this point in a student's development of becoming more energetically sensitive, the book lost some of its importance.

Takata's idea of how to teach new students was to simply have them treat all the organs each time a treatment was given. The 12 standard hand placements she organized did just that and are much easier to learn and more practical than having to look up hand placements in a book. In teaching the

---

297  These positions changed over time. Based on the notes given to Doris Duke by Takata, est. circa 1950's and found in Appendix 5, she taught four standard positions on the abdomen plus the treatment of the kidneys. In the early 1970's Takata would teach three positions on the head and four positions on the front of the body in Takata's foundation treatment. These seven positions are described in both Iris Ishikuro's notes and in John Harvey Gray's book, *Hand to Hand,* 93. Later Takata would expand this foundation treatment to include 12 positions. Takata also taught many optional treatment positions for certain conditions.

298  Translations have been published in Gray and Gray, *Hand to Hand,* as well as in Petter, Yamaguchi, and Hayashi, *Hayashi Reiki Manual.*

hand positions this way, there would be only a few cases where some optional hand positions, in addition to the standard 12, would be needed to treat the illnesses and diseases listed in Hayashi's manual.

The name of Hayashi's healing guide is **Ryōhō Shishin** or "*Healing Method Guideline*." This is the same name that is on the hand placement guideline section of the Reiki Ryoho Hikkei, which Hiroshi Doi received from Mrs. Koyama, the sixth president of the Usui Reiki Ryoho Gakkai.

The information found in these healing guides is also very similar to the guide written in a book published in 1930 entitled, *Te-no-Hira Ryōchi*, by Koshi Mitsui. Mitsui was a Master student of Toshihiro Eguchi, and Eguchi was a student of Usui.

Takata also knew about the technique *Hatsurei-hō*. She mentions these in her diary entry dated December 10, 1935 (edited for grammar and for insertion of Japanese words in brackets). Her diary reads, "Meaning of 'Leiki' [Reiki] Energy within oneself, when concentrated [condensed] and applied to patient, will cure all ailments ... "It is natures greatest cure, which requires no drugs. It helps in all respects, human and animal life. In order to concentrate [condense], one must purify one's thoughts, and words and to meditate to let true 'energy' come out from within. It lies in the bottom of your stomach about 2 inches below the navel [*tanden*]. Sit in a comfortable position, close your eyes, concentrate [focus]on your thoughts [Jōshin-ho]and relax. Close your hands together [Gasshō] and wait for the sign [Reinetsu and Reiha]. Kindly and gently apply the hands starting from head downward. The patient who is about to receive this treatment must purify one's [his or her] thoughts, feel comfortable, and [have] a desire to get well. One must not forget to feel grateful. Gratitude is a great cure for the mind. In all cases, the patient could be diagnosed just by the touch of [the] hand [Byōsen]."

From a translation of the 1933 book *Reiki To Jinjutusu – Tomita Ryu Teate Ryōhō*, by Kaiji Tomita, on page 62 it states, "After Seiza[299], do Gassho now. The posture of this practice is gathering the Reiki energy, power of mind, to both the hands." After the posture of *Gasshō-Seiza* is done, it recommends chanting some of the poetry of the Meiji Emperor to help purify one's thoughts. This is called *Jōshin-ho*. On page 24, it reads, "While practicing Jōshin-hō, the body and mind get calmed down and purified. This feeling should be kept all the time when practicing. As the mind being purified naturally, the warmth and heat may be felt in both the palms. It is called Reinetsu (spiritual heat).

---

299   This simply means sitting on the floor or a mat, with your buttocks resting on your heels and your back straight.

While the body and mind has increased its harmony, the sensation may be felt like electric waves, which is called Reiha (spiritual wave). A combination of Reinetsu and Reiha is the motion of Reiki, which is the theme of the Teate ryōhō [Hand Healing Method]. At the beginning, the sensation from the palms may be weak. After practicing Seiza longer, the sensation of Reiki becomes stronger. Also, as your body and mind become more harmonized, you will be more sensitive to Reiki; on the other hand, when your body and mind aren't in harmony, your sensitivity will disappear."

As one can see, Takata describes in detail the technique for Hatsurei-hō very much like Kaiji Tomita, who was another early practitioner of Reiki.[300]

In my own research, I discovered that although Barbara Weber Ray later changed the system of Reiki as she learned it from Takata from a three degree system to a seven-level system in 1984,[301] she initially kept intact most of what Takata had taught her.[302] Despite her actions later, she did hold true to the teaching of Takata in her early years of teaching Reiki (from 1979 through 1983). This is why I was very fortunate to have done a Master-level training exchange with Marcia Halligan, who received her Master training with Barbara Weber Ray in 1983. A very detailed manual containing many of the aforementioned techniques in this chapter was published by Barbara starting in 1982 in the first edition of *The Official Reiki HandbookThe Official Reiki Handbook*. This manual is one of the best I have ever seen for a First Degree student. Old copies can sometimes be bought online from bookstores.

There are also many books written about a system of energy work called Te-no-Hira Ryōchi. This system is very similar to Usui Reiki Ryōhō, as the founder of this system was a student of Usui named Toshihiro Eguchi. Eguchi went on to found his own school named Te-no-hira Ryōchi Kenkyūkai (Palm Healing Research Association), shortly after Usui died.[303] These books are not yet available in English, so it is good to have friends who can read both old

---

300  It is not currently known who taught Kaiji Tomita Reiki. Kaiji Tomita mentions learning Reiki and mentions Usui in the book but doesn't specify exactly who taught him Reiki. By the date of the book, 1933, it would appear that if Usui didn't teach Kniji, then it probably was one of Usui's Master students.

301  The third, 1984 edition of *The Official Reiki Handbook* specifically mentions the system having seven levels (p. 65). Prior editions, including the 1982 and 1983 editions, makes mention that there were levels beyond the Third Degree, although it seems that students whom I've interviewed were taught that there were just three levels. I can only conclude that either this extra material referred to was how to initiate another master, as Barbara stated only she knew how to do, or that Barbara simply was planning on expanding the system beyond the traditional three level system but hadn't yet decided on just how many levels to add onto the system and so didn't write in specific terms. Today, many of the additional levels that have been added were simply parts of the Second Degree class that had been broken up and spread across many "levels." For example, Takata taught three Reiki symbols in the Second Degree class, both the names of the symbols and how to draw them. I have audio recordings of Takata teaching her Second Degree students this way, which would contradict those who insist otherwise. It seems that in Barbara's later style of Reiki, the Second Degree symbols were taught but the names were not given until higher levels.

302  She also changed her name from Barbara Weber to Barbara Weber Ray.

303  One book is called *Tenohira Ryōchi Nyūmon (Introduction to Healing with the Palms)* co-written by Eguchi and Mitsui. Thanks to Bronwen Stiene for this information.

and new Japanese. As one can imagine, there are a lot of similarities between Eguchi's system and Usui's system; and, as I have shown in this chapter, between Usui's and Takata's systems of Reiki. By comparing all three systems[304], one comes to a greater understanding of the traditional Reiki system and its practices and can see how little information changed from Usui to Takata and her students over the years.

However, not all of Takata's students felt the need to hold the system of Reiki intact as was done for the first three generations of Reiki Masters (Usui-Hayashi-Takata). Now this system is in danger of being lost due to the vast majority of misinformation being circulated. This has been one of the biggest motivating factors in publishing this book and has also been a big motivation for me in the decision to start training Masters in this tradition.

It is my opinion that Takata was a genius in her way of presenting Reiki to our Western culture. In my Traditional Chinese Medical practice of acupuncture and Chinese herbal medicine, I am confronted with the same dilemma every day. I cannot tell a patient that they have a diagnosis of liver qi overacting on their spleen qi and expect them to understand what I mean by that. I have to do my best to translate this Chinese medical diagnosis into something that the patient will understand. So you see, I don't practice acupuncture or herbal medicine differently from how I was taught to diagnose, but the way I present and explain it to my patients would seem funny or changed to another practitioner of Chinese Medicine.

This chapter was written to present some of the teaching components of the Reiki system as passed down from Usui to Hayashi to Takata. It is meant to be informative but not all-inclusive.

---

304   Usui Reiki Ryōhō, Usui Shiki Ryoho and Te-no-Hira Ryōchi

# *Chapter* THIRTEEN

## *Finding a Reiki Master Teacher*

# CHAPTER
# 13

*Finding a Reiki Master Teacher*

To be able to practice Usui Shiki Reiki Ryoho, we need to first receive an initiation from an Usui Shiki Reiki Ryoho Master/Teacher. In the First Degree of Reiki, also called Shoden or the Introductory course[305], there are four Reiki initiations. In Second Degree—Okuden—there is one Reiki initiation, and at the Master/Teacher level there is one more Reiki initiation.

Finding a good teacher is important in this process. You may want to interview a potential teacher before deciding to train with him or her. A good teacher will be able to easily answer the following questions.

1. What system of Reiki do you teach?[306]

2. How long have you been practicing Reiki?

3. Why did you get involved or started with Reiki?

4. How did you get involved or started with Reiki?

5. What was your own Reiki training like?

   a. Did you receive your training in person or some other way?

   b. How long did your training take?

   c. Was there time between each level of Reiki, or was it taught all in one weekend?

6. How often do you give yourself a Reiki treatment?

7. Do you frequently treat others with Reiki?

---

305   Takata used the terms "Introductory Course," "Intermediate Course," and "Advanced Course" for First, Second, and Third Degree, respectively.

306   There are specific names for the systems of Reiki such as Usui Shiki [Reiki] Ryoho, Gendai Reiki ho, Komyo Reiki, Jikiden Reiki, Karuna Reiki, etc. An answer of "Usui Reiki" is not the name of any particular system of Reiki and might indicate the teacher does not know the name of the system they are teaching.

8. Do you know your entire Reiki lineage?

9. Can you please tell me about the Five Reiki Precepts?

10. When you teach, do you teach only the system of Reiki, or are other things added in or discussed as well?[307]

11. How much time is allotted for hands-on practice in the class?

12. Do you require or advise a waiting period between each degree of training?

Reiki training is passed down orally from Master/Teacher to student. That doesn't mean that there can't be any written notes—it means that both the teacher and the student are present together.[308]

Some things, like the hand positions, are best shown and practiced together during a Reiki class. Classes that provide lots of time for hands-on practice allow students to feel confident that they can go home and practice on their own. Also, this allows the students to discover what it feels like to receive a full-body treatment.

Finally, having time between each degree for practice is advised. I want my own students to have practiced what they have learned in First Degree before moving on to Second Degree. I typically require three months of practice between the First and Second Degrees. When Takata taught in an area that she wasn't going to get back to for a while, like Canada, she would allow students to take both the First and the Second Degree class without waiting in between. Takata herself learned First and Second Degrees without a waiting period.[309] Mastership requirements depend greatly on the individual, but a dedication to the system of Reiki is a key component.

Takata asked her students not to change the system of Reiki and to practice and teach the system of Reiki as they were taught it. Takata said that to mix in another system or to add things from other systems was to cheapen Reiki.[310] She stated that making changes, or adding things to it, says that Reiki isn't good enough to stand on its own.

There are many styles of the system today and even more hybrid styles. The majority of these systems originated from Usui Shiki Reiki Ryoho. Stu-

---

307    See the chapter titled "Traditional Reiki System Practices."

308    Occasionally Takata would teach students remotely by having conversations over the phone and doing the initiations remotely. See Appendix 5 for further information.

309    Takata's First and Second Degree certificates are both dated December 13, 1935. See Chapter 5 for further information.

310    Hawayo Takata, *Takata Speaks: Volume 1, Reiki Stories.*

dents interested in learning more about Usui Shiki Reiki Ryoho can contact The Reiki Preservation Society (www.TheReikiPreservationSociety.org) or The Reiki Alliance (www.ReikiAlliance.com).

# Chapter FOURTEEN

## Lineage

# CHAPTER
# 14

## *Lineage*

*"Lineage doesn't make you superior or inferior...
your actions, deeds, and behavior determines this."*
~ Hyakuten Inamoto

In Takata's day, the aspect of lineage was very simple. She learned the Reiki system from Chujiro Hayashi, who was a Master student of the founder, Mikao Usui. Today, however, things have changed. Lineage and the accompanying teachings are not as straightforward as they once were.

One of the motivating factors in writing this book was to help others along their Reiki path. Only after I received my first Reiki training did I find out that it was not entirely traditional Usui Shiki Reiki Ryoho. It was this very reason that inspired me to begin research on the original elements of the Reiki system. I am grateful for this experience now, although in the beginning of this quest I became worried, angry, and definitely not grateful that what I had originally received was not strictly the Reiki system. In short, I had utterly failed to uphold the Reiki principles.

Today I look at these events as opportunities to practice the Reiki principles. Because I first had non-traditional training, it led to my desire to find the traditional teachings of Takata. This, in turn, has led me to learn so much more about Reiki and its history than I would have otherwise. As a result, I was able to meet with so many wonderful Reiki Masters and practitioners from the early days of Reiki in the United States and Canada.

Remember, it isn't just a matter of who taught whom. Lineage is the embodiment of Reiki, its teachings, and how they interplay, affect, and fulfill our lives with peace, joy, happiness, and a sense of connectivity with all things. This is what matters. This is the Reiki system.

One of my Master students, Liza Binford, put it this way: "A person's Reiki lineage is the historical, traceable, line of teachers and the knowledge which one receives, through a direct transmission from teacher to student."

When looking at my Reiki lineages, I don't want my own students or anyone else to get the misguided impression that a person needs to train with a lot of teachers. I did this because I wanted to get to the truth about some of the history of the Reiki system and its teachings. I needed to cross-train in different lineages to double-check, triple-check, or more, the information I was given, in order to see the commonalities in the teachings, which I could then deem as reliable. I looked at all the teachings I learned with a critical eye, until I could verify them through another lineage or source. I write more about this approach to research in Appendix 1entitled "Researching Logic 101." This need to verify and cross-check information simply stemmed from the fact that I had first learned nontraditional Reiki teachings and I wanted to make sure I learned the system of Reiki as practiced by Takata.

Knowing your lineage is important. It is a way of honoring your teachers along this path. Unfortunately, people are under the impression that a shorter lineage is better than a longer lineage. There are even many cases of people making up their own Reiki lineages as they see fit. And while it is true that with a longer lineage there are more opportunities for people to make changes in a system, realize that it takes only one Master to do this.

Remember, lineage does not make you nobler or better than anyone else. So, when we try to judge others based on lineage, we are showing our own ignorance. In the future, lineage may not seem as important as it once did. Direct contact with the source (Reiki) is what matters. Once initiated, you don't *need* to be reinitiated. If you're connected with source, you're connected with source. The only reason necessary to be initiated again is to be initiated into a new form of practice, i.e. a new lineage.[311]

I would like to express my own viewpoints on passing on a Reiki lineage. First is that it should be done clearly; this is a matter of honor to me. This means, if you list different Reiki teachers in your lineage, it is a matter

---

311  Note I used the words "necessary" and "need" in these sentences. I am not discounting that there may be other benefits to receiving the initiations repeatedly.

of honor to also list what degree(s) of training you studied with them.

I train Masters over a period of time and in stages. There are those Masters who have been trained and initiated to teach the Practitioner levels (the First and Second Degrees) and those who have been trained and initiated to teach the Teaching levels (each aspect of the Third Degree). Only the latter are trained, initiated, and recognized to pass on my *teaching* lineage by training another Third Degree (Shinpiden) student. It is through this line of Dai Shihans that the continuation of my own lineage is ensured; these individuals are therefore designated as "lineage holders".[312]

Because some Reiki lineages and schools do not have a Master initiation, in those cases the Master lineage is considered to be from the person who taught you how to do the Reiki initiations. For example, it would be dishonorable for me to use John Harvey Gray as my teacher in my teaching lineage like this: Usui-Hayashi-Takata-Gray-Fueston. I was trained and initiated by John in the First and Second Degrees, and John claims there originally was not a Master initiation in his lineage. But I learned the initiation methods from one of his Master students, Stephen Comee. So my lineage in this example would be Usui-Hayashi-Takata-Gray-Comee-Fueston.

I spend a lot of time, one to two years, with Master Candidates (Shihan-kaku and Shihan students), thoroughly training them in how to teach the Practitioner Levels (First and Second Degrees) of the Reiki system, and they spend a lot of time and money for the training I provide. I spend even more time with individuals whom I train to carry on my teaching lineage (Dai Shihan students). Contrast this with someone who has taken Second Degree with me, which is normally between nine and twelve hours and typically taught over two days. To use me as their teaching lineage or as their energy lineage would be to misrepresent the nature and level of our relationship and of their training with me. In other words, this would be breaking the fourth Precept, "Just for today, do your work honestly."

This is my opinion, and not all Reiki schools or teachers need to share my opinion.[313] I have given my own reasons here, and they have to do with

---

312  Shihan-kaku and Shihans can pass on the practitioner levels. Therefore, if no Dai Shihans are trained in a lineage, the lineage will become extinct after the last person who was trained as a Dai Shihan in the lineage goes into transition.

313  For example, Hyakuten Inamoto and Tadao Yamaguchi use their teacher Mrs. Yamaguchi's Second Degree Reiki lineage of Usui-Hayashi-Chiyoko Yamaguchi. Since Hyakuten was my teacher, I will honor his decision. However, I know some Reiki Masters who took the First and Second Degrees with Mrs. Yamaguchi. If one of these Masters then later learned the initiation process from Tadao or Hyakuten, but simply used their Second Degree lineage from Mrs. Yamaguchi (leaving Tadao or Hyakuten out of their teaching lineage), I wonder if they would be okay with this? Hiroshi Doi, with whom I have also trained, uses his Gakkai lineage, one in which he had not officially received Master training. However, since his instructions were to use this lineage of Usui-Taketomi-Koyama-Doi, I will do so.

what I think of as having honor and integrity. I am simply stating what is true for anyone in my own lineage, now or in the future. I can decide for myself the honorable way I want my lineage to be represented. I am making this statement as clear as possible here so that my wishes and my reasoning are understood by the future generations of Reiki teachers in my lineage. I list the teachers I have trained, including their level of training, on The Reiki Preservation Society's website: www.TheReikiPreservationSociety.org

## Usui-Hayashi-Takata-Fran Brown-Mary Goslen-Robert N. Fueston[314]

I completed the First Degree, Second Degree, and part of the Third Degree training as a Master Candidate with Fran Brown.[25] This training with Fran really helped me confirm and verify information I learned in other Master lineages after having heard it directly from one of Takata's master students. I completed my Master training in Fran's lineage with one of her Master students, Mary Goslen.

*Robert Fueston and Fran Brown*

---

314 Mary Goslen also completed her Third Degree and Fourth Degree training with Takata's Master student Barbara Weber Ray prior to going to Fran Brown for training in each level.

*Mary Goslen and Robert Fueston*

*John Harvey Gray, Robert Fueston, Lourdes Gray*

*Marcia Halligan and Robert Fueston*

*Hyakuten Inamoto, Hiroshi Doi, Robert Fueston*

*Glenda Fern Johnson and Robert Fueston*

The information below is for reference only regarding my past training.

**My other Reiki Master lineages**:

- Usui-Hayashi-Takata-Barbara Weber Ray-Marcia Halligan-Robert N. Fueston

- Usui-Hayashi-Takata-John Harvey Gray-Stephen Comee-Robert N. Fueston (Note: I had trained in both the First and Second Degrees with John Harvey Gray and his wife Lourdes prior to this training.)

- Usui-Hayashi-Takata-Barbara McCullough-Helen Borth-Robert N. Fueston

- Usui-Hayashi-Takata-Mary McFadyen-Gail Johnston-Kathy Rose-Glenda Johnson.

Glenda was a member of The Reiki Alliance for three years, starting in 1991. Mary McFadyen checked Glenda's initiation process upon joining The Reiki Alliance.

- Usui-Hayashi-Takata-Barbara Weber Ray-Brigitte Byrd[315]-Light and Adonea.

- Usui-Hayashi-Takata-Virginia Samdahl-Viola Ebert-Timothy Mc-Namara.

This was a Master-level exchange of information, including how to do the initiation procedures. I later contacted Viola Ebert to clarify some of what Timothy had taught me.

- Usui-Hayashi-Takata-Phyllis Lei Furumoto-Carell Ann Farmer-Leah Smith-William Rand-Light and Adonea.[316]

- Usui-Hayashi-Takata, Phyllis Lei Furumoto, Pat Jack, Cherie Wine-Prasuhn, DeVonna Simpkins-Michael Frazier-Shelah Sara-von-Rev. Jone Eagle.

**Non-Takata lineages:**

- Usui-Hayashi-Chiyoko Yamaguchi-Hyakuten Inamoto[313]

Chiyoko Yamaguchi studied the First and Second Degrees with Chujiro Hayashi. However, it was Mrs. Yamaguchi's uncle, Sugano Wasaburo, who was a master student of Hayashi, who trained her at the Master level. Hyakuten has named his system Komyo Reiki.

- Usui- Kan'ichi Taketomi-Kimiko Koyama-Hiroshi Doi[313]

Mikao Usui was the first president and founder of the Usui Reiki Ryoho Gakkai. Kan'ichi Taketomi was the third president, and Kimiko Koyama was the sixth president. Hiroshi Doi is, or was, a member of the Gakkai.

Hiroshi Doi claims to have originally taken all the levels of Reiki training in the following lineage: Mikao Usui-Kan'ichi Taketomi-Ayako Sasaki-Hiroshi Ohta. Ohta-sensei's teacher, Sakaki-san, was a Gakkai member and in charge of the Hiroshima chapter of the Gakkai. He had taught full Shinpiden to Ohta-san, who in turn passed all this on to Doi-sensei as simply "téaté" (a generic term for hands on healing). Years

---

315  Brigitte told my teacher Adonea that she was trained by Barbara Weber Ray. But when I spoke with Brigitte, she told me that she had taken the First and Second Degrees with Blanche Hanks (lineage Takata-Weber Ray) and "3a" (Third Degree part 1) with Marvelle Carter (originally her birth name was Marvette Carter, then she became Marvelle Carter, and later Marvelle Lightfields). Back in those days it was not uncommon for a teacher to train someone at the Master level, but then have the teacher's teacher do the initiations. So it is quite possible that Brigitte received the Master initiation directly from Barbara Weber Ray. It is my understanding that Brigitte taught an early form of Barbara Ray's Radiance Technique, but since she did not want to sign Barbara Weber Ray's contract she thought she could not teach it. However, folks convinced Brigitte to share her knowledge, so she taught as an independent Reiki Master. Until very recently, only Barbara Weber Ray was allowed/supposed to teach the Third Degree and above in her system of Reiki (The Radiance Technique).

316  Light and Adonea also studied at the Master level with many different Reiki Masters and Reiki lineages.

later, Doi-sensei discovered Sasaki-sensei's position in the Gakkai and realized he had already received Reiki in 1982.

Ayako Sasaki was a formally certificated Gakkai master. Just after World War II, the Gakkai, as well as any other organizations consisting of military personnel, were banned from having meetings by the Allies, and the Gakkai masters were separated. Ayako Sasaki taught Hiroshi Ohta at that time, without formal certification from the Gakkai. That is, Ohta-sensei was allowed by Sasaki-sensei to teach Reiki, but Ohta-sensei was not a Gakkai member and was not certificated by the Gakkai. Ohta-sensei, who was not a formal Gakkai master, taught Reiki to Doi-sensei. Therefore, Doi-sensei is allowed by Ohta-sensei to teach Reiki but Doi does not want to say that he received "Shinpiden", to avoid confusion. If Doi-sensei uses the word "Shinpiden", some will get the misunderstanding that Doi-sensei has Shinpiden in the Gakkai. Doi-sensei says, "The current Gakkai teachers agree that my energy lineage is definitely the one from Usui-sensei." When Doi-sensei was taught the above, he was not aware it was Reiki.[317]

---

317   Rick Rivard, presentation at Usui Reiki Ryoho International conference, November 9-11, 2001, Madrid, Spain.

# *Appendix* ONE

---

## *Researching Logic 101*

# APPENDIX
# 01

## *Researching Logic 101*

*"A conclusion is the place where you got tired of thinking."*
~ Martin H. Fischer

I remember one incident when a reporter wanted to interview me for the local newspaper and I consented. However, after reading the finished article already in print, I was shocked to discover the reporter had made changes to my story. For example, I had told the reporter that my wife and I met in Colorado while we were both in acupuncture school. I had also mentioned that I had just returned from France from some Master training with Fran Brown at a Tibetan Monastery. The reporter however, decided to modify a few of my stories and stated my wife and I met when I was in France training with Fran Brown at a Tibetan Monastery. I called up the writer to tell her about the mistake and she explained to me that she changed the story on purpose to make it more interesting. That possibility had never crossed my mind.

A researcher needs to determine if the information received is accurate and the likeliness that it is true. This is critical, and frequently the validity of the information is either not known or understood and certainly not verified by many authors (books, magazine, websites, etc.). People tend to take the stance that something is true unless proven otherwise, which is like the "innocent until proven guilty" approach the American justice system takes. But this approach does not and cannot work when doing research and it is an inappropriate philosophy to utilize. In fact, taking this approach isn't research at all; it is simply repeating hearsay.

198

Approach A, below, is an example of hearsay presenting itself as "research".

| Approach A |
| --- |
| Piece of information posted by Mr. X |
| Relay of Mr. X's information by Mrs. B |
| Someone, Mr. D, doing "hearsay research" finds Mrs. B stating the information. Mr. D then concludes that it must be "true." |
| Mr. D reposts and passes on the information as "true" AND as valid "research." |

I recall one experience when a person wanted me to convince him that Iris Ishikuro, one of Takata's Master students, wasn't Takata's cousin. He had read they were cousins, and I was stating that they were not.

I later found out that he thought they were cousins to begin with because the source of his information had used some misinformation I had posted on my *own* website years before. I was originally told by a *reliable* source, Fran Brown, that Iris and Takata were cousins. I had no second source of information to verify this claim, but I posted it as fact because it came from what I deemed a reliable source. Other people took my word for the truth, just as I had taken Fran's word as the truth. Later however, when I spoke with Iris's daughter, a much more reliable source, I found out they were not cousins and I updated my website. In other words, I was guilty of being "Mr. D" as in my example above.

So, for me, this was an ironic situation. This person believed these two were cousins only because I had written it on my website years before; and now he wouldn't believe the newer information on my website even though I knew it had come from a more reliable source. In a way, this is good. It shows how both this man and I had grown over the years to think critically. He simply wasn't going to believe me, or my website, that this piece of information was true unless he, himself, spoke with Iris's daughter. I have learned to ensure I have several sources to verify information before stating that they are true, or likely to be true.

A little bit better, but still with its flaws, is this research example in approach B:

| | Approach B | |
|---|---|---|
| | Piece of information posted by Mr. X | |
| Relay of Mr. X's information by Mrs. A | Relay of Mr. X's information by Mrs. B | Relay of Mr. X's information by Mrs. C |
| | Someone, Mr. D, doing hearsay research finds all these sources (Mrs. A, B, and C) stating the same information. Mr. D then concludes that it must be "true." | |
| | Mr. D reposts and passes on the information as "true" AND as valid "research." | |

Mr. D needed to find out the **source** of Mrs. A, B, and C's information. If he had done so, he could conclude that Mr. X likely stated this piece of information (as three persons claimed he did). But we still don't know for sure if what Mr. X stated to begin with is true. Mrs. A, B, and C all used the same source for their information, so we can only conclude that it is very likely that Mr. X stated this information.

Approach B can work, or is useful, for some types of research. For example, on my own Reiki journey I wanted to know how and what Takata taught as the Reiki system. So, based on speaking with those people who knew Takata and took training from her, I could objectively look at the information I received, noting the similarities and differences in the information.

The similarities in the information received indicate that it is likely true that Takata taught this piece of information. However, we must not jump to conclusions that the differences in information are either true or untrue.

With differences, we must simply wait until more data is gathered to see if in the future some new information will back up a single piece of information that currently has no confirmation to back it up.

In the case of my research on the Reiki system as taught by Takata, I was able to go a few steps further. It is great to have people stating the same information, as in approach B, which is what I call "soft evidence" because one cannot absolutely prove with 100 percent accuracy whether the information is true. One can only state the relative probability that a piece of information is true. The chance that a piece of information is true is greater with more and more reliable sources giving similar information.

It is absolutely wonderful when you can get "hard evidence." Hard evidence is nearly undisputable evidence, as in the case of audio recordings, pictures, and video recordings. Hard evidence, in other words, is physical evidence that has "signatures" of authenticity on it; for example, audio recordings of Takata teaching. I can tell that the voice on the recordings is the same person speaking. However, I cannot assume that the person's voice is Takata speaking. I have never met Takata, so I do not know firsthand what her voice sounded like. Therefore, I need to use logic and research to determine the likelihood that it is Takata's voice on the audio recordings.

At first, I had only one audio recording of "Takata" speaking. I deemed the source *somewhat* reliable, because other information I had obtained from this person was not always found to be accurate or true. Luckily I was able to obtain additional and different audio recordings from other people who all stated the recordings were of Takata. These recordings contained the same voice as the previous recording I had. None of the sources for these audio recordings had any relationship to each other. The likelihood that all these independent sources, who didn't know each other, could get the same woman to record different pieces of Reiki information on audio recordings was next to none. Still, one could argue that an "unscrupulous genius" could have made many different audio recordings supposedly narrated by Takata. Theoretically, this "genius" could then have secretly given the different recordings to various Reiki people who did not know each other. Therefore, however unlikely this scenario is, we cannot know with 100 percent certainty that the person on the recordings is Takata. We can only state that the probability is extremely high that the person speaking on the recordings is Takata.

One source of the audio recordings, John Harvey Gray, was a Master student of Takata's. John found these recordings while cleaning out his ex-wife's garage. His ex-wife, Beth Gray, was also a Master student of Takata's and reportedly had made about 20 tapes of Takata teaching Reiki classes. John, of course, would recognize his own teacher's voice. In fact, on one audio recording I have, I can recognize John's voice on the recording during one of Takata's classes. Someone even says his name, John, in the audio recording of the class. I also have confirmation from another Takata Master student, Fran Brown, that the voice on the recordings is that of Takata. This is an example of research and hard evidence.

One might say that the lengths to which a researcher goes to get verification of information area little bit extreme. I say, as a researcher, that it is not only necessary but is the definition of "good research"! In today's world, with so many websites discussing the various systems of Reiki, it seems that most authors take "Approach A" for their information. This is passed along as "research" and, unfortunately, the general public doesn't question it.

There have been several cases in Reiki history where a "Mr. X" simply made up information, stating that he had "hard evidence." However, Mr. X would not let anyone else view or confirm his "hard evidence." Documents he supposedly owned, or Reiki Masters he had supposedly studied with, were not made available for a third party (an independent source who has no inherent interest or ulterior motivation) to verify the claims.[318] In at least one case, the "Mr. X" in question has admitted to his deception. There will always be "Mr. X's" in the Reiki world who will fabricate stories to sway students to take their training.

In 2012, in the beginning of my lecture at the New York Reiki Conference, I said, "I don't expect anyone to believe anything that I am about to say." I said this because despite the evidence I was about to give, (information that I knew to be from different reliable and verifiable resources), I had to view myself from the audience's perspective. To the attendees, all this information coming from me was going to be new. I wanted them to think about that before believing something as factual.

I had done this research into the history and practice of Usui Shiki Reiki Ryoho for my own sake, so that I would know the history and how Takata had taught Reiki. I wanted to know and verify the practice so I could pass

---

318  It is for this reason that I am willing to provide evidence, "if and when it is needed" regarding some of the materials I have that are not freely available or easily found. I am willing to do this so that the materials can be verified by a third party who is approved by both the Reiki community and by me. This does require that the third party travel to my location as the materials are not, and will not be, copied in any way. The materials can be verified and the third party can report back to the community. I am a custodian of this material. I have the honor of being entrusted with it and I take this responsibility seriously. In the tradition I follow, some of this material is to remain within the followers of Usui Shiki Reiki Ryoho and therefore it is inappropriate to distribute to outsiders. Third party verification is the acceptable compromise and I feel is the balance between those who wish to have materials verified and those of us who hold sacred the materials and teachings in Usui Shiki Reiki Ryoho.

on to my own students the Reiki system as taught by Takata. It has been a pleasure to share some of what I have learned with other Reiki practitioners who were interested in my Reiki research.

# *Appendix* TWO

---

## *Chronologically Ordered by Master Training Date*

# APPENDIX
# 02

## *Hawayo Takata's 22 Master Students*
### *Chronologically Ordered by Master Training Date*

I spent hundreds, if not thousands of hours over the past 19 years researching Takata's 22 Master students. Other Reiki practitioners I knew wanted to know more about these Masters and I was happy to share my original research. I posted this information on my website starting in the late 1990's.

I was correct about the interest in this topic and others started to share and re-post the material from my website. However, at some point, web links back to my original research and attributing the credit for the research to me, were dropped. While I was happy to share my research, it seemed ungrateful to me for people to pass off another's hard work as one's own. Furthermore, without web links back to my original site, readers would not be directed to where my most current research was published. I was raised in a home where I was taught good manners and to give credit to people where credit was due. We all like being recognized for our work. This is also true of authors; otherwise, they would write books anonymously.

This idea was reinforced during my academic graduate level training in Library and Information Science. It is the professional standard to cite one's source of information, and it is unprofessional to plagiarize another person's work. While the Internet community in general might not hold themselves to such high standards, Reiki practitioners are suppose to live by a code of honor. Our code of honor is the five Reiki Precepts, one of which is doing one's work honestly.

For the foreseeable future, I have taken down my web pages concerning Takata's 22 Master students. This chapter represents the latest, most up-to-date version of my research. As I have literally thousands of pages of research regarding all aspects of the system of Reiki, what I am writing here should not be construed as all the information I would like to share on this subject. Rather, this is simply the stopping point of my writing on this subject at the moment.

I hope you enjoy this chapter as much as I have enjoyed writing it to share with you. A picture of each of Takata's 22 Master students can be found throughout this book.

Note: The original URLs (Web links) for the websites are given here. Websites with broken links can sometimes still be accessed by using the Internet Archive to view the Web pages: http://archive.org/web/web.php

## Photo of attendees at the 1982 meeting in Hawaii.

*Names from left to right:*

3rd row: Leo Bernard Samdahl (Virginia Samdahl's husband), Marta Getty, Barbara West, Carell Ann Farmer, Paul Mitchell, Susan Mitchell, Vincent Elmore (Mary McFadyen's husband)

2nd row: Rick Bockner, Adair Samdahl (Virginia Samdahl's daughter), Bunny Sjogren, John Harvey Gray, unknown person's shoulder, Fran Brown, Bethal Phaigh

1st row: Virginia Samdahl, Beth Gray, Kay Yamashita, Phyllis Lei Furumoto, Ethel Lombardi, Dorothy Baba (just behind Ethel), Jiro Baba (Dorothy Baba's husband)

## *Kay Yamashita*

**Born:** Unknown

**Transition:** Unknown

**First Degree and Second Degree:** Most likely in the late 1930s or early 1940s.

The First and Second Degrees were most likely learned together over an approximately 5 day period with the training cost being $300. [319]

**Third Degree:** 1975

Takata had her first heart attack in 1975. Afterwards, she decided to train her sister Kay Yamashita as a Master, in the event she died before training a master.

**Reiki Organization Affiliations:**

It is possible she was a member of a branch of the Hayashi Reiki Ken-kyūkai ("Research Society") on the Hawaiian Islands.

In John Harvey Gray and Lourdes Gray's book entitled *Hand to Hand: The Longest-Practicing Reiki Master Tells His Story*, John states on page 178, "My first training in Reiki Mastership was learning the procedure and attunements for the First Degree class. Then Takata had to go back to Hawaii. Before she left, she said to me, 'When I come back in three months I will tell you about the Second Degree." Well, 'I answered, 'I've already paid the standard fee for mastership training. What will happen if you die?' Takata became flustered and angry. 'My sister in the Hawaiian Islands knows the procedure and could train you if I died', she said. She then gave me the contact information for her sister."

---

319   See chapter 10 for more information.

## M. Virginia Walker Samdahl

**Born:** 1918[320]

**Transition:** March 4, 1994

**First Degree:** August 25, 1974[321]

**Second Degree:** 1975[322]

**Third Degree:** June 5, 1976[321] with Takata.

Was retrained and initiated as a Master by Barbara Weber in 1981. She was certified to teach the First and Second Degrees by the A.R.A./A.I.R.A. before she left the group in 1983.

**Reiki Organization Affiliations:**

A.R.A./A.I.R.A.

Founding member of The Reiki Alliance

**Resources:**

*Virginia Samdahl: Reiki Master Healer* by Barbara D. Lugenbeel, a biography of Virginia Samdahl, was written in 1984.[323]

*The Reiki Handbook* by Larry Arnold and Sandy Nevius, two of Virginia's students, wrote this as a First Degree manual and Virginia checked its accuracy.

Virginia Samdahl lived in Chicago, Illinois. Before beginning her Reiki training, Virginia was a psychic healer. Virginia was the first non-Asian Reiki Master to be trained. She introduced her own Reiki student, Barbara Weber, to Hawayo Takata.

Virginia first joined the American Reiki Association, headed by Barbara Weber. In 1983, upon its founding, she also joined The Reiki Alliance, originally headed by Phyllis Lei Furumoto. Virginia tried to be the peacemaker between these two organizations.

Virginia trained, or helped train, the following people as masters:

- Adair Samdahl, now Adair Seeman. Virginia's daughter, Adair, was trained as a Master before the others although Virginia knew Adair

320  Date from Virginia Samdahl's gravestone.

321  According to Takata's ledger book. Personal collection of Phyllis Furumoto. Note: dates listed in the ledger book are when a receipt for payment was written by Takata. The dates may not be the exact dates of training or dates listed on certificates.

322  The dates for all three degrees of her training are stated in Lugenbeel, *Virginia Samdahl,* 80.

323  I've heard from several of Virginia's students that Virginia wasn't entirely happy with the content of this book. Virginia thought it overemphasized supernatural events.

didn't want to teach Reiki.

- Viola R. Ebert was trained by Virginia but Barbara Weber completed the final training and initiation. Virginia and Viola[324] were both certified to teach the First and Second Degrees by the A.R.A./A.I.R.A. Viola did her A.R.A./A.I.R.A. apprenticeship with Virginia.

- Barbi Lazonby was trained by Viola Ebert, but was initiated by Virginia Samdahl as Master. Barbi started practicing Reiki in 1986, was the founding director of The Reiki Center of Florida, and was a member of The Reiki Alliance. She was initiated as a Master in 1990 and died July 4, 2001.

- Richard Pinneau was trained by Viola Ebert, but was initiated by Virginia Samdahl as Master.

- Barbara Thompson.

Virginia retired from teaching Reiki in 1989. She was a smoker and died as a result of emphysema.

Virginia's obituary from the *Chicago Tribune* appears below. It was taken from: http://articles.chicagotribune.com/1994-03-27/news/9403270001_1_reiki-energy-field-master-teacher

---

### *Art Master Martha Samdahl, 76*

March 27, 1994 | By Michael A. Lev, *Tribune Staff Writer.*

Martha Virginia Walker Samdahl, 76, a longtime Chicago-area resident who was a master of the Japanese healing art known as reiki, died March 4 in a Huntsville, Ala., hospital.

Mrs. Samdahl, who lived in Park Forest for 30 years until moving to Florida in 1986, was the first non-Asian person to become a master teacher of the Usui system of reiki, said her daughter, Adair Seeman.

According to the beliefs of reiki, the body consists of one large energy field that is interrupted when illness or injury occurs. Reiki holds that using certain methods of hand placement restores the energy field to its natural flow.

Mrs. Samdahl, who learned of reiki when an Asian master visited Chicago about 30 years ago, traveled the world teaching the system

---

324   Viola is listed as a teacher in *The Reiki Review*, 3:3 (Summer 1983), 11.

to others, her daughter said.

She was also an ordained minister in the Church of Antioch and a teacher.

A graduate of the University of Wisconsin-Stout in Menomonie, Mrs. Samdahl taught high school in Chicago in the late 1940s and helped establish the home economics department at American University in Heidelberg, Germany, in the early 1950s.

Other survivors include a brother and five grandchildren.

A graveside memorial service is planned for May 28 in Halverson Cemetery in Menomonie.

## *Ethel Lombardi*

**Born:** 1922 or 1923

**Transition:** October 14, 2009, at the age of 86

**First Degree:** September 16, 1974[321]

**Second Degree:** 1975

**Third Degree:** June 11, 1976[321]

**Reiki Organization Affiliations:** None

Ethel was already a well-known healer living in Chicago, Illinois, when she met Takata. Ethel stopped teaching Reiki shortly after Takata's death due to the Reiki politics going on at this time.

Ethel taught Reiki from 1976 to 1983 and was one of the Reiki teachers with the most students at the time.[325] She was one of the most successful Reiki teachers, having 100 or more students in her classes at a time. Other Masters helped Ethel to initiate the large number of students in these classes. The photo below is provided by Marta Getty and is published with her permission.

Back row, left to right: Beth Gray, Helen Borth, Phyllis Furumoto, Shinobu Saito, Fran Brown

Front row, left to right: Ethel Lombardi, Patricia Bowling (Ewing), Barbara McCullough, Dorothy Baba, Marta Getty

---

325   The others were Virginia Samdahl and Barbara Weber Ray.

In 1983 Ethel stopped teaching Reiki and created her own system of energy work called Mari-El.[326]At this time she disengaged from her Reiki identity and clearly named and pursued her own system rather than tie it to the Usui System by trying to interweave the two.[327] "Mari" represents Mary, mother of Christ, and "El" one of the names of God. It is believed that the Mari-El system of healing is no longer being taught. After Ethel stopped teaching Mari-El, she began teaching a system called "The Next Step."

---

326  Personal communication with many of Ethel's students.

327  Technically, Ethel had added one new technique, a "pulling out" technique, when teaching Reiki before she changed the name of her system to Mari-El.

## John Harvey Gray

**Born:** April 10, 1917

**Transition:** January 12, 2011

**First Degree:** June 12, 1974 [328]

**Second Degree:** Unknown.

Most likely the date would be February 1, 1975; the same date found on Beth Gray's certificate.

**Third Degree:** October 6, 1976 [329]

**Reiki Organization Affiliations:**

Founder of the Usui-Gray Integrated System®

**Resources:**

*Hand to Hand: The Longest-Practicing Reiki Master Tells His Story* by John Harvey Gray and Lourdes Gray.

Website: http://www.learnreiki.org

John taught more than 700 Reiki classes. John's first wife, Beth Gray, would later also become a Master student of Takata's. John's second wife, Lourdes, became John's successor.

---

328   *Hand to Hand: The Longest-Practicing Reiki Master Tells His Story* (Xlibris: 2002), 29.
329   *Hand to Hand: The Longest-Practicing Reiki Master Tells His Story* (Xlibris: 2002), 32.

## *Iris A. Ishikuro*

*Iris Ishikuro is sitting on the far left and Takata on the far right. The others were Iris Ishikuro's students. Photo taken at Takata's retirement party on May 29, 1977.*

**Born:** Unknown

**Transition:** 1984

**First Degree:** 1968 [330]

**Second Degree:** Unknown

**Third Degree:** November 1976 [331]

**Reiki Organization Affiliations:**

Universal Light Center in California

According to Arthur Robertson, Iris was told by Takata to train only three people as Masters. Iris offered three people the training: her daughter Ruby, her husband (who declined the training), and Arthur Robertson.

Arthur Robertson was responsible for adding the Kanji Hand Positions

---

330  According to Iris's daughter, Ruby.

331  According to her own flyer, she was trained as a Master in November 1976. Takata's ledger book shows her first payment as a Master was July 15, 1977. Personal collection of Phyllis Furumoto It is possible that Iris was trained in November 1976 but didn't make a payment to Takata until July 15, 1977, and therefore why she was not included in Takata's 1976 retirement letter.

(mudras), the Johrei Symbols, "Reiki Master Spinal Therapy," "Kidney Breathing" and Antahkarana symbols to the system of Reiki. Arthur named his own system Raku-Kei Reiki. [332]

Iris was trained by Hawayo Takata for the fee of $10,000 and, according to Arthur, Iris asked him never to charge that amount, but to make it more affordable to people of sincere aspiration who could not afford the traditional fee. I received a lot of material that once belonged to Iris via her daughter. Ruby sent me an Antahkarana board, made by Arthur Robertson, and told me that Iris did use these boards under her Reiki table. However, she did not include them in her Reiki training for her students.

Iris charged $100 for the First Degree in 1977, and by 1984 she was charging $125.[330]

---

332   Ruby said that Arthur made lots of changes to the Reiki system. According to Iris's own notes and Ruby's review of Arthur's materials and manuals I sent to her, she stated she had never seen most of the material Arthur was teaching in his Reiki system.

## Harry Masami Kuboi

**Born:** 1930 (exact date unknown)

**Transition:** October 19, 2013

**First Degree:** April 28, 1974 [333]

**Second Degree:** October 27, 1975 [333]

**Third Degree:** April 18, 1977 [333] (He was offered to be trained as a Master in 1976 but waited a year to decide.)

**Reiki Organization Affiliations:** None

**Resources:**

*All of Reiki Book I* and *All of Reiki Book II* by Harry Kuboi.

A third book *All of Reiki Book III* was partially written but never published. The book was to be a manual for the Second Degree students. It included, "A detailed explanation on how to do distant Reiki treatment, Reiki symbols, and how to properly write them, and how to protect oneself before doing distant treatment."[334]

An unpublished book entitled, *Knowledge Beyond the Earthly Realm* was written.

Website: at http://byguy.com/harrykuboi

Harry Masami Kuboi was born during the Great Depression on Oahu in the Hawaiian Islands. He was the oldest child of Alma and Isami

---

333   Date on Harry Kuboi's certificate.
334   "Forthcoming Publications," in Kuboi, *All of Reiki: Book Two* (Honolulu: Hawaii Reiki Center, 1996).

Kuboi. He was a retired mason, and an Army veteran who served in the Korean War. [335]

Harry explains, "Reiki energy comes through a channel. It enters through your solar plexus (near your belly button), travels up to the heart area and from there it moves to the shoulder joints. It flows down the arms and when it reaches the wrists, it fills the entire palms of the hands." Harry goes on to explain, "Reiki energy does not enter through your head." [336]

This is slightly different from how Takata described the Reiki channel. As described by Takata in Chapter 7, Reiki enters the crown first before entering the "solar plexus". (Both Takata and Harry used the term "solar plexus" to describe the lower *tanden*.)

In a letter I received from Harry and in our phone conversations, he explained that most people were being attuned where the energy enters the hands and travels down the body and exits the perineum (*Hui Yin*) — therefore, it is negative (implying that people are sucking energy out of the person they are treating.

Harry said he stopped teaching the system of Reiki around 2002, but in fact he still taught on occasion. Harry taught classes of four students or fewer throughout his career.

Harry focused more on doing exorcisms, including changing people's "negative" Reiki into "positive" Reiki. He did this by first energetically removing the person's incorrect Reiki initiations and then reinitiating the student properly.

Harry trained two Reiki Masters to carry on his lineage. They are in order of training date:

- Judy C. Lau (now Judy C. Byrd). Judy has retired from teaching the system of Reiki.
- Dick Giles

In another letter I have from Harry, he stated that in 1985, after about two months of channeling, Eitoku (Mikao Usui) came down during one of his channeling's and gave him the title of "Reiki Master of Masters." He also said that he could not teach other people Reiki exorcism, because this requires the ability "to channel with father in the spirit world."

---

335   http://obits.staradvertiser.com/2013/11/14/harry-m-kuboi/ accessed February 17, 2015.
336   Kuboi, *All of Reiki: Book Two* (Honolulu: Hawaii Reiki Center, 1996), 15, 82.

## Barbara Lincoln McCullough

**Born:** November 20, 1924

**Transition:** June 16, 2000

**First Degree:** 1975

**Second Degree:** 1976

**Third Degree:** June 25, 1977 in Keosauqua, Iowa[321]

**Reiki Organization Affiliations:** None

Barbara was a legal secretary and lived with Parkinson's disease for many years. She trained a few Master students including:

- Helen Borth on December 21, 1980
- David G. Jarrell on August 5, 1981
- Judy Carol Stewart on January 22, 1985
- Laryl Fett on June 18, 1986, in Martinsburg, West Virginia. A Unitarian Universalist minister.

## <u>Dorothy Baba</u> (born <u>*Aiko Kajita*</u>)

**Born:** June 9, 1917

**Transition:** December, 1985

Dorothy was in a severe car accident and died a few days later as a result of the injuries she sustained.

**First Degree:** May 6, 1976 [321]

**Second Degree:** September 18, 1976 [321]

**Third Degree:** July 10, 1977 [321]

**Reiki Organization Affiliations:** None

Dorothy Baba was a social worker who lived in Stockton, California. [337] She never trained a Master student.

---

337   Information provided by a personal correspondence with John Harvey Gray.

### Ursula Baylow

**Born:** 1911

**Transition:** October 21, 1996[338]

**First Degree:** July 7, 1976,[339] in Summerland, British Columbia (along with Barbara Brown[340]).

**Second Degree:** August 25, 1978[339]

**Third Degree:** August 1978 in Penticton, British Columbia.

Originally Ursula was secretly trained as a Master immediately after taking the Second Degree.[341] However, she was told by Takata not to tell anyone she had been trained as a Master.[342] When Takata returned a year later, Ursula received a certificate showing she had completed the advanced course (Master/Third Degree) on June 11, 1979.

**Reiki Organization Affiliations:**

Founding member of The Reiki Alliance

Ursula was the first Reiki Master in Canada, and Takata stayed at Ursula's home in Penticton, BC, several times on her trips to Canada. The most commonly shared photo of Takata was taken by Ursula's husband, Gunter, in their garden in Penticton (photo found in Chapter 5).

---

338  Personal correspondence with Sarah Baylow (Ursula's daughter). July 5, 2004.
339  Date on Ursula Baylow's certificate, given to me by Sarah Baylow.
340  Twan, *Early days of Reiki,* 1.
341  Personal correspondence with Phyllis Furumoto and Sarah Baylow, who also confirmed it with Fran Brown.
342  I speculate that this unusually condensed training format was because Takata was unsure if she would return to Canada in the future.

Ursula practiced Reiki and reflexology from around 1976 until 1989 (at age 77). *"After a stroke in 1989, Ursula was no longer able to treat clients, but continued to share her healing with family and friends. Ursula Baylow died of a heart attack in her sleep, peacefully. She experienced Reiki as one of the most meaningful aspects of her life, and used it in her daily life at every opportunity. She lived the Reiki principles. Many of her clients viewed her as a healer, with great improvement in serious and chronic conditions."*[338]

## Frances "Fran" Walker Brown

**Born:** March 10, 1924

**Transition:** April 12, 2009

**First Degree:** June 15, 1973 [343]

**Second Degree:** 1976 from John Harvey Gray [344]

During Fran's Third Degree training with Takata, Takata confirmed Fran's Second Degree training with John by giving her a Second Degree certificate dated January 11, 1979. [343]

**Third Degree:** January 15, 1979, in Keosauqua, Iowa [343]

**Reiki Organization Affiliations:**

The Reiki Alliance

**Resources:**

*Living Reiki: Takata's Teachings* by Fran Brown

http://www.reikifranbrown.com

home.pacbell.net/revfranb

Fran stated: *"In 1997 I was asked to come to Japan and teach Hayashi's system and in 1999 it was my privilege to meet with members of the group founded by Usui, the Usui Reiki Ryoho Gakkai, as well as students and masters taught by Chujiro Hayashi. We compared teachings and initiations and were delighted to find them to be similar. Hayashi organized the hand placements taught by Usui so that it was easier to teach Reiki. Takata says that he never changed any of the teachings and asked her not to change them either, nor have I."* [345]

During this 1999 meeting Fran met with Chiyoko Yamaguchi, a woman who had taken the First and Second Degrees with Chūjirō Hayashi and later the Master level with her uncle, Wasaburo Sugano (a Master student of Hayashi's). Chiyoko Yamaguchi recognized Fran as teaching the authentic Hayashi method as taught to Takata.

Fran lived in San Mateo, California.

---

343   Dates found on Fran's certificates. However, Takata's ledger book shows Fran's First Degree class payment was on June 2, 1974.

344   Personal e-mail correspondence from Fran Brown to author March 16, 2000.

345   www.reikifranbrown.com/bio.htm accessed February 17, 2015

## *Phyllis Lei Furumoto*

**Born:** August 22, 1948

**Transition:** N/A

**First Degree:** Certificate dated April 15, 1977

First initiated during childhood.

**Second Degree:** Certificate dated May 1, 1978

**Third Degree:** Certificate dated May 10, 1979. (Initiation in April, 1979)

**Reiki Organization Affiliations:**

Founding member of The Reiki Alliance. Recognized by The Reiki Alliance as a Grand Master, lineage bearer, and successor to Hawayo Takata.

Office of the Grand Master

The Reiki Foundation International

Reiki Home

**Resources:**

http://www.usuireiki-ogm.com, http://www.usuishikiryohoreiki.com/

*"Phyllis Lei Furumoto, Mrs. Takata's granddaughter, grew up in the Midwest of the United States. Initiated into Reiki at an early age, it was her duty to treat her grandmother when she came to visit the family. Her conscious journey with the Usui System of Reiki Healing, Usui Shiki Ryoho, did not begin until many years later. After studying psychology at college, Phyllis worked in a psychiatric hospital and later as a university administrator. At the age of thirty, she decided it was time to dedicate her life to a meaningful purpose and accepted an invitation to travel and work with her grandmother. She was initiated as a master at the start of their trip in April 1979. For the next year and-a-half Phyllis apprenticed with her grandmother, as Takata gave treatments, taught first and second degree classes, and trained and initiated masters."*[346]

---

346   http://www.usuireiki-ogm.com/mastery_p.html accessed April 17, 2015. Reproduced with permission.

## Barbara Jean Drum Weber (Ray)

**Born:** September 1, 1941

**Transition:** Unknown or N/A

**First Degree:** Certificate dated August 20, 1978 [347]

**Second Degree:** Certificate dated October 2, 1978

**Third Degree:** Certificate dated September 1, 1979

**Reiki Organization Affiliations:**

Founder of the American Reiki Association and subsequent incarnations

**Resources:**

*The Reiki Factor* (later versions have different titles) by Barbara Weber Ray

*The Official Reiki Handbook* by Barbara Weber Ray

Barbara Weber obtained her Ph.D. in humanities at Florida State University. In the early 1980s she took on a new spiritual last name, "Ray". She is the founder of The Radiance Technique™.

According to the back of the expanded editions of *The Reiki Factor*, she was a licensed astrologer and had a radio show called "Star-Talk," which aired in Atlanta, Georgia. She also was a practicing clairvoyant, since 1973, and a reader of the I Ching. Since 1984 Barbara held retreats called The Awakening Journey®.

---

347  Originally trained by Virginia Samdahl.

## Bethal Phaigh

**Born:** July 2, 1914

**Transition:** January 3, 1986

**First Degree:** June 16, 1979. (Certificate dated July 15, 1978.*)

**Second Degree:** Certificate dated October 10, 1979

**Third Degree:** October 12, 1979,[348] but her Master certificate is dated October 7, 1980.

Bethal initially paid Takata $5,000 and sent the rest of the Master fee as she made money teaching classes.[349] Takata issued the Third Degree certificate to her students upon receiving final payment.

Trained in Cherryville, British Columbia along with Wanja Twan and Barbara Brown.[348]

**Reiki Organization Affiliations:**

Founding member of The Reiki Alliance

**Resources:**

*Gestalt and the Wisdom of the Kahunas* by Bethal Phaigh

*Journey into Consciousness* by Bethal Phaigh. This is her unpublished autobiography and it was written during her last few years.

*Takata would sometimes incorrectly write dates on the certificates she gave out. This is partly due to the fact that Takata did not travel with the certificates; they were made out later and mailed to the students. In addition, sometimes Takata would only give out First Degree certificates to those students who completed the Second Degree. Due to the time lapse between these classes, the dates on the First Degree certificates were not always accurate.

Bethal took the Third Degree training just a couple of days after the Second Degree, just as Ursula Baylow had done in 1978. She wrote in her book *Journey into Consciousness*, "Now I have to drive two hundred miles back to the Slocan to get the money and then back again to Lumby, be initiated as a Master. All this and second degree within a few days!"[349] She also wrote, "The lessons (in life that I needed to learn) may have been particularly painful because my initiations had been timed so closely together. I had left Hawaii that spring not knowing of Reiki. I return this winter as a Reiki Master, a very green one."[350]

348   Twan, *Early days of Reiki*, 7.
349   Phaigh, *Journey into Consciousness*, 130.
350   Phaigh, *Journey into Consciousness*, 132.

## Barbara Brown

*(From left to right: Barbara Brown, Hawayo Takata, Wanja Twan, Phyllis Furumoto. Photo courtesy of Rick Bockner)*

**Born:** Unknown

**Transition:** April 23, 2000, approximately 85 years old. (The information I have on her age comes from a statement she made in 1999, "I am 84 and still traveling.")

**First Degree:** July 7, 1976, in Summerland, British Columbia (along with Ursula Baylow[340])

**Second Degree:**1978, most likely sometime in late August or early September, just after Ursula Baylow was trained in Second and Third Degree.

**Third Degree:** October 12, 1979

Trained in Cherryville, British Columbia along with Wanja Twan and Bethal Phaigh.[348]

**Reiki Organization Affiliations:**

Founding member of The Reiki Alliance

**Resources:**

*Early Days of Reiki: Memories of Hawayo Takata*, by Anneli Twan. This book is a series of interviews with Takata's Master students Wanja Twan and Barbara Brown as well as a few other students of Takata's.

## Wanja Twan

**Born:** Unknown

**Transition:** N/A. Retired from teaching Reiki.

**First Degree:** Late summer or early fall of 1978[351] around the same time Barbara Brown was taking her Second Degree class.

**Second Degree:** June 1979[352]

**Third Degree:** October 12, 1979

Trained in Cherryville, British Columbia along with Barbara Brown and Bethal Phaigh.[348]

**Reiki Organization Affiliations:**

Founding member of The Reiki Alliance

**Resources:**

*Early Days of Reiki: Memories of Hawayo Takata*, by Anneli Twan, 2005. This book is a series of interviews with Takata's Master students Wanja Twan and Barbara Brown as well as a few other students of Takata's.

*In the Light of a Distant Star* by Wanja Twan, 1995

*Looking in Boxes and Other Stories* by Wanja Twan, 2006

*Winter in the Red House: Canadian Tales from Super Natural British Columbia* by Wanja Twan, 2006

*The History of Reiki in Canada*, DVD, 2012

*Sasquatch Stories or Story with Wanja Twan*, DVD, 2012

---

351  Twan, *In the Light of a Distant Star: A Spiritual Journey Bringing the Unseen into the Seen*, 21.

352  Twan, *In the Light of a Distant Star: A Spiritual Journey Bringing the Unseen into the Seen*, 100. Wanja mentions that at this time her daughters Anneli and Kristina would take their First Degree training with Takata. Anneli, in an interview on Phyllis Furumoto's Reiki Talk Show states that this was in June, 1979. http://www.reikitalkshow.com/shows/view/28

## Beth Kathelin Gray

**Born:** April 11, 1918

**Transition:** May 13, 2008

**First Degree:** Certificate dated June 12, 1974[353]

**Second Degree:** Certificate dated February 1, 1975

**Third Degree:** Certificate dated October 28, 1979

**Reiki Organization Affiliations:**

Trinity Metaphysical Center (her church where she practiced and taught Reiki)

**Resources:**

http://www.bethgray.org

**Location:** Woodside, California

Beth Gray was first trained by her spouse at the time, John Harvey Gray, how to do the Reiki initiations. This situation was later resolved and Takata recognized Beth as a Master.[354]

Beth had a stroke around 1993 that left her paralyzed. Afterwards, because she could not speak well, she stopped teaching Reiki.

Beth trained two Masters:

Barbara McGregor in Sydney, Australia

Denise Crundall (who made her transition on June 30, 2002) in Melbourne, Australia.

---

353  The date on her certificate isn't exactly accurate. Beth had taken the First Degree a few weeks before this. *Hand to Hand: The Longest-Practicing Reiki Master Tells His Story* (Xlibris: 2002), 28-29. However, as discussed previously, Takata did not always write the correct dates on certificates.

354  Personal conversation with Fran Brown.

## *George Araki*

*(From left to right: Marta Getty and George Araki. Photo used with permission from Marta Getty.)*

**Born:** January 11, 1932, in Oakland, California

**Transition:** June 29, 2006, at the age of 74

**First Degree:** Unknown

**Second Degree:** Unknown

**Third Degree:** November 1, 1979[355] (together with Paul Mitchell)

**Reiki Organization Affiliations:**

Founding member of The Reiki Alliance

George Araki became a professor at San Francisco State University in 1962.[356] He was head of the school's department for alternative healing when he became a Reiki Master. George became a Master in order to do a research study on Reiki. However, it was too difficult to set up the protocol. George taught Reiki only a few times. He sent his students and others to learn from Fran Brown and Shinobu Saito.[357] For personal reasons, he didn't want his name listed among the other Master students of Takata's in the "Grey Book" compiled by Alice Furumoto, Takata's daughter.

San Francisco State University has several Web pages of information

---

355  Personal conversation with Paul Mitchell. September 9, 2013.
356  http://www.sfsu.edu/~bulletin/current/faculty2.htm accessed February 17, 2015.
357  Personal conversation with Fran Brown and Shinobu Saito.

about George Araki, cited and quoted below:

*"George Araki received his doctorate in biological sciences from Stanford University doing work in ecological physiology. He began biofeedback studies in 1969 at SFSU. He became the Director of the Center for Interdisciplinary Sciences and founded the holistic health program in 1976. He retired Spring 1999.*

*Dr. Araki was a visionary leader, who touched many people with his integrative thinking and his caring ways. Every year, since his retirement, IHHS faculty have selected a top Holistic Health student to receive the George S. Araki Achievement Award for Academic Accomplishment and Outstanding Contribution to Holistic Health. This award reflects the academic and service achievements characterized by George Araki. Each year we honor him and an outstanding student with this award.*

*Donations in his memory will be targeted for student scholarships and service awards. Donations can be made to: The Holistic Health Learning Center, c/o George S. Araki Student Awards, San Francisco State University, 1600 Holloway Ave., San Francisco, CA 94132."*[358]

*"Holistic Health (HH) and the Institute for Holistic Healing Studies (IHHS) evolved out of a courses taught through the Center for Interdisciplinary Science (CIS) at San Francisco State University. Established in 1974, CIS was a pioneering effort exploring new interdisciplinary perspectives in physical and biological sciences in the then School of Science. The founding Director of CIS, Dr. George Araki initiated two courses in holistic health in 1976, "New Approaches for Health and Self-Regulation", and "Research Seminar in Holistic Health". These courses introduced the new field of biofeedback which became an early catalyst for interest in holistic health."*[359]

---

Title of Article:

## *George Araki, Who Discovered Significance of Angel Island Carvings, Dies*

From the *NichiBei Times* Weekly July 13, 2006

By KENJI G. TAGUMA
NichiBei Times

---

358  http://www.sfsu.edu/~ihhs/popup/araki.htm accessed February 17, 2015.
359  http://www.sfsu.edu/~ihhs/index.htm?history.htm-right accessed February 17, 2015.

George Araki, who helped to discover the rich history carved into the former Angel Island Immigration Station barracks in the 1970s and who founded San Francisco State University's holistic health program, died on Thursday, June 29, 2006 at the Marin General Hospital. He was 74.

He died of complications from an aggressive form of colon cancer, said daughter Lianne Araki.

A long-time biology professor, Araki was also a key organizer of the Center for Japanese American Studies, which was founded in 1969 and held a monthly lecture series on a wide range of topics relating to Japanese American culture and history, Japanese language classes, and an annual mochitsuki (rice pounding) event that continues to this day.

"He was one of the key persons behind the scenes," said Karl Matsushita, executive director of the Japanese American National Library, which emerged out of the Center for Japanese American Studies. "He was one of the instrumental persons who put the Center for Japanese American Studies together."

According to Matsushita, most of the early planning meetings for the Center were held at Araki's San Francisco home.

The Center also established the Center Players, which put on plays involving local playwrights such as Hiroshi Kashiwagi and Philip Gotanda. The plays were not only performed in San Francisco but in other parts of the state as well.

According to Jim Hirabayashi, the first dean of the College of Ethnic Studies at San Francisco State University, Araki was also part of a student-faculty group that developed the first Japanese American studies curriculum in the country. The Japanese American Curriculum Planning Group met in San Francisco's Japantown right after the ethnic studies strike.

## Carvings at Angel Island

Much has been documented about the tens of thousands of immigrants *from Asia who entered the West Coast through the Angel Island Immigration Station between 1910 and 1940, but the immigration barracks were nearly forgotten and their history nearly destroyed until one day in 1970, when a student of Araki's stumbled upon carvings in the walls. California State Park Ranger Alexander Weiss saw the carvings etched in the walls and alerted Araki, who identified them as poems. Along with Araki's colleague Mak Takahashi, they arranged to photograph the walls.*

*Shortly thereafter, Asian American studies students were taking trips to Angel Island and began to spread word about the poems.*
*"(George) alerted the Chinese American community, initially Professor Kai Yu Shu of the Asian Language Department at SF State," recalled Hirabayashi, who noted that in addition to carvings by Chinese and Japanese immigrants, there were also carvings by Japanese prisoners of war during World War II as well.*

*Bay Area Asian Americans, sparked by the discovery, then formed the Angel Island Immigration Historical Advisory Committee to study how to best preserve the station for historical interpretation. In 1983 the barracks were opened to the public and the Angel Island Immigration Station Foundation was established to continue the preservation and education efforts regarding the site.*

*The Angel Island Immigration Station was declared a National Historic Landmark by the National Park Service in 1997.*

*The Angel Island Immigration Station Foundation is currently conducting a massive renovation of the barracks, attempting to preserve the remaining buildings and their carvings.*

### Oakland Native

*George Shoichi Araki was born on Jan. 11, 1932 in Oakland, Calif. He had been residing in San Rafael, Calif.*

*During World War II Araki, like some 120,000 other persons of Japanese ancestry on the West Coast, was forcibly removed and herded into a wartime concentration camp. He was incarcerated at the Topaz (Central Utah) concentration camp.*

*Araki had a lot of interests, recalled daughter Lianne Araki of San Mateo.*

*"He did a lot of woodwork for family and friends," she said. "He really enjoyed working with wood."*
*His last project, which he finished in May, was a display case for Lianne.*

### Long-Time SF State Faculty

*Araki, who earned his doctorate in biological sciences from Stanford University, was an expert in the study of cells.*

*At San Francisco State University, where he held a variety of administrative positions, Araki supported the aims of those involved in the tumultuous strike for ethnic studies — which led to the establishment of the first ethnic studies program in the country.*

*During a one-year sabbatical from 1970-71, Araki was an exchange professor for the California State University system at Waseda University in Tokyo, where in addition to teaching he advised foreign students there. "The whole family was there," recalled daughter Lianne, who attended public school in Japan during that time.*

*He was the chair of the Cell and Molecular Biology Department, and became the director of the Center for Interdisciplinary Sciences and founded the holistic health program in 1976, retiring in 1999.*
*The holistic health minor degree program included students in the nursing program at SF State.*

*"He introduced various aspects of Asian medicine, like acupuncture, shiatsu, herbal medicines and also meditation," said Hirabayashi. "And because of the influence of George and people like him, we have the introduction of alternative health methods into our mainstream medical system."*

*Araki also assisted late human rights activist Dr. Clifford Uyeda, who passed away in the summer of 2004 after a long bout with prostate cancer, during his final days.*

*"He did a lot when Clifford was sick," said long-time friend Jane Horii, who co-wrote the landmark book of Japanese American culture "Matsuri: Festival" with Araki's ex-wife Nancy Araki. "He went out of his way to help."*

*Uyeda didn't have any other relatives nearby, and Araki would help Uyeda with tasks such as paperwork or computer issues.*

*"He felt compelled to help him," said daughter Lianne Araki. "It probably has to do with his compassion for people."*

*Friends recalled the thoughtful and generous nature of Araki.*

*"I can't see a **mochitsuki** without him," said Horii. Araki is survived by his wife Camilla Jewel; ex-wife Nancy Araki; children Lianne (Edward Hattyar) Araki of San Mateo, David (Lisa) Araki of New York City and Kathy (Todd Hotchkiss) Araki; granddaughters Ayumi and Kiyomi Araki-Beaucage of Albuquerque, New Mexico; step-son Alex Sherman of Santa Fe, New Mexico; brother Kai of Sacramento; a nephew; nieces and cousins.*

*A memorial service celebrating the life of George S. Araki will be held on Sunday, July 30, from 1 to 3 p.m., at the Mill Valley Community Center, 180 Camino Alto, Mill Valley, CA 94941."*[360]

---

360  Kenji G. Taguma, *"George Araki, Who Discovered Significance of Angel Island Carvings, Dies,"* NichiBei Times Weekly July 13, 2006 https://web.archive.org/web/20061123173455/http://www.nichibeitimes.com/articles/stories.php?subaction=showfull&id=1152820800&archive=&start_from=&ucat=1&

## *Paul David Mitchell*

**Born:** June 21, 1946

**Transition:** N/A

**First Degree:** Summer 1978

**Second Degree:** 1979

**Third Degree:** November 1, 1979[361] (along with George Araki at Paul's house in San Francisco, California)

**Reiki Organization Affiliations:**

Founding member of The Reiki Alliance

Office of the Grand Master

"Paul Mitchell grew up in California and entered the Catholic seminary at fourteen with the desire to become a priest. At 24, he left the seminary, feeling that life called him to some other form of service. He continued his education and earned a degree in philosophy at the University of San Francisco. In 1978, Paul was teaching religion in a boy's [sic] Catholic high school and studying for a master's degree in education when he heard Hawayo Takata give a talk on Reiki. Driving home that morning, Paul says, 'I had this very clear thought: "This is what I have been looking for." And then I realized I didn't know I had been looking for anything.' Paul took first degree Reiki from Mrs. Takata that summer. The following year, he studied the second degree. Shortly thereafter, Takata initiated him as a master and he embarked on a career of offering treatments and teaching Reiki classes. Paul began to work with Phyllis Furumoto in the early 1980s and was a founding member of The Reiki Alliance. He was recruited to teach in the Self-Assessment Program, a training program established by Phyllis to prepare Reiki Master candidates. Paul is the author of the student book, The Usui System of Natural Healing, published in nine languages. His articles on the Usui System have been published in journals around the world. As a master student of Mrs. Takata, Paul is committed to carry, practice, and teach Reiki as she brought it to the Western world. Through personal contact at international gatherings, workshops, and in his Reiki classes, Paul gives students a direct connection with the teachings of Hawayo Takata and with the Usui System."[362]

---

361   Personal conversation with Paul Mitchell.
362   http://www.usuireiki-ogm.com/mastery_p.html accessed April 17, 2015. Reproduced with permission.

## Shinobu Saito

**Born:** Unknown

**Transition:** April 10, 2015

**First Degree:** 1976

**Second Degree:** 1978

**Third Degree:** May 1980 in Palo Alto, California

**Reiki Organization Affiliations:**

Member of The Reiki Alliance

Shinobu was born in Japan and was a survivor of the atomic bomb dropped on Hiroshima. Hawayo Takata hoped she would help take Reiki back to Japan. Shinobu only trained Reiki masters in Japan.[363]

---

363   Personal conversation with Shinobu Saito.

## Patricia Bowling (Ewing)

**Born:** Unknown

**Transition:** N/A

**First Degree:** May 10, 1976[321]

**Second Degree:** Unknown

**Third Degree:** September 7, 1980 in Oregon

**Reiki Organization Affiliations:** Unknown

She later got married and changed her name to Patricia Ewing.

Patricia had retired from teaching Reiki by 1989. She never trained a Master student. Patricia was into meditation, soul retrieval, channeling and other modalities. I believe she was the youngest of all Takata's Master students.

## Mary Alexandra McFadyen (born Mary McFadyen)

*(Photo courtesy of Kathy Gaston)*

**Born:** August 18, 1931, Leeds, England

**Transition:** February 19, 2011 (presumed). This date was the last time anyone heard from Mary. A missing-person report has been filed with the police department in Austin, Texas, where she lived.

**First Degree:** December 1979 by John Harvey Gray

**Second Degree:** July 1980, by John Harvey Gray

**Third Degree:** September 7, 1980 in Oregon

**Reiki Organization Affiliations:**

Started Reiki Outreach International

Member of Reiki Alliance (resigned prior to her death)

**Resources:**

http://www.annieo.com/reikioutreach

*Die Heilkraft des Reiki. Lehren einer Meisterin* by Mary McFadyen. Available only in German.

*Die Heilkraft des Reiki. Mit Händenheilen. Schnellbehandlung* by Mary McFadyen. Available only in German.

## *Rick Bockner*

**Born:** September 19, 1948

**Transition:** N/A

**First Degree:** October 10, 1979 [364]

**Second Degree:** October 20, 1979 [364]

**Third Degree:** October 12, 1980 [364]

**Reiki Organization Affiliations:**

Member of The Reiki Alliance

In October 1980, Rick Bockner arranged a large class of approximately 54 students for Hawayo Takata to teach at the Grey Creek Hall in British Columbia. It was Canadian Thanksgiving weekend, and they had a large potluck following the class. His actual Master initiation was done a few days later at Bethal Phaigh's cabin in the Slocan Valley.

Rick is also a professional guitar player, singer, songwriter, and carpenter.

---

[364]  Personal e-mail to the author, March 19, 2000.

## *Appendix* THREE

*Two Articles from the Sunday Mainichi,*
*March 4, 1928*

# APPENDIX
# 03

*Two Articles from the Sunday Mainichi,*

*March 4, 1928*

*In the early 2000s, thanks to the websites of James Deacon and Richard Rivard, Westerners interested in Reiki history became aware of a 1928 newspaper article on Usui Reiki Ryōhō by the playwright and theater critic Matsui Shōō, who had been a student of Hayashi Chūjirō. This article is a unique artifact in that it is the most extensive public account of Usui Reiki Ryōhō by a Japanese practitioner in the pre-war period. Matsui describes that the publicly promotion of Usui Reiki Ryōhō was forbidden, and said that his contemporaries might think him a "heretic" for writing so openly about it, but that the benefits of this therapy are so great, he can no longer be silent. The details in this article are invaluable to our knowledge of the thoughts of an Usui Reiki Ryōhō practitioner in the 1920s.*

*What many people may not have known is that, directly under this article was a second article written by an anonymous reporter who received a treatment from Mr. Matsui. To my knowledge, this second article has never before been translated. As it goes into much more detail regarding how Usui Reiki Ryōhō was actually being practiced, it is at least as important of a document as the first article.*

*The Japanese text was transliterated into post-war characters by Tanaka*

Satoshi *(taken with permission from his website: http://homepage3.nifty.com/ faithfull/), and edited by Hirano Naoko. We are reproducing this transliterated Japanese text side-by-side with my original English translations. I hope that you find these accounts of how Usui Reiki Ryōhō was practiced in the 1920s as fascinating and inspiring as I have.*

- Justin Stein

「隻手萬病を治する療法」
松居松翁
『サンデー毎日』
昭和3年3月4日
14-15頁

　読者の注文　一月三十日発行の大毎本紙書物紹介ページに載せられた、松居松翁氏の隻手萬病を治する療法を照会せられたし、（朝鮮稲岡瀧治郎）。

　読者の御希望というのなら、喜んでお話し致します。
ーーこの隻手万病を治する療法なるものは、霊気療法という名の下に、或る特殊の人々によって行われているものである。これを発見したというか、または創見したとでもいうか、ともかく、その療法の開祖ーーこのグルウプでは肇祖といっているーーは臼井甕男という人で、すでに三年ばかり以前に他界し、今は、その弟子であった人々が治療所を持ち、或いは、その療法の伝授をも行なっている。しかし、隻手よく万病を治するほどな療法でありながら、未だ余り世間に知られていない。何故かといえば、この臼井なる人が特にこれを吹聴することを嫌ったから、その末流を汲む人々もまたなお宣伝することを避けているがためである。

"A Therapy that Heals All Disease with a Single Hand," MATSUI Shōō, *Sunday Mainichi*, March 4, Shōwa 3 [1928], pp. 14-15.

Reader's request: I would like to know more about the healing method introduced by MATSUI Shōō in the book section of this paper's January 30th issue (Korea, INAOKA Takijirō).

Because it is a reader's request, I would be delighted to speak [about this].

This therapy that heals ten thousand diseases with a single hand goes by the name Reiki Therapy (*reiki ryōhō*) and is practiced by certain special people. It was discovered—or should I say created?—anyway, the founder of this therapy and group was a man named Usui Mikao. It's already been three years since he passed away. Now, his students have a clinic [for treatments] or to give instruction* in this therapy. However, despite being able to heal the ten thousand diseases with a single hand, this therapy is still hardly known to the public. For some reason, this Usui especially disliked making it public, so those trained in his schools also still avoid advertising.

しかし、わたしは、その宣伝嫌いがどうしても判らない。耶蘇教には今も宣教師があり、仏教にも宣伝使がある。畏くも勅宣、院宣の文字もある様に、「威徳を中外にひろめる」のが宣という字の意味だ。宣伝の原語 propaganda も、真理信仰を拡充する場合に用いられたのが初めだ。苟くも、そのことが真理で人類の幸福に寄与するものがあらば、これを宣伝するが、人間としての義務ではないか。だからわたしは、この療法について、他人から尋ねられれば、親切に宣伝をする。雑誌新聞から寄稿を求められれば、わたしは喜んで書くーーだもんだから、わたしに対して相当に反対があるそうだ。或いは、異端者の様に思われているかも知れぬ。しかし、こんな立派な療法が世にありながら、これを一般に知らしめないということは、頗る遺憾千万な話だと思っている。道徳的にも、世間的にも、如何にも惜しいものである。そこでわたしは多くの人々のため、喜び勇んで宣伝をするのであるが、特に、大毎東日ほどな大新聞の読者から、この療法について質問されて、「いや、てまえの療法は宣伝が嫌いですから、何事も申上げられません」と断わったら、記者諸君なり、読者諸君なりは、それこそ霊気療法を山師の仕事と思うかもしれない。「あらゆる病気を癒すなどと広言を吐いても、さあという時には、責任を負った発表が出来ぬじゃないか」といわれても仕方がない。だからわたしは、霊気療法そのもののためにも宣伝するーー真理を公表する。この意味で喋るのだから、わたしの態度は、本療法関係者の意志に基づくものではない。

However, I do not understand this distaste for advertisement. Even today, Christianity and Buddhism have missionaries. The emperor's words are also made public. This is the meaning of the saying, "solemn virtue should be spread at home and abroad." The original meaning of the word "propaganda" was "to spread the true faith." If any truth contributes to human happiness, isn't our duty to humanity to promote it? That is why, when others ask me about this therapy, I kindly publicize it. If asked to contribute to a magazine or newspaper, I happily contribute something. For this reason, I hear that there is considerable opposition to my actions. Perhaps I am thought a heretic. However, I think that it is simply too deplorable that this splendid therapy exists but is not generally known. Morally and socially, it is such a pity. Therefore, for the sake of the masses, with joy and courage, I publicize it. Especially as I was asked by the reader of such a large paper as the *Daimai Tōnichi*, if I were to say, "No, we dislike publicizing our therapy, so sorry," regarding our therapy, you journalists and readers might think that Reiki Therapy is a sham. Couldn't they say things like "They say it is able to heal every disease, don't they have a responsibility to be able to present it?" That is why I am publicizing it—making the truth public. This is my own attitude, and is not based on the wishes of other practitioners of this therapy.

全然わたし一個の思考から独自の立場にあって、あえてこれを発表するものである。病魔に悩む多くの人々のため、わたしは、どう考えて見ても、この口を緘してはいられない、わたし自身について見ても、この療法を知って以来のわたしの気持は、とても凝乎として芝居なんか書いていられない様なーー実際を告白すれば、まあ、そんな風な気持になっている。わたしが一生懸命にこの療法を宣伝して、自分の理想を実現する時が来れば、日本は実に極楽になるのだ。いや、延いては世界中が無病息災のパラダイスになるのだ、ああ、一人にでも多く宣伝したい。

　所で、この霊気療法は、発見されて以来すでに十数年になるが、治療所は極めて少数である。私が伝授を受けたのは林忠次郎という海軍大佐で、極めてまじめな、人情深い、如何にもこの仕事に生まれついた様な人である。午前中は一般の治療に応じ、月の五日間は療法の伝授を行なっている。しかし、世間には霊の字のついた療法が非常に多い、それで、矢張りまたあの霊気療法かと、十把一からげにされて軽蔑されている。それでも宣伝したくないというのだから、この偉大なる道が行われないのも是非がない。

My original position comes completely from my own individual thoughts, but I'm going to present it anyway. Thinking of the large number of people worried about illness, seeing them—for their sake, I cannot remain silent. Now that I know about this therapy, I feel as though I no longer care about writing another play—to confess the truth, this is how I feel. With all of my ability I will publicize this therapy and, when my dream is realized, Japan will become a paradise. No, not only Japan, but the entire world will become a healthy paradise, free of disease. Ah, even if I could only reach just one more person.

Well, this Reiki Therapy was discovered some decades ago, but its clinics are still extremely few in number. My instruction* was given by a Navy Captain named HAYASHI Chūjirō, an extremely serious and profoundly warm-hearted man who seems to have been born for this work. Generally, he gives treatments throughout the morning, and five days a month he gives instruction in the therapy. However, since there are so many therapies in the world that use the character *rei*, as one would expect, our Reiki Therapy is lumped together with all the others and held with contempt. Still, because [practitioners] do not want to publicize [Reiki], it is no wonder that this great path is not practiced.

　この療法は、少なくともわたしが研究した数種の療法の中で、最もユニックな、最も効力の顕著なもので、全く万病を医することが出来る。一知半解の徒は、その名によって直に「神経的な病気に利くか」などときっというが、そんな神経的なものに限られてはいない。内臓の諸症でも、負傷、やけど、リウマチス、神経衰弱、内科でも、外科でも——お望み次第だ。

　霊気療法は、その名の示す如く、少なくともスピリチュアルなものとして考えられているが、わたしが今までに百人以上を治療した経験からいえば、むしろ、わたしはフィジカルなものじゃないかと思っている。或る人は、これを以てキリストや釈迦が人の病を救った奇蹟と等しいものの様に考えているが、少なくともわたしは、彼等の如き偉大な人間でもなければ、またそんなものを行ない得る人格の所有者でもない。

　一体世の中には、あらゆる世間のあらわれを霊的に解釈して、人間の霊の方面のみを見つめながら世を送っている人があるが、同時にまた反対に、世界の事件の表現を散文的に、フィジカルに、プラクチカルに考えて、すべてそういう方法で解決をつけてゆく人もある。わたしはその後者に属する、卑俗凡庸な人間であるから、人間のフィジカルな治療をするのに、急に、スピリチュアルな野心を起こす必要はない。少なくとも今の所では、わたし自身のやっている療法だけは、決して超自然的なものではない。極めてノーマルなもの、極めて生理的なものだと解釈している。

This therapy is the most unique and the most effective out of all of the ones that I have studied. Its effectiveness is so remarkable, it can heal all of the ten thousand diseases [i.e., every disease]. Those with superficial knowledge, hearing the name, right away ask, "Does it work on nervous disorders?" and the like, but it is not limited to nervous disorders. Even various internal organs, injuries, burns, rheumatism, neurasthenia, internal medicine, surgery—whatever you desire.

As the name Reiki Therapy indicates, it can be considered a spiritual thing, but if I were speak from my experience of having treated over a hundred people to date, I think it is a physical thing. Some people think it is equal to the way that Christ and the historical Buddha miraculously relieved people's illnesses, but I am not a great man like them, and I also do not have great character [yet I can heal].

In general, there are people who go through this world transfixed by the spiritual side of things and interpret every social phenomenon in a spiritual fashion. At the same time, there are those who prosaically regard the world's events physically and practically, and by this method solve everything. I am in this latter group. I am a vulgar, commonplace person, so treating people physically does not require any spiritual ambitions. At the very least, the treatment I do is not in any way supernatural. I explain it as an extremely normal thing and an extremely physiological thing.

理論はぬきにして、先ず実例から話してみよう――。

　最近の方では、今月初めに、浦和のある高等学校の教授が、四歳になる娘を或る人の紹介でつれて来た。その娘は片眼がつぶれ、同時にまた他の片眼にも移ろうとしているので、方々の博士の所を渡りあるいた、だが一向に癒らぬ。それでわたしの所に来た。わたしは、単に眼ばかりでなく、全身のどこかに欠陥があるのじゃないかと考えたから、第一に全身を診た、胃腸が悪い、鼻が悪い、腎臓が悪い、種々な点を綜合して考えると、全身的な疾患が最も強く眼に現われたものらしい。そこでわたしは、わたしの療法を試みた所、五六回ばかりで眼が見える様になって来た。勿論のこと他の疾患も漸次快復して来た。その父親は「この娘のためには、自分の眼球をくり抜いても惜まぬ」といっていた。今その父君は自ら今月より入門して、自分でその娘の病を癒そうとしている。

Leaving theory aside, first let's speak from some examples.

Recently, at the beginning of this month, someone brought a high school teacher from Urawa and his four-year-old daughter to my clinic. His daughter couldn't see out of one eye, and she was going blind in the other eye as well. The father had brought her to various doctors' offices, but they were completely unable to heal her. That is why they came to my clinic. It appeared to me that the problem wasn't only in her eyes, but I thought there were deficiencies in other parts of her body, so first I examined her. Her stomach, nose, and kidneys were all bad, and I thought it seemed that these points came together in such a way as to strongly manifest in her eyes. Thus, I tried my therapy just five or six times, and she became able to see. Of course, those other ailments also gradually improved. Her father, who had previously said "I would pull out my own eyes for my daughter," has just become a student [of Reiki Therapy] this month himself so that he is able to heal her illness himself.

　次は、昨年十二月初旬のことであった――知名の画家〇氏が
三時間の時に死んで終うと宣告された。すでに二時間は経過し
て、あと一時間の生命であるというので、夜中にその娘さんか
ら電話がかかった。そこでわれ等夫婦は、郊外駒沢に一時間余
を費して自動車を飛ばした。馳せつけた時にはもう三時間半の
後であったが、門前にわれ等を待ち受けている家人の話によれ
ば、一時間も前に人事不省に陥ったというのだ。われ等夫婦は
直ちに心臓へ手をかけた、そうして心臓弁膜症のために心臓麻
痺に陥っていた〇氏は、われ等夫婦が、六時間半、一滴の茶も
飲まずにその胸に手を置いた結果、とうとう、医者は〇氏が安
全区域にたち戻ったことを宣告し、その次の夜には、平熱に下
がって脈搏も八十位を打つ様になって来た、――わたしは公言
する、大抵の場合、百二十位を打っている脈搏の人を、二三時
間で八十位までにすることはさまで困難なことでないことを。

　また、「穏田の神さま」といわれる飯野吉三郎君が重体の時
は、有力な博士が四人もかかっていた。彼は四度も死の宣告を
受けたが、その最後の朝、その家族達が袂別の水を彼の唇にし
めした後、わたし達はその蘇生を受け合った。そうして彼は死
線を越えた、宿直のお医者さん達は退散した。

　こんな、奇跡的な実例は腐るほどにある。しかし、実は、そ
れは奇跡でも何でもない、簡単に生理的な治療が施されたに過
ぎない。

The next example was from the beginning of last December—the re-nowned painter Mr. O was given three hours to live. Already two hours had passed and with one hour of life remaining, at midnight, his daughter called me. My wife and I got in the car and flew to the suburb of Komazawa, but it took an hour, and although we hurried, by the time we got there it had been three-and-a-half hours. At the gate, the family was waiting; they told us he had become unconscious one hour earlier. My wife and I placed our hands on his heart. Because of damage to one of its valves, Mr. O had suffered a heart attack. My wife and I laid our hands on his chest for six-and-a-half hours, without a drop of tea, and as a result, finally, the doctor announced that Mr. O had returned to a safe zone. The following evening, his temperature went down to normal and his pulse went down to eighty. I can declare that, most of the time, in two or three hours [of treatment] a strong pulse of one-twenty will come down to eighty without difficulty.

Also, when "the god of Onden," IINO Kichisaburō [1867-1944, religious leader and military advisor who started a new religion in the Tokyo neigh-borhood of Onden, Shibuya], was seriously ill, they brought four prominent doctors. He received four death announcements, but the final morning, after his family had brought water to moisten his lips [a Japanese ritual performed just after someone dies], we assured we would resuscitate him. And he came back from the brink of death and we sent the round-the-clock doctors home.

Such miraculous examples are countless. However, in truth, they are not really miracles. We simply gave physiological treatments, nothing more.

　では、如何にしてわたしは病気を治療するかというに、ただ患者の患部に手を載せて置くだけだ。押しもしない。叩きもしない、そこにこの療法の妙味があるものとわたしは思っている。ただこの療法の強味は全身的に診察してその病源を悉く探知し、その部分に治療を加えるから、治療の効果が顕著で迅速なのだと思う。そんなら、如何にして病源を発見するかというに、患者の全身どこにでもわたしの手をかければ、その悪い所においてのみ、わたしの掌が痛むからである。掌の痛む程度は勿論病気次第で違う、といってそれは病気の軽重によって強弱が比例するものかどうか、未だわたしには秩序的に解っていない。しかしながら患者自身が悪いという場所に限り掌が痛むというのではなくその病源において掌に痛みを感ずるのであるから従ってまた容易に発見せられる訳である。多くの場合お医者さんは、病人の訴えによってのみその患部が判る。ところが、わたし達には病人からの告白はいらない、のみならず病人はこんなことで癒るものかと思っていてもよい。否でも応でも、三十分乃至一二時間の後にはきっとその病所に、革命が現れるのだから仕方がない。

Well, in what way do I treat with my therapy? All I do is place my hand on the affected part. I neither push nor pat; I think this is the charm of this therapy. But the strong point of this therapy is that we examine the entire body to completely detect the *byōgen* ("source of disease"), then increase treatment of these areas, so the treatment's effectiveness is remarkably quick. I discover the *byōgen* by placing my hand over the patient's entire body, and when I reach a bad spot, my palm hurts. Of course, the degree to which the palm hurts changes depending on the type of disease, but we haven't yet systematically worked out whether its relative strength corresponds to the severity of the disease. However, my hand doesn't only feel pain at the place where the patients themselves feel badly, but they also hurt at that *byōgen*. That is why I can easily discover [the treatment points]. Often, doctors know the afflicted area based on their patients' complaints. However, we don't need our patients' confessions. Besides, let the patients think that we are not healing that area [that they complain about]. Anyway, after a period from thirty minutes to an hour or two, the affected area will be completely transformed so there is nothing they can say [because they will be better].

例えば、ここに心臓のひどく悪い男がある。これを医学的に見ても八十五六位しか脈搏が打っていないとする、それでも彼は、その胸が苦しくなるのを感ずる、医者も心臓の狭窄症だという——この場合、わたしが彼の心臓に手をかけても、わたしの掌は痛みを感じない。そこで胃腸と腎臓との部分に手をかけて見る、わたしの掌は非常に痛む、すなわちわたしはその部分を癒すことに努力する。すると間もなく心臓の圧迫も取れてしまう。新派俳優の泰斗、河合武雄の場合が丁度それであったのである。

そこで疑問が起きる。

——なぜそうなるのか、なぜ掌が痛むのか、それが問題だ。なぜ医者の手放したものが癒るのか、それが不思議といえば不思議だ。ただ手を置きさえすればそれで癒るものは癒るのだから、そこが霊的に解釈されるゆえんかも知れぬ。しかし、わたしの考える所では、わたしの手には、林氏の伝授を受けた刹那から、自分の全体を通じて異常な血液の活躍が促されて来たらしい。しかして、末梢神経の指端において、これが最も急激に、微妙に、素晴らしい活躍をするのかも知れぬ。さらば、林氏の伝授が、わたしにこの力を与えてくれたのであるか——それはチョッと公表しがたい。

For example, there is a man with a seriously bad heart. His pulse is only eighty-five or eighty-six, but still he feels chest pain. The doctor says he has cardiac stenosis—in this situation, I put my hand on his chest, but I don't feel any pain in my palm. So I try putting my hand on his stomach and his kidneys, and my palm becomes extremely painful. That is, I have to work hard to heal those areas. Once I did this, the pressure on his heart quickly disappeared. This was exactly the case of the authoritative actor of the "new school" [*shinpa*; modernist theater], KAWAI Takeo (1877-1942).

Now, a question arises.

Why does this happen? Why do the palms hurt? These are questions. It is indeed mysterious that cases which doctors give up on can be cured. If you lay hands, they are cured, so it tends to be explained spiritually. However, in my opinion, from the instant I received instruction* from Mr. Hayashi, it was as though abnormal levels of blood were stimulated in my hands, through my entire body. And now it seems that the peripheral nerves of my fingertips suddenly, subtly, have marvelous activity as well. Whether Mr. Hayashi's instruction gave me this power—that is a little difficult to say.

　兎に角、そういう血液の活動して居る指端が、患者の病所に置かれた時、わたしの血液の波動が患者の血液の波動を促す、つまり、ブラッド・カレントが一つになる、波長が一つになるゆえであるかも知れぬ。それで患者の充血、鬱血、或いは貧血したために起こった病患が、段々にノーマルな状態になって、病気は自然に癒って来るという理屈であると信ずる。この意味において、輸血療法、淋疾のカテーテル療法、その他種々な医術的療法も相一致するものがあると思う。

　もし、仮に治者被治者のブラッド・カレントが合致するという解釈が、この事実を説明し得たとしても、何人といえども、皮膚を隔てて果して左様なことが出来るかどうか、この疑問を抱くに相違ない。しかし、梅毒のために鼻柱の落ちた人も、今日の進歩した医学によって造鼻術が行われる、膝の肉や皮やを取って来てそれを欠けた鼻の上に植えつければよいのだ。ところがその膝の肉は少なくとも一時間は死んだものだ。それが自分の、或いは他人の鼻の上で癒着して、血液も通うし、神経も働くことになる。これから考えれば、皮膚の隔たり位は何でもあるまいではないか。

At any rate, when those fingertips with that blood activity are placed on the diseased areas of the patient, the vibration of my blood stimulates the vibration of the patient's blood. In other words, maybe it is because our "blood currents" and their wavelengths become one. That is why I believe in the theory that says that sicknesses that originate in the patient's congested blood, stagnant blood, or blood deficiencies, gradually normalize and the sickness naturally heals. This is why I think that it works in a similar way to blood transfusion therapy, gonorrheal catheter therapy, and other medical therapies.

If, for argument's sake, we can explain [this healing] by the "blood currents" of the ruler and the ruled becoming unified, it is certain that many people will embrace doubts about whether it can work although [the two people's blood] is divided by the skin. However, it is just like how today's advanced medical science can build noses for syphilitics whose septums have fallen off by taking flesh from places like the knee and growing it over the lost nose. The flesh from the knee is dead for at least an hour but, in fact, our noses adhere, the blood flows, and the neurons also work. After this, the skin barrier isn't really anything, is it?

　この話をすると、世間の半可通は直に「動物電気だろう」などという。しかし、「電気とは何ぞや」の定義すら、今日の科学では未だ決定されていない。あの大エヂソン、大マルコニーのプラクチスは驚くべきものがあるが、電気の本質的説明は出来ていない――だから、この問題はそう簡単には断定が出来ない。が、わたしのぼんやりした感じからいうなら、或いはエーテルの作用ではないかと思うけれど、エーテルの研究はなお出来ていない今日だ、無学なわたしなどが、こんなことをいったら他人様はお笑いになるだろう。ただわたしがこの療法を人にアプライする時に、大体においてエーテルの法則に従って説明するのが一番近い様に思うのだ。といってわたしは、微分積分も知らぬ人間だから、はっきりしたことはとても言い得ない。いずれ、これから高等数学でも習って研究的に実験してゆくうちに、或いは説明の出来る時機が到来するかも知れぬが、兎に角今のところでは、応用の方面で偉大な効果のあることだけで、まあ、満足しているより外はない。

When I tell these stories, people with superficial knowledge say things like, "Isn't it animal magnetism?" [literally, "animal electricity"] However, in today's science, the definition of "what is electricity?" has yet to be determined. The practices of great Edison and great Marconi are surprising, but electricity's essence is inexplicable—thus, this problem cannot be easily concluded at this time. From my indistinct feelings, I feel that another possibility is the concept of ether, but at this time, the study of ether is still not possible. When illiterate people like me say things like this, it probably makes others laugh. But when I apply this therapy to people, for the purposes of explanation, I think the laws of ether are generally the closest [thing to it]. However, I am a person who does not know differentials or integrals [i.e., calculus], so I really cannot say it clearly. Maybe if I studied high-level mathematics I could conduct scholarly experiments or have the opportunity to explain. At any rate, I am completely satisfied just with the great results that I get from the field of practical application [of this therapy].

　わたしも、初めはこの療法を鼻先で笑って見たものである。

　或る日、わたしは友人に向って「どうも身体が快くないからゴルフでもやろうと思うがどうか」といったものだ、友人は「それならゴルフよりこんな良いものがある」といって、この療法の存在を教えてくれた。その友人の父はかつては日本銀行の総裁であった人、その友もまた英国に留学して来て今は立派な実業家だ。こんな人から勧められたものだから、わたしもその気になって、妻と子供と三人で直に入門した、だが、真実をいえばまだその時ですら信じてはいなかったものだ。ところが間もなく、西條八十、宮島新三郎両君等と講演旅行に出かけ、その旅先で、鯉こくを食ってその骨を喉に立てて、ぎくしゃく泣いてる男を見た。わたしは何の気なしに療法を試みたところ、不思議にも痛みが取れた。この時、わたしは初めて療法の「こつ」を悟った。これ以来わたしは、もう鼻先で笑えなくなったのである。

I also laughed derisively the first time I encountered this therapy.

One day, I said to my friend, "My body hasn't been feeling right, so I've been thinking about taking up golf – what do you think?" He said, "If that's the case, there's something better than golf," and he told me about this therapy. His father was the president of the Bank of Japan, and he himself had studied in the UK and is a fine businessman. Because it was recommended by such a [great] person, I too became interested and, along with my wife and child, became a student [of Reiki therapy] right away. However, to tell the truth, even at that time, I didn't believe in it. Shortly after that time, I went on a lecture tour with SAIJŌ Yaso [poet and lyricist (1892-1970)] and MIYAJIMA Shinzaburō [literary critic and scholar of English literature (1892-1934)]. During that trip, we saw a man who was crying because he had been eating *koikoku* [carp with miso sauce] and a bone got stuck in his throat. I tried out the therapy on him, and right away his pain mysteriously disappeared. That's when I became aware of the "art" of the therapy. Since then, I can no longer laugh derisively [at Reiki].

　わたしは、或る人の紹介で林氏の元に入門した。この療法を伝授されるについては、相当な金を払って伝授されたもので、それには初伝とか奥伝とかあるのだが、わたしは未だ奥伝にはいれぬ程なぺえぺえに過ぎぬ。だから、委しい事はよく知らない、その門下には種々な階級もある様だ。こんな善事を宣伝することすら嫌うほどの謙譲な人々の集まりで、階級を設けたり、入門金を取ったりするのも変な様ではあるが、しかしそれは、この人々の特権であるから、何人もその既得権は認めねばならぬ。またそれが徳義でもある。この意味でわたしは、その伝授と療法とについて、もっと詳しく発表するの自由をもたないことを遺憾とする。それはその人々の生活にまで危害を加えることであるから。

Through an acquaintance's introduction, I became a student of Mr. Hayashi. In order to be instructed* in the therapy, I paid a substantial sum. There is an introductory level [*shoden*] and an advanced level [*okuden*], but I am so untalented that I haven't reached the advanced level. I do not know all the details, but it seems that there are various ranks of students. It seems strange that a group of people so modest that they dislike publicizing their good deeds, would do things like establish ranks and collect enrollment fees. However, this is their privilege, and everyone must respect their rights to do so. It is moral. It is regrettable that I cannot freely give a more detailed presentation of the teachings* and the therapy, but it is because I do not want to harm the lives of these people.

但し、これだけはいって差し支えあるまい。一日一時間半位
の程度に、五日間の稽古であるが、人によっては、最初に伝授
を受けたその日から、もう他の人を癒すことが出来る、それほ
ど問題は簡単至極なものだといえる。人間の誰にでも、第六感
となって潜んでいる或る意識が、この稽古によってその発動を
促され、その間に習得されるものであるらしい。ともかく、極
く簡単な方法で教えられるもので、一言にしていえば、人類全
体に共通な力で、小児でさえなければ誰にでも出来ることだ。
方法としても、単にその患部へ隻手を置けばよいのだから、実
際これ位な治療法は世の中にあるまい。これを特に恵まれた人
々にのみ限らず一般に公開したら――という熱情が、日夜わた
しの心の底に湧いて来る。だが、或る特殊な事情によってそれ
が許されない。せめてこんな療法が存在することだけでも、一
人にでも多く知らしめたいというのが、わたしの今日の溢るる
が如き熱情だ。

　最後に、最近におけるわたしの愉快な報告を、もう一つ二つ
つけ加えさせて頂きたい。

But, I think I could just talk about this one thing without a problem. [At the beginning,] one practices for ninety minutes a day for five days, but it's different from person to person. Some people can heal others from the very first day they receive instruction*. To that extent, one could say that the therapy is exceedingly simple [to learn]. All humans have an aspect of consciousness that is hidden as our sixth sense. It seems that [Reiki] practice stimulates that faculty, so that during training, one acquires the ability. Anyway, it is taught in an extremely simple way. To put it briefly, it is an ability that is common to all humans so that, with the exception of babies, anyone can do it. The method is simply to place a hand on the affected area, so, come to think of it, no simpler treatment method exists. To be able to open it to the public and not have it for an especially privileged group—day and night, this passion rises up from the bottom of my heart. However, because of particular circumstances, this is not permitted. The very least I could do is to simply speak of the existence of this therapy so that, even if I reach just one more person, I want make it as well known as possible. Today I overflow with this passion.

Finally, I would like to add a few of my recent wonderful stories.

　わたしは今月にはいってから、福島県の或る富豪の未亡人の瀬死の床を見舞った。これはわたしが青年時代に丁稚奉公をしていた家の主婦であるが、昨年の夏その地方へ往った時、二回手をかけたところが、頭痛が非常に楽になったので、是非かさねてわたしの治療を受けたいというのであった。わたしは、報恩の意味で忙しい東京から六日間のがれて、一日七八時間ずつ治療をしたが、死の影はもうその病室から去って終ったらしい。その時その一家でわたしは、矢張り昨夏手をかけた患者に遭った。それは四十年来掌の皮が非常に荒れる病症だ。労働者の踝といえどもこんなにあつく、硬く、ひび荒れはしないと思うほどになっている。それも夏も末で、しかも手の甲は極めてすべっこい。これはこの辺の風土病と見えて、その頃わたしが逗留していた飯阪の旅館の姪にも同じ疾患があった。これは八度福島病院でレントゲンをかけて貰ったが何の効もなかったというのだ。わたしは自分の力では、とてもこんな難病は癒るまいと思いながら、ただほんの経験のために手をかけて見ると、双方とも、十分位でやわらかな、綺麗な手にかわった。そして今度行って見ると従来は一層烈しく荒れ爛れる運命を見ていた冬の最中に、依然として綺麗になっていた。わたしもびっくりした、人々も驚いていた。

　（記者註、この二つの事実は福島の新聞が写真入で特報している）

From the beginning of this month, I went to Fukushima Prefecture to visit a wealthy widow on her deathbed. She is the housewife of a family for whom I served as an apprentice in my youth. When I visited her last summer, I put my hands on her twice, and it really relieved her headaches, so she definitely wanted to receive my treatments again. I was busy in Tokyo but, because I owe her a great debt, I spent six days treating her for seven or eight hours a day, and the shadow of death left the sickroom and seemed to be finished. At that time, I met another patient whom I put hands on last summer. This patient had terribly ruined skin on the palms for forty years. They had become thicker, harder, and more cracked than the heels of a physical laborer. In addition, at the end of the summer, the backs of the hands were extremely smooth. This illness could be commonly seen in that area and, where I stayed, the innkeeper's niece had the same affliction. She had been to Fukushima Hospital eight times and received radiation, but with no results. I thought that my ability could not cure this intractable disease, but because of my experiences, I tried placing my hands. In both cases, after ten minutes, their hands became beautiful. Now, it is mid-winter, in which inflamed, chapped skin is our lot, but their hands are still beautiful. I was surprised, and others around them are surprised as well.

(Reporter: These two cases were reported along with pictures in a Fukushima newspaper.)

手の話が出たから、もう一つ自慢話を――。

　それは去年の暮れのこと、或る知名な建築家が、永年の職業上、製図に必要な二本の指が硬直して、遂に満足に数字が書けなくなった。二行位も書くと鉛筆はこの建築家の指から抜けて落ちた。或る博士に三ヶ月もかよった。病魔は思う様に退散しない。そこで私の所に来た、この時も私には自信はなかったが「まあ、やって見よう」というので、十分ばかりも建築家にとっては偉大であるべき二本の指を私は掴んだ。一つの暗い人生を隻手に握ったのである。所がどうだろう、その指は間もなく動き出した、生活があるき出したのだ、そして三回もやったら完全に昔の指になったではないか。

　しかしこんな自慢話はいくらしたって、信じない人には信じられない。また話だけでは信じない方が道理だ。あなた自身病気があるなら目前で直しましょう。しかし軽い病気は癒してもつまらない。お医者さんでも癒せる。お医者さんで癒せない病人があったらつれて行らっしゃい。つれて来られない重病人なら、こっちから出かけてもよろしい。といっても御承知のごとくわたしは忙しい身体だ。来月は二つの劇場の脚本三つをこれから一週間で書くのだ。そう沢山はいけない。ただわたしの隻手療法の実力を試験するために適当と思う重患の人を一人だけやって見ましょう。

　（二月某日文責在記者）

I have one more boastful story about the hands.

It was the end of last year, and a well-known architect had two fingers that he had used to draft for so many years, but had stiffened to the point that he could no longer satisfactorily write numbers. If he wrote two lines, the pencil would fall from his hand. He went to the doctor for three months, but the disease did not leave, so he came to my clinic. I was not confident, but I said "Well, let's try," and for just ten minutes I grasped those two fingers that should be an architect's greatest treasure. In one hand, I held a man's sadness [literally, "a dark life"]. But, how is it? Soon those fingers began to move, his life began to progress, and after three more treatments his fingers were perfectly as before.

However, no matter how many of these boastful stories I tell, suspicious people cannot believe them. And it is reasonable not to believe mere stories. If you yourself are ill, I can cure it before your very eyes. However, it is boring to heal minor illnesses. Doctors can also heal those. Please bring patients whom doctors cannot heal. For seriously ill patients whom you cannot bring, I can go to them. However, as you know, I must say that I am busy. Next month, I have to write three scripts for two different theaters in one week's time, so I cannot do much. However, in order to test the merit of my one hand therapy, I will try it out on one patient with an appropriately severe illness. (February, the editor reworded the article)

* The Japanese word *denju* is interpreted in this translation as "instruction," as this seems to be the way it was used at that time. However, it can also be used to mean "initiation."

「隻手療法実験のため　自ら患者となるの記」
あさき生

『サンデー毎日』
昭和3年3月4日
15-16頁

隻手療法なんて、そんな莫迦な――少なくともモダアンのモの字でも識る人間なら、隻手で万病を治するてえな夢を、誰が見るものか、多分、松翁先生が劇作のかたてまに、何事か皮肉な遊戯でも考案したんだろ、何を莫迦なとばかり、雪の日、長崎町のお宅に出かけたもんだ。

　先づ一通り話を聞く、――驚いたことには、先生は頗る真面目である、むしろ謹厳な態度で療法談が続けられる。もとより彼は、やじ馬気分で先生の門を叩いたのではないけれども、さりとて彼は、奇蹟に近い事実が行われていようとも予想しなかった。所が、話しは正しく奇蹟の上を歩いている。彼の饒舌な心は忽ち沈黙した。実は、奇蹟を信ずるよりも、彼は松居その人を信じたのである。また、もち屋がもちを食わぬと同様に、芝居道の大家が、医者の真似をするに何の不思議もあり得ない。

　で、富樫じゃないが問答無益、いざ、彼自身の万病を目の前で癒して見よう、見事なおして見るか、見るぞよ、なんでもないことてな訳で、別室に支度がされる、支度といって横臥の場所をつくるだけで、聴診器も薬も無用なのである。所で彼の病気は？山ほどある、大病でもなく、寝つくほどでもない、ぴんしゃんした病気ではあるが、曰く軽度でびっこの乱視、曰く胃腸の持病、曰く鼻、曰く神経衰弱、曰く……等。

"For the Sake of Testing Single-Hand Therapy: A Personal Account of Becoming a Patient," Asaki (pseudonym), *Sunday Mainichi*, March 4, Shōwa 3 [1928], 15-16.

Single-hand therapy? What a fool… Who could know the syllable "mo" in "modern" and also dream of healing the ten thousand illnesses with a single hand? Maybe this is just an ironic game that Matsui-sensei came up with in his free time from playwriting. It's just absurd. I visited his house in Nagasaki Town [present-day Toshima-ku, Tokyo] on a snowy day.

For starters, I've heard his explanation—it is surprising, because [Matsui] *sensei* is quite serious. Rather, in his strict manner, he continued to discuss this therapy. From the beginning, I wasn't knocking on *sensei's* gate with the feeling of a curious onlooker. I had no expectation of witnessing any miracles. However, [Matsui-*sensei's*] stories sound truly miraculous. My talkative spirit was instantly silenced. Actually, rather than believing in miracles, I believed in Matsui the man. Just as mochi makers do not eat mochi, it is no wonder that this expert on the "way of theater" could play a doctor.

Now, I am no Togashi, but talk is cheap [a reference to a famous kabuki scene in which one character interrogates another]: let's try it out. Would it amaze you if I healed your ten thousand [i.e., all of your] ailments before your eyes? Can you show me? You will see. It will be easy. There is a place where one can lie down, but I assure you, they don't use either stethoscope or drugs. By the way, what illnesses did I have? There are a lot. I'm not gravely ill or laid up in bed, it's not serious, but I had an astigmatism, chronic stomach problems, nasal problems, neurasthenia, etc.

　そのうち最も病気らしい胃腸と眼、この二つを治療してもらうことにして、やがて別室に舞台は移された。彼は裸体に近くなった。仰向けに寝た。羽根ぶとんが上からやさしくかけられた。先ず血圧を計り心臓を診た上で先生は左半身に、奥さん（かつ子夫人）は右半身に、河村さん（看護婦）は両眼に、三人がかりで、腹部と顔面とに手は置かれた。

　読者の注文は、如何にして満足されるか、彼は、恰も俎上の鯉の如く、息を殺して身動きもせず、診察？の結果を待った。最早少しの疑いをも抱く訳にゆかない。何だか原始的な治療を受けている様な気だ。反対に、隻手療法とは如何にするものか、まるで、甲賀流の道場に忍術でも盗みに来たかの様に、頻りに好奇心が活躍を始めた。

　と、間もなく――

「どうだ、このお腹のひどいことは！」

と先生が。

「何だか、腎臓でも悪い様ですよ」と奥さんが。

「此方もよく出ますよ」と河村さんが。

Out of these, the worst seemed to be my stomach and my eyes. They decided to treat these two ailments, and soon the scene shifted into the treatment room. I stripped down, nearly nude, and lay face up. I was gently covered with a feather quilt. First *sensei* checked my blood pressure and examined my heart. He then laid hands on my left side, his wife (Mrs. Katsuko) on my right side, and Kawamura-san (a nurse) on both eyes, so that I was amidst three people laying hands on my abdomen and face.

How can I satisfy your curiosity? I was just like a carp on the cutting board, not breathing, not moving, awaiting the results of the "examination". At this moment, it was impossible to harbor even a little suspicion. For some reason, it felt like receiving a primitive treatment. On the other hand, I became curious how the one hand therapy works, just like we might want to steal the techniques of the Kōka-ryū *ninjutsu*.

And soon, *sensei* said, "How can this stomach be so bad!"

His wife: "The kidneys seem somewhat bad as well."

"It's coming out a lot over here as well," added Kawamura.

　彼の病状について最初の報告である。「出ますよ」とは、患部が血液を要求するとの意味で、掌に反応を感ずることだ。つまり掌が痛むことを指す。ふん、べらぼうめ、ひとの腹の上に手をおいて、こちらは痛くも痒くもないに、やれ掌が痛むの出ますの候のと、ひとをこけにするも程があらあ、さては松翁先生夫妻は発狂でもしたか——といやあ話はお終いだ、松竹の人、歌舞伎の役者、みんな発狂したことになる。では、どんな風に痛むのか、——ぢりりと来る、びりっと痛む、刺すように痛む、時には、焼けたフライパンの底でこすられる様な痛みを感ずることがあるとの話だ。おかしな現象だ、しかも、患者は療法を疑っていても治療に支障はないとある。霊気療法とはいえ事実上霊的なものでないのだから。

　そこで彼は先生に話しかける、先生は奥さんにいう、河村さんがあいづちを打つ。或いは、癒った人々から来た礼状が見せられる、帝展の審査員であった洋画家Ｓ氏、日本唯一人の大実業家の息で、また、相当な実業家である所のＳ氏、そんな人々の筆跡を彼は寝ながら読んだ。こんな先生の私交にまでおよびたくはないが、その意志に叛いても彼は読者に満足を与えたいが腹一杯なのである。この間およそ約二時間、会話をしながら手は頻りに動かされて患部が索られている。が、松翁先生夫妻の身体は坐ったまま動かない。芝居王国の責任者として忙しい人に、こんな仕事をただの物好きで出来るものじゃない。終に彼は大病人になった様な気がして来た。

This was the first information about my condition. "It's coming out" meant that the affected area needs blood, which is felt in the palms. In other words, it indicated that their palms hurt. Well, morons, I don't care if you hold your hands over my stomach and say your palms hurt and "it's coming out"? I don't feel anything. Aren't Mr. and Mrs. Matsui just insane and making a fool out of me? The stories [of their patients]—the Shōchiku [theater and film company for whom Matsui had worked] man and a kabuki actor—they must have gone mad as well. In what manner did their hands hurt? It came like little electric shocks, sparks, and stabbing pains. Sometimes, he said, it felt like being rubbed with the bottom of a hot frying pan. This was strange, and yet, patients' suspicions of the therapy were no obstacle for their cure. That's because, although it is called Reiki Ryōhō, it's not actually psycho-spiritual (*reiteki*).

At that time, I spoke with *sensei*, he spoke with his wife, and Kawamura-san agreed. Additionally, I was shown letters of thanks from people healed [by Matsui]. Mr. S, a painter of *yōga* [a Japanese modern art movement] who had been a judge at the Imperial Exhibition, and Mr. S, son of the biggest businessman in Japan. I lay there and read this businessman's letter. I do not intend to violate the privacy of his personal correspondence but I wanted to completely fulfill the readers' curiosity. This went on for about two hours. The whole time, *sensei's* hands frequently moved looking for affected areas. Matsui-*sensei* and his wife sat without moving. As supervisor of the kingdom of theater, he is a busy man, and does not do this work as mere whimsy. In the end, I felt I was a serious case.

　これで第一日の治療は終った。むしろ切り上げられた。胃腸と腎臓が非常に悪い。意外にも肝臓まで悪い。それが癒れば眼も自然に視力を回復するとのことだ。驚いたことには、十七八年も前に手術した鼻の話はしないのに、河村さんが「ここによく出ますよ」といって、それを摘発したではないか。好奇心が不思議な物に跳びついたまま動けなくなった心持である。

　彼は、降り積む雪の中を戻りながら、へたな碁打ちみたいに、あの手はどうか、この手はどうだったかと、手のことばかり考えさせられた。仕掛けもやある、呼吸もやあると首を捻って見たところで、この場合無から有は出ない。反対に有から無にでもなるか、頭が軽くなって、目先が明るくなり、何となく爽快な気持がして来た。彼は眼鏡を外して歩いてみた。

　翌日は休んで容態を観察した。眼はやや疲労を覚え、腹は徒にふくれ上がる様な感じで、それ以外別に異常はない。自重しておかゆを喰ったら珍しや軽い下痢をしたばかり。

　第二日は約三時間、型の如く治療を終った。内臓が混乱したらしい感覚が強烈に襲うて来た。或る軽快さで腹中が鳴りわたる。下腹部が膨れて来たが重苦しさを伴わない。やや全身的に疲労が感ぜられる。

With this, the first day of treatment ended. In fact, we had to stop early. The stomach and the kidneys were both extremely bad. It was also surprising how bad the liver was. If they could heal these areas, the eyes and, naturally, the eyesight would recover. Surprisingly, even though I didn't tell them I had surgery on my nose seventeen or eighteen years ago, Kawamura-san found out when she said, "it's coming out a lot over here." My curiosity about this mysterious phenomenon grew so that I felt that I could no longer continue my disbelief.

As I returned home amid the accumulating snow, I felt like an inferior player of *go*. Why had I made that "move"? What was I thinking? I was made to think of my "moves". They had no tricks or covert signals? I wondered. I did not want to make something out of nothing at this point, but on the other hand, how could nothing come out of something [i.e., Matsui's results]? My head became lighter, I immediately brightened, and for some reason I became exhilarated. I took off my glasses and began to walk.

The next day I rested and they observed my condition. My eyes were a little tired and my stomach felt bloated, but aside from that, nothing abnormal. I took it easy and just had some rice porridge. The only strange thing was some light diarrhea.

On the second day, the treatment model ended after three hours. I was assailed with the feeling that my insides were in chaos. And then, my stomach began to feel better. There was no heavy feeling of bloating in the lower abdomen. My entire body was weary.

　第三日となった。

「これだけ手がけて、なおかつ凱歌をあげられぬとは心外だ」といいながら、松翁夫妻は彼の難症に突撃せんばかりの意気である。手先は方々に転戦する。間もなく先生は叫んだ。「ほっ、やった、ここだそ、加勢しろ加勢しろ！」先生の手の上に奥さんの手が来た、その上にまた川村さんの手が重ねられた。病魔の巣を発見して総攻撃をするのだ。「痛い！うう痛い！」と先生は顔をしかめた、「待ってくれ、もう敵わん、右手と取り換えるから」

　重ねられた手の下で、彼の腸はぐず、ぐずと鳴った、霜柱が溶け崩れる様に——。恐らく鬱血でも散る音なのか、気味が悪い、この時彼は、この療法の開祖が飯野吉三郎や太霊道と共に、日本三やま師の一人といわれたことを思い出した。

　その日、彼は小山にでも登った様な疲労を覚えた。家で横になると心臓が早くどきどき打っている。胃も弱ったらしい兆候がある。入浴の後また横になると前後不覚に仮寝の夢、何だか鼾をかいてる夢だ。一時間ばかりして好い心持で目を覚まし、聞けばとても大きな鼾をかいたそうだ。醒めての気持は今までにない愉快さである。

It became the third day.

While saying, "it's regrettable that this is all that we're handling, and still can offer no victory song," Mr. and Mrs. Matsui had the spirit of soldiers on the front lines of my incurable illness. Their fingers were fighting in numerous battles. Just then, *sensei* cried out. "Oh, I did it! It's here. Backup, backup!" His wife's hands moved atop *sensei's*, and Kawamura's piled atop theirs. They had discovered the nest of the demons of disease and launched a general attack. "It hurts! Ow, it hurts!" *Sensei* frowned. "Wait, I can no longer bear it, I'm going to change my right hand."

From under the piled hands, my stomach grumbled like ice needles melting and crumbling. Perhaps it was the sound of blood stagnation dissolving. It was creepy. [And yet,] at that time, I recalled the founder of this therapy, who is said to be one of Japan's three fraudulent wizards, together with IINO Kichisaburō and Taireidō [founder TANAKA Morihei].

That day, I was weary as though I had climbed a hill. When I went to lie down at home, my heart was beating rapidly. My stomach also seemed weak. When I lay down again after my bath, I passed out for a bit, slightly snoring. After just an hour, I opened my eyes, feeling good. I was told that I was snoring very loudly. When I woke, I felt more pleasant than I ever had before.

　第四日には、腹がくうくう鳴り出した。治療を始めて以来いつも腹一杯食っている気で、しかも喰えばいくらでも食える状態にあったが、この日は腹中もやや整って来た様な感じで空腹感が漸く湧いて来る。が、眼はまだ眼鏡なしには疲労する様だ。

　以上の如き経過で、胃腸に何等かの革命が起きたことは事実だ。俗に「動じ」という奴か、反動的に一時悪くなったか、ともかく、反応のあったことはわかる。しかし、果して癒るかどうか更に続けて見ねば確答は与えられまい、ただ報告を急ぐため不満足ながら、実験記はこの程度にしておくが、なお治療はして頂く約束である。

　最後まで索ってみたが、隻手には何の秘密も何もないらしい。それとなく奥さんをねらっても「このお腹ん中に種が仕入れてあるんですよ」とばかり、笑って答えない、松翁先生も笑っていた。

　信ずるか、信じないか、――それは個々人の見識にあることで、報告は単に報告に過ぎないことを特に附記しておく。

On the fourth day, my stomach cried out that it was empty. From the time the therapy started, I had the feeling of having stuffed myself [i.e., being bloated]. Moreover, this was no matter how much I actually ate. That day my stomach felt a little more orderly, and I finally began to feel hungry. However, my eyes still got tired without glasses.

And so, my stomach had really transformed. I could tell there was some reaction because of that thing commonly called "distress" (*dōji*): that is, that I reacted by temporarily feeling poorly. However, without seeing whether the healing continued as expected, we cannot give a definitive answer. But to rush the report would be unsatisfying. This is the extent of the experiment records, but I have an appointment for further treatment.

I looked thoroughly, but there seems to be no secret to the single hand. When I indirectly asked Mrs. Matsui, she just replied, "We learned that the cause was in the stomach," laughing. Matsui-*sensei* laughed too.

If you believe, if you don't believe—that is a matter of personal opinion. I just add my notes, and a report is nothing more than a report.

# *Appendix* FOUR

---

## *Selected Articles from the Hawaii Hochi, 1937-1938*

## Selected Articles from the Hawaii Hochi, 1937-1938

In preparation for a trip to Honolulu to go through a significant amount of microfilm at the main research library of the University of Hawaii looking for mentions of Hawayo Takata, I realized that their collection included a significant number of Japanese-language newspapers. While my reading skills were not sufficient at the time to engage in the time-consuming task of skimming through reels of microfilm in Japanese, I suggested to my colleague Hirano Naoko that she might be able to find some coverage of Hayashi Chūjirō's teaching tour in the Islands between October 1937 and February 1938.

Ms. Hirano was able to uncover a treasure trove of twenty-three articles (although some are quite short) about Usui Reiki Ryōhō and twelve adver-tisements for training courses offered by Hayashi and Takata. She graciously transliterated these hard-to-read microfilm scans for me into post-war characters (and corrected these initial texts with cleaner copies of these articles she has since located at a library in Japan).

Translations of all of these articles will be posted on my website, but for now I am proud to present original translations of these two historic articles that have never before been reproduced. Footnotes with asterisks are my own, whereas numbered ones are Robert Fueston's. All transcription was by Hirano Naoko and the articles are reproduced with the permission of the Hawaii Hōchi.

- Justin Stein

1937 年 9 月 30 日

## 「霊気療法の林忠次郎氏来布　令嬢キヨエさん同伴　土曜日秩父丸で」

霊気療法の大家として著名の東京四谷東信濃町林霊気研究会々長林忠次郎氏は令嬢キヨエさんを同伴来る土曜日入港の秩父丸にて来布する由当地の知友に通知があった。霊気療法に就いては布哇では未だ広く一般に知られていないがヒロ市の牧師樋口貫氏夫妻並びに日本語学校々長田原仲亮氏等は昭和八年五月に霊気療法の伝授を受けて居り、最近では加哇島カパアの高田ヒロミ夫人が伝授を受けた。高田夫人は夙に東京の研究会から通信講習を受けていたが遂に今年六月日本に行って講習を受け今月二十四日帰布した熱心家である。こうした関係上林氏の来布は予てから希望されていたもので、又林氏の令嬢キヨエさんも結婚前に是非一度布哇を見たいと熱望していたところから今回来布となった由である。林氏は当地に於いて希望者があれば講習会を開いて霊気療法を伝えたいと希望している。又キヨエさんは茶の湯、生花に通暁しているのでこれ又希望者には教授を惜しまないという。因に霊気療法の肇祖は臼井甕男氏で生物生活に必須の「エネルギー」を霊気と呼んでその霊能を疾病治療上に活用したものであると云う（写真は林忠次郎氏）。

*The Hawaii Hochi*, September 30, 1937, p. 7

### "Reiki Ryōhō's Hayashi Chūjirō Comes to Hawaii—Accompanied by his Daughter Kiyoe—Arrives Saturday on the Chichibu Maru"

A close friend of Hayashi Chūjirō, head of the Hayashi Reiki Kenkyūkai in Tokyo's Higashi Shinanomachi (Yotsuya) and celebrated expert of Reiki Ryōhō, reports that he will arrive on Saturday on the Chichibu Maru, accompanied by his daughter Kiyoe. Reiki Ryōhō is not yet widely known in Hawaii but the Rev. and Mrs. Higuchi Kan* of Hilo and Tahara,** head of the Japanese language school, received instruction (*denju****) in May of the 8th year of Shōwa [1933]. Recently, Mrs. Takata Hiromi from Kapaa, Kauai, [also] received instruction.*** Long ago, Mrs. Takata received training from the Tokyo Kenkyūkai, but at last, this June, she went to Japan for a training and she returned to Hawaii on the 24th of this month as an enthusiastic practitioner. It was hoped for some time that her teacher Mr. Hayashi would come to Hawaii, and as Mr. Hayashi's daughter Kiyoe also eagerly longed to see Hawaii before she was married, they are coming together. Mr. Hayashi hopes to teach Reiki Ryōhō by holding some training courses here if people are interested. In addition, Kiyoe is well acquainted with tea ceremony and ikebana, so she would also be willing to teach those to interested persons. Incidentally, Reiki Ryōhō's founder, Mikao Usui said that Reiki is an energy that is essential to life, and this psycho-spiritual ability (*reinō*) can be used practically to treat disease. (Photo is of Mr. Hayashi Chūjirō)

* Higuchi Kan was the minister of the Hilo Japanese Christian Church.

** Possibly Tahara Hiroshi, principal of the Papaikou Japanese School on the Papaikou plantation on the Hamakua coast, about five miles north of Hilo.

*** The word denju 伝授,, here translated as "instruction", can also mean "initiation", which is how it is used in contemporary Japanese Reiki. It was also used to refer to the initiation ritual of the Te-no-Hira Ryōchi healing technique of Toshihiro Eguchi (another student of Mikao Usui) in the 1930s. However, Naoko Hirano of Waseda University believes this usage is closer to "instruction" or, more specifically, "being formally taught the important teachings by a master" (personal e-mail to Justin Stein, April 16, 2014).

1938 年 2 月 22 日

## 「皆様の御厚情に衷心より感謝す　林氏の告別放送」

　　左は去るサンデー朝ケージー・エム・ビーから放送された臼井霊気療法の林忠次郎氏帰国告別挨拶

　私はご紹介に預かりました臼井霊気療法の林忠次郎であります。昨年十月以来当市に滞在中でありましたが、明後二十二日初の龍田丸で帰国いたしますので、一言ご挨拶を述べさせて頂きます。

　霊気療法は人の体から自然に湧き出る霊気と云う力を以て自分の身体は勿論、他人の病気や性質を何の工夫もなく直す方法で少しも六ケしい修行もいりません。只五六日間毎日三時間位の講習を御聞きになれば、初めの日から驚く程の効果を顕わすことができます。十二三才以上なれば男女の区別なく誰にでもたやすく出来ます。布哇全島で三百五十名の会員が出来ましたが、其中には全く日本語の分らぬ白人、布哇人、支那人なども居られますが、皆様能く御分りになって、色々の病気を直して大変喜んで居られます　布哇島、馬哇島の地方に此喜びをお分けすることの出来なかったのは誠に遺憾に存じます。

　日本には会員が約五千名程居られますが、其中から此療法の伝授に適すると認めましたお方十三名を推薦致しましたが、当市の高田はわよ夫人は其一人で、布哇及米国を通じて伝授者は高田夫人只一人であります。外には居りません。

　**伝授**をお望みのお方や又は病気で悩むで居られるお方は高田夫人又は治療主任青山文記氏にご相談ください。ヌアヌ街グローブ・ホテルに居られます。

　高田夫人は加哇生れの第二世ですが、一昨々年の冬東京の私の治療所で約半年の間熱心にこの法を修行して一昨年七月加哇島に帰り同地で治療と伝授を始めました処、会員五十余名に達しました。昨年七月夫人は突然私の宅を訪れ私に布哇観光を勧めましたので私は是に応じ娘を伴い十月二日ホノルルに上陸し、四日加哇に渡り同地の会員に御面会しましたが、皆様から心なる御歓待を受けましたことを茲に感謝いたします。

十月下旬再び当市に帰りまして**有志諸君のお望みにより**今日迄に十四回の講習会を開きました。毎回多数の入会者が御座いまして何れも能く御理解下さいまして、御自分は勿論近親の病気をやすやすと直されて健康の幸福を感謝して居られます。

私の当市滞在が案外に永引きましたので日本の希望者が大分待って居られますので明後二十二日此の思い出多き地を後にして帰国致します。滞在中は会員諸君を始め皆様方の一方ならぬ御歓待を頂きまして誠に愉快に、少しも旅の淋しさなどを感ぜず、五ヶ月の長い月日を一日の如く過ごさせて頂きましたことは私等親子の終生忘れられぬ喜びでありまして皆様の御好情を深く深く御礼申し上げます　皆様の御健康と幸福を切に祈り申し上げましてごあいさつを終ります。皆さん御機嫌よう……左様なら。

*The Hawaii Hochi*, February 22, 1938, p. 8

### "I Appreciate Everyone's Kindness From the Bottom of My Heart—Mr. Hayashi's Farewell Address"

The following is Mr. Hayashi's farewell address on returning to Japan, broadcast last Sunday morning on KGMB.

I am pleased to have the opportunity to speak today. I am Usui Reiki Ryōhōs Hayashi Chūjirō. I have stayed in this city since last October but, since I am returning to Japan on the 22nd on the Tatsuta Maru, please allow me to say a few words

Reiki Ryōhō is a therapy that heals disease and corrects personality [flaws] in oneself or, of course, in other people, without the use of any devices or difficult austerities, but by means of a power called Reiki that naturally gushes forth from the body. Training courses are usually five or six days long, three hours a day. Those who attend tend to express the extent to which they are astonished by the efficacy from the first day. From the age of twelve or thirteen years old,[365] anybody can do it easily, with no distinction between

---

365  My understanding of Hayashi's statement specifying this as an appropriate age comes from my years of studying and practicing Traditional Chinese Medicine which found its way into Japan around the sixth or seventh century and is called *kanpō*. In Japanese meridian theory, the energetic system of a person isn't fully developed until the teen years. Therefore, in Japan children are treated not with acupuncture but with what is called Sho Ni Shin. I believe that Hayashi made this statement for this reason. More evidence for this reason is shown by Larisa Stow whom Takata initiated as a child, while she declined to initiate Larisa's friend. This is because Takata stated that her friend's energetic system was not yet fully developed, so the initiations could harm her. See http://www.reiki-healing-touch.com/&art_takata for the article by Larisa.

men and women. There are already **three hundred**\* and fifty members in the Hawaiian Islands, and among them are whites, Hawaiians, and Chinese who understand absolutely no Japanese language. Yet everybody has learned well and is very happy to be able to heal various diseases. It's truly unfortunate that I was unable to share this joy with the islands of Hawaii [Big Island] and Maui.

In Japan there are about five thousand members, but out of this number there are thirteen\*\* who have received the approval to give the initiation for this therapy. However, this city's [Honolulu's] Mrs. Takata Hawayo is alone: Mrs. Takata is the only instructor throughout Hawaii and North America. Aside from her, there is no one.

Those who want **instruction**\* (*denju*\*\*\*) or who are troubled by illness, please consult Mrs. Takata or the treatment manager (*chiryō shunin*) Aoyama Bunki at the Grove Hotel on Nuuanu Avenue.

Mrs. Takata is a Nisei\*\*\*\* born in Kauai, but three years ago [1935], in the winter, she spent about six months enthusiastically training in this method at my Tokyo clinic. Two years ago, she returned to Kauai in July [1936], where she started healing and teaching; her students numbered more than fifty. Then, last July [1937], she suddenly came to my home, suggesting that I travel to Hawaii, so I agreed, and with my daughter[366] as my companion, I landed in Honolulu on October second. On the fourth, we traveled to Kauai, where I met with the members there, and I am grateful for the warm reception I received from everyone.

At the end of October, we returned to Honolulu, and due to the wishes of the **interested**\* ladies and gentlemen, we held fourteen training courses between then and now. Each time, many new members attended, they understood well, and, of course, they painlessly healed the diseases of their close relatives and were grateful for the happiness of health.

My stay in this city has been unexpectedly long, and the people wishing to study with me in Japan have been waiting, so the day after tomorrow, the twenty-second, I will leave these memorable places and return to my country. During my stay, I have been truly happy to receive an extraordinarily warm welcome from all the new members, and not once in my travels have I been felt lonely at all, so that the five long months have seemed as though they were but a single day. My daughter and I will never forget this place. We are delighted. It is late, but thank you for your goodwill. I conclude with words

---

366  Note from Robert Fueston: Hayashi's daughter's name was Kiyoe Hayashi.

of prayer for everyone's health and happiness. Everyone, farewell… goodbye.

    \* These words were printed in the original in a larger, boldfaced font.

    \*\* In this text it isn't clear who trained these thirteen people. However, in another article, dated January 11, 1938, it specifies that these thirteen people were trained by Mr. Hayashi.

    \*\*\* The word denju 伝授,, here translated as "instruction", can also mean "initiation", which is how it is used in contemporary Japanese Reiki. It was also used to refer to the initiation ritual of the Te-no-Hira Ryōchi healing technique of Toshihiro Eguchi (another student of Mikao Usui) in the 1930s. However, Naoko Hirano of Waseda University believes this usage is closer to "instruction" or, more specifically, "being formally taught the important teachings by a master" (personal e-mail to Justin Stein, April 16, 2014).

    \*\*\*\* i.e., second-generation Japanese American.

# *Appendix* FIVE

---

# *Remote Initiations*

# APPENDIX

# 05

## *Remote Initiations*
### *First Degree Notes Given to Doris Duke by Hawayo Takata*

Takata, on occasion, performed remote initiations on students. Takata would teach classes to students over the phone and/or through letters and then do the initiations remotely. I discovered this while researching at Duke University in 2014.[367]

It is somewhat common knowledge that Takata knew Doris Duke. The archives at Duke University contain a wealth of information regarding their relationship. From this information, I realized that Doris was a First and Second Degree student of Takata's. What was very interesting was that Doris learned the Second Degree remotely, over the telephone. I have permission to publish the following letter from the Doris Duke Charitable Foundation Archives, with acknowledgment to the Rubenstein Library at Duke University. This is one of the many documents I scanned while researching there.

Below is a copy of a letter, pages 2-4, written by Takata to Doris, envelope stamped December 19, 1978. I follow the Reiki tradition of not publishing symbols for public viewing and teaching them only as part of a class. Therefore, I edited out page one, part of page two, and part of page four. Page four contained the name of the first symbol taught in the Second Degree class.[368]

*after talking to you on the phone, I realized, that the symbol is easy to master, but the important thing is, your hands should be initiated to make it work — So that is the problem —*

---

367 Thanks to Justin Stein, who gave me the lead about checking out Duke University's archives.
368 Another letter containing all three Second Degree symbols was also found in the Doris Duke Charitable Foundation Archives. This is substantial proof that Takata did end up finishing Doris's Second Degree training.

I must contact you (3) by short wave and do the initiation by remote control, which I have done in the past to reach patients or students in the hospitals or far away — If you wish to do this, then please call 319 - 293 - 3974 — to set the time, so I can reach you in 30 seconds and initiate you in 10 minuts — Then your hands a ready to use

— It increases your power into 100 horse power, so the treatment results are faster — If you wish to try, There is no such thing as failure, you call me — Otherwise you will have to waite until we can get together some where some time, and then, person to person initiation.

Best Wishes for The Season and a Happy New Year.

Love, Hiromi

It is important to consider the context in which Takata's remote teaching occurred. Takata explained that she only used remote initiations when it seemed absolutely necessary. In her letter to Doris, Takata specified she had given remote initiations when the recipient was in the hospital or was far away and in obvious need. Clearly this way of teaching was the exception rather than the norm.

After making this discovery at Duke University, during a discussion with Marta Getty she told me she had a conversation with Takata regarding remote initiations. I asked her to write something about this conversation to include in this book.

Marta writes, "*Having met Mrs. Hawayo Takata, Sensei, during my Reiki practice well before becoming a Reiki Master, it was especially a privilege in the time we had together in October 1980 that she was willing to answer my many questions. Some of those questions seem banal now. The answers meant little to me at the time but have had much valuable impact after all these years when I wanted to know those certain answers.*

*One day, talking with Mrs. Takata (and asking my usual questions), I asked her if since it is possible to do distant or absent healing for others, would it also be possible to do the Reiki Initiations at a distance. She looked at me*

*with surprise, and I thought perhaps she wouldn't answer my question. Instead, she said it is possible, and that she had done it on emergency occasions, but she didn't like doing it at all because one of the central values in Reiki, Usui Shiki Ryoho, is the oral tradition, and to have direct contact between student and Master in the transmission of energy, information and stories.*

*What I have understood from her response, after the passage of many years in my practice as a teacher, is that because something can be done, does not mean that it is the best way of doing it, nor the best service to the student or to Reiki."*[369]

### First Degree Notes Given to Doris Duke by Hawayo Takata

I hesitated whether or not to include these notes in this book. However, in the end, I felt that they represented a small sample of how detailed the treatment methods in Usui Shiki Reiki Ryoho are. The many details regarding the hand positions used to treat different disorders were given orally or in print by Takata to her First Degree students: in other words, beginning students without treatment experience. But she always mentioned to pay attention to what the practitioner's hands were sensing on any given position (Byōsen). These hand positions cover the most likely places in the body that are the cause of the particular disorder. The reasoning behind the hand positions are based on Traditional Chinese Medicine and the personal experiences of Takata and Hayashi.

I would like to point out during this time in which Doris Duke received her First Degree training, it appears the only hand positions used every time in the standard treatment were the four abdominal positions and the kidneys. As written in the "Grey Book," the treatment was said to begin on the head. I think the set of standard hand positions evolved naturally over time based on experience. Before a standard set of hand positions was developed, all hand positions used were based entirely on the particular disorder and by sensing Byōsen. Hayashi would give a small booklet of positions to treat based on the illness. We can see over time the evolution of Takata's standard set of hand positions used in treatment.

By the mid-1970s and later, Takata would normally give 12 standard hand positions to be used during each treatment. They included positions on

---

369  Email from Marta Getty to author dated May 19, 2015.

the head, abdomen, and back. Sometimes Takata would say to start treatment on the head, and at other times she stated to start the treatment on the abdomen[370] – it makes no difference therapeutically. By using these 12 standard hand positions all the major organs and glands of the body would be treated. Therefore, there would be fewer additional hand positions to teach students for the treatment of specific disorders, making it easier for students to learn. In addition, it gave new students a systematic way to provide therapeutic treatments even if they could not yet sense *Byōsen* (areas of need) in the body.

These notes given by Takata to Doris are reprinted here with permission.[371] An essay written by Takata, later published in the "Grey Book", contains similar notes.

---

370    It seems that while teaching in California, Takata recommended starting treatment on the abdomen and then treating the head. So, if you *really* believe there is a difference as to where to start, I'll recommend that you start treatment on the head, unless you happen to be in California.

371    Hawayo Takata to Doris Duke, Doris Duke Papers, Doris Duke Charitable Foundation Historical Archives, David M. Rubenstein Rare Book & Manuscript Library, Duke University.

## REIKI - JAPANESE PALM HEALING

Always treat basic #1, 2, 3, 4, and kidneys.

### Head

Hair - Falling hair - Treat #1, 2, 3, 4, Kidney long time then head.

Headache - Treat eyes, side and back of head, ear, gall bladder and liver.

Migraine - Women - Treat #1,2, 3, 4, and 4 (Ovaries) longer. Also check sinus, All of head. No ovaries, treat gall bladder, Thyroid.

Migraine - Man - Treat #1, 2, 3, 4, then prostate. Also check sinus, Treat all of head. No prostate, treat gall bladder, Thyroid.

### Eyes

Cataract - Glaucoma Etc. Treat #1, 2, 3, 4, Kidney, Eyes ½ hour.

Almost blind - Treat #1, (,Pancreas) long time, then #2, 3, 4, treat eyes for ½ hour.

Squint or Cross Eye - Exercise - Look to left top corner till eyes get tired, then straight ahead and close eyes. Next right top, lower left, lower right. Do that five times each. Treat eyes ½ hour.

Dizzy - Out of balance  Put hand on both side of head, one inch above and one inch forward of ear.(Pituitary) Also for growth.

### Ears

Anything - Buzzing, Ringing, Draining. Treat chest (Upper) two side Blood pressure point, all of head. Treat ear ½ hour.

### Sinus

Upper - Apply fingers over eyes and at the same time on forehead. Also treat side of head by ear and back of head.

Lower - Apply hand on cheek, both side.

### Nose

Bleeding - Pinch bridge of nose, tilt head slightly back, treat back of neck at base of skull.

Broken blood vessel - Put ice in towel and hold in back of neck. Same time treat bridge of nose.

Plugged nose - Treat nose and chest.

Hay Fever - Treat two side of chest, throat, nose and eyes.

### Mouth

Tongue - Cold sore, burn or anything in mouth. Treat sole of feet.

Lip - Blister, sore, dry lip, rash around mouth. Treat mouth and stomach (Acid)

Stutter - Treat #1, 2, 3, 4, throat, head, mouth and sole of feet.

Tooth Ache - Pain - Apply hand on affected area.

Tooth Extraction - Bleeding - Try treating gum. If it doesn't stop, treat Pancreas. Person could be Diabetic.

Mumps - Woman - Treat #1, 2, 3, 4, and ovary. Treat neck to take away pain.
 Man - Treat #1, 2, 3, 4, and testes. Treat neck to take away pain.

Thyroid - Lump - Treat #1, 2, 3, 4, Kidney, Thyroid, head and heart.

High Blood Pressure - Treat side of neck below ear ½ hour.

Low Blood Pressure - Treat same as above. Then treat down both legs.

Voice box - Treat voice box.

BODY

Pneumonia - Treat #1, 2, 3, 4, Kidney, Heart area, Left chest. Treat back by right shoulder blade. Do not turn sick person.

Asthma - Treat #1, 2, 3, 4, Kidney, Heart area, Whole chest, side of ribs, all of back.

Breast - Tumor or lump - Treat #1, 2, 3, 4, Ovaries ½ hour and breast ½ hour.

Engorgement - Treat #1, 2, 3, 4, Thyroid, brain and breast ½ hour.

Heart - pain - Treat #1 long time then #2, 3, 4, then heart. Never at heart first. Could be gas traped in chest cavity.

Stomach - Ulcer - Treat stomach. Cabbage juice for pain.

Gall Bladder - Treat gall bladder area (Right side below ribs) then treat right shoulder blade area.

Pancreas - Diabetic - Treat #1, 2, (Left side below ribs) then #3,4, Drink - String beans, watercress, cabbage, little water. Blender and drink.

Hernia - Pain - Treat #1, 2, 3, and #4 longer.

Uterus - Womb Cramp - Treat #1, 2, 3, and #4 longer. Five days before and five days during period.

Pregnant - Morning Sickness Treat #1 ( Stomach)

Epilepsy - Treat #1 long time then #2,3, 4, Chest, all of head and back.

Hiccup - To treat, make person lay down and put arms straight above head and treat #1 till hiccup goes away.

Bed Wetting - Urinate - Treat #1,2, 3, and #4 longer.(Bladder) Treat Kidney. Exercise Urinate - Urinate, stop, hold a while, Urinate a little. Repeat 3 times then let it all out.

Leukemia - Treat #1,2, 3, 4, Go back liver area (Below right ribs) and treat spleen.

Arthritis - Gout - Treat #1,2,3,4, Kidney ½ or more. Then site last.

Water Knee - Treat #1,2,3,4, Kidneys then knees.

Sweat - Hand - Treat #1,2,3,4, and kidneys good.

Back

Back ache - Treat #1,2,3,4, Long time. Then treat back and Kidneys.

Nervous Break Down - Treat whole body, Head. Then left shoulder blade area. All of back down to Kidneys.

Kidneys - Urinate often - Treat #1,2,3,4, and bladder longer. Treat Kidneys ½ hour.

Prostate - Treat #1,2,3,4, and apply hand over tail bone area.

Hemorrhoid - Man or Woman - Treat #1,2,3,4, Then put fingers on rectum ½ hour or more.

Whip Lash - Treat #1,2,3,4, Neck and complete head. Back. Treat adrenal for shock.

Broken Neck - Treat whole body and head.

Burns - Regular - Apply hand on burn.

Skin Peeling - Keep hand ½ inches or more above burn.

Bite Insect - Apply hand on bite for 15 to 20 minutes.

Skin Disease - Treat stomach, Kidneys and effected area.

Breath - Bad Breath - Treat stomach.

Mole - Treat mole with finger.

Wart - Treat wart with finger.

Shock - Treat adrenal gland right above kidneys ½ hour or more.

Stroke - Do not treat before 21 days to a month. After that treat whole body. Limbs and joint on affected side.

Lock Jaw - Treat #1,2,3,4, till person can release gas. When jaw opens treat jaw to take away pain.

# *Bibliography*

Bibliographic note about the "Grey Book": The "Grey Book" was compiled by Hawayo Takata's daughter, Alice Furumoto, after Takata's death. It contains excerpts from Takata's diary, photographs, a copy of Takata's Dai-Shihan certificate, articles by Takata, and the above- mentioned Japanese-language Hayashi manual of hand positions used to treat different illnesses. Takata's 22 Master students each received a copy, as well as a few other early Reiki Masters. I was lucky enough to have Iris Ishikuro's, on loan from her daughter. Harry Kuboi told me he regretfully gave his copy away because he couldn't read Japanese. Truth be told, the Japanese section is simply a list of medical diagnoses and where the practitioner should place his or her hands, given the diagnosis. The most enlightening part of the "Grey Book" is Takata's own diary and thoughts on Reiki, which are written in English.

## Works Cited

Arnold, Larry and Sandi Nevius. *The Reiki Handbook*. Harrisburg, PA: PSI Press. 1982.

Beatles, The. "We Can Work It Out." By Paul McCartney and John Lennon. In *We Can Work It Out / Day Tripper*. Capitol, 1965.

Brown, Fran. *Living Reiki: Takata's Teachings*. Mendocino, CA: LifeRhythm. 1992.

"Clarification." *The Reiki Review* 2:4 (Fall 1982), 3.

"Explanation of Instruction For the Public." *The Reiki Threshold*. http://www.threshold.ca/reiki/URH_Explanation.html last accessed December 1, 2014.

"FAQ." *Usui Shiki Ryoho*. http://www.usuishikiryohoreiki.com/ogm/faq/ last accessed December 1, 2014.

Fischer, Martin H. "Fischerisms." In *Encore: A Continuing Anthology (March 1945)*, edited by Dent Smith. Hoboken, NJ: Encore Press. 1945.

Fujimoto, Ruth. *Chapters of My Life*. Large print edition. CreateSpace Independent Publishing. 2011.

Graham, Vera. "Mrs. Takata Opens Minds to 'Reiki.'" *The Times* (San Mateo, CA). May 17, 1975.

Gray, John Harvey and Lourdes Gray with Steven McFadden and Elisabeth Clark. *Hand to Hand: The Longest-Practicing Reiki Master Tells His Story.* Xlibris. 2002.

Gray, Lourdes. "The Sacred Keys." *The John Harvey Gray Center for Reiki Healing Newsletter.* September 2011. http://hosted.verticalresponse. com/245353/59232afaa5/1410027123/13ce55ae81/ last accessed December 1, 2014.

Haberly, Helen J. *Reiki: Hawayo Takata's Story.* Olney, MD: Archedigm Publications. 1990.

Hammond, Sally. *We Are All Healers.* New York: Harper & Row. 1973.

Hayashi, Chūjirō. "I Appreciate Everyone's Kindness From the Bottom of My Heart—Mr. Hayashi's Farewell Address." *The Hawaii Hōchi.* February 22, 1938, 8. http://thescienceofsoul.wordpress. com/2014/04/19/1937222/ last accessed December 23, 2014

Ishikuro, Iris. Unpublished class notes. 1978.

Jacobs, Susan. "Reiki: Hands-On Healing." *Yoga Journal.* (May/June 1984), 40-43.

Johnson, Paul V. Letter to William L. Rand dated March 14, 1994.

Kathar Rinpoche, Ven. Khenpo. *Dharma Paths.* Ithaca, NY: Snow Lion. 1992.

Klatt, Oliver. *Reiki Systems of the World: One Heart—Many Beats.* Twin Lakes, WI: Lotus Press. 2006.

Kuboi, Harry M. *All of Reiki: Book 1.* Honolulu: Sirius Books. 1995.

Mitsui, Koshi. *Te no Hira Ryōchi.* Tokyo: Vortex. 2003 [1930].

Mitsui, Mieko. "Reiki Trip to Japan." *The Reiki Journal* 5:1 (March-May 1985), 10.

———. "Tracing the History: A Japanese Book on Reiki." *The Reiki Journal* 5:3 (October-December 1985), 9.

Lazonby, Barbi. *Reiki: Transforming Your Life, Volume 1: Healing with Your Hands*. Self-published.

Lugenbeel, Barbara Derrick. *Virginia Samdahl: Master Healer*. Norfolk, VA: Grunwald and Radcliff. 1984.

Mitchell, Paul. *Reiki* (a.k.a., *The "Blue Book"*). Revised edition. Coeur d'Alene, ID: Reiki Alliance, 2012 [1985].

National Archives and Records Administration. Washington, D.C. *Passenger Lists of Vessels Departing from Honolulu, Hawaii, compiled 06/1900 - 11/1954*. National Archives Microfilm Publication: A3422, Roll: 167. *A3510*, Roll: *133*. In *Records of the Immigration and Naturalization Service, 1787 – 2004*. Record Group Number: *RG 85*. Series M1410, Roll 362.

Ogawa, Fumio. "Everybody Can Do Reiki." Self-published.

"Our Organization." *Reiki Alliance*. http://www.reikialliance.com/the-reiki-alliance/founding-statement last accessed December 1, 2014.

Petter, Frank Arjava. "FAQ." *Reiki Dharma*. http://www.reikidharma.com/en/index_en.html last accessed December 1, 2014.

————. *This Is Reiki: Transformation of Body, Mind and Soul—From the Origins to the Practice*. Twin Lakes, WI: Lotus Press, 2012.

Petter, Frank Arjava, Tadao Yamaguchi, and Chujiro Hayashi. *The Hayashi Reiki Manual: Traditional Japanese Healing Techniques from the Founder of the Western Reiki System*. Twin Lakes, WI: Lotus Press, 2004.

"Purposes of A.R.A." *The Reiki Review* 1:3 (Fall 1981), 1.

Ray, Barbara. *The Official Handbook of The Radiance Technique®*. Santa Monica, CA: American-International Reiki Association. 1987

Ray, Barbara Weber, and Yesnie Carrington. *The Official Reiki Handbook*. Third edition. St. Petersburg, FL: American-International Reiki Association. 1984.

Ray, Barbara Weber, and Nonie Greene. *The Official Reiki Handbook*. First edition. Atlanta: American-International Reiki Association. 1982.

Ray, Barbara Weber, and Yesnie Greene. *The Official Reiki Handbook*. Second edition. Atlanta: America-International Reiki Association. 1983.

Ray, Barbara Weber, Nonie C. Greene, Virginia W. Samdahl, and Barbara St. John. Letter to John Latz dated March 7, 1983. Private collection.

"Reiki Ryōhō's Hayashi Chūjirō Comes to Hawaii—Accompanied by his Daughter Kiyoe—Arrives Saturday on the Chichibu Maru." *The Hawaii Hōchi*. September 30, 1938. p. 7. http://thescienceofsoul. wordpress.com/2014/04/09/19370930/ last accessed December 23, 2014.

"Reiki Ryōhō's Mr. Hayashi Chūjirō Arrived in Hawaii – Ex-Naval Surgeon and Captain – Will Stay Until December," *The Hawaii* Hōchi, October 2, 1937. http://thescienceofsoul.wordpress. com/2014/12/25/1937102/ last accessed December 25, 2014.

Stewart, Judy-Carol, *Reiki Touch: The Essential Handbook*. Second edition. Houston: Reiki Touch Institute of Holistic Medicine. 1995.

Stiene, Bronwen, and Frans Stiene. "Levels of Reiki." *International House of Reiki*. Published August 23, 2002. http://www.ihreiki.com/ blog/article/levels_of_reiki, last accessed December 1, 2014.

Straub, Mary. "Reiki – Japanese Method of Healing Could Spark Public Interest Similar to Chinese Acupuncture." *The Tinley Park Times Herald*. November 13, 1974. p. 13.

Takata, Alice, editor. "Grey Book." Self published. 1982.

Takata, Hawayo. Audio recording. August 24, 1979. Private collection.

———. Audio recording of a First Degree class. 1980. Private collection.

———. Letter to Alfred Beck dated September 30, 1956. Doris Duke Papers. Doris Duke Charitable Foundation Historical Archives. David M. Rubenstein Rare Book & Manuscript Library. Duke University.

———. Letter to Doris Duke dated November 16, 1954. Doris Duke Papers. Doris Duke Charitable Foundation Historical Archives. David

M. Rubenstein Rare Book & Manuscript Library. Duke University.

———. Letter to Phyllis Furumoto dated February 1, 1980. Private collection.

———. Letter to Rick Bockner dated March 1, 1980. Private collection.

———. Letter to Mr. S. L. Hawkins and Thomas Perkins dated June 24, 1956. Doris Duke Papers. Doris Duke Charitable Foundation Historical Archives. David M. Rubenstein Rare Book & Manuscript Library. Duke University.

———. Letter to Wanja Twan, available for viewing at the 2013 Reiki Alliance Meeting. Private collection.

———. "Statement of Mrs. Hawayo Hiromi Takata, Senior Citizen." In *Problems of the Aging: Hearings Before the Subcommittee on Federal and State Activities of the Special Committee on Aging. United States Senate Eighty-Seventh Congress, First Session, Part 12—Hilo, Hawaii, December 1, 1961.* Washington: U.S. Government Printing Office, 1962, 1601-1603. Available at http://www.aetw.org/reiki_takata_special_committee.html, last accessed December 1, 2014.

———. *Takata Telling the Stories of Dr. Hayashi, on CD.* Reiki Visions. com. 2003.

———. *Takata Telling the Stories of Dr. Usui, on CD.* Reiki Visions. com. 2003.

———. *Takata Speaks: Volume 1, Reiki Stories.* Audio recording. Rindge, NH: John Harvey Gray Center for Reiki Healing,

———. Unpublished autobiography draft, typed by Nonie Carrington Greene.

Takata, Hawayo and Beth Gray. "Questions and Answers with Hawayo Takata." *The John Harvey Gray Center for Reiki Healing Newsletter.* November 2008. http://learnreiki.org/newsletters/2008-11-Reiki-Newsletter.htm last accessed December 1, 2014.

Twan, Anneli. *Early Days of Reiki: Memories of Hawayo Takata.* Hope, BC: Morning Star Productions. 2005.

U.S. Geological Survey, "Historic Earthquakes," http://earthquake. usgs.gov/earthquakes/world/events/1923_09_01.php last accessed December 1, 2014.

Yamaguchi, Tadao, *Light on the Origins of Reiki*. Twin Lakes, WI: Lotus Light, 2007.